D0368705

Women Writers of Latin America

The Texas Pan American Series

Women Writers of Latin America

✣ ✣ ✣

INTIMATE HISTORIES

by Magdalena García Pinto

Translated by Trudy Balch
and Magdalena García Pinto

Illuminations by Karen Parker Lears

UNIVERSITY OF TEXAS PRESS, AUSTIN

Printed in the United States of America

First Edition, 1991

♾ The paper used in this publication meets the minimum requirements of American National Standard for Information Sciences—Permanence of Paper for Printed Library Materials, ANSI Z39.48-1984.

The Texas Pan American Series is published with the assistance of a revolving publication fund established by the Pan American Sulphur Company.

Library of Congress Cataloging-in-Publication Data
García Pinto, Magdalena.
[Historias íntimas. English]
Women writers of Latin America : intimate histories / by Magdalena García Pinto ; translated by Trudy Balch and Magdalena García Pinto ; illuminations by Karen Parker Lears. — 1st ed.
p. cm. — (The Texas Pan American series)
Translation of: Historias íntimas.
Includes bibliographical references and index.
ISBN 0-292-73862-5. — ISBN 0-292-73866-8 (pbk.)
1. Women authors, Spanish American—20th century—Interviews. 2. Spanish American literature—Women authors—History and criticism. 3. Spanish American literature—20th century— History and criticism. 4. Women and literature—Latin America. I. Title. II. Series.
PQ7081.G3613 1991
860.9'9287—dc20 90-23146
CIP

Undergrad

To my grandmother María Teresa and
to celebrate the memory of Marta Traba

Contents

Preface

THIS PROJECT began in 1983 as a consequence of my having discovered women's culture and its literary expressions. Some feminist friends and colleagues, Dorothy Haecker in particular, introduced me to important feminist ideas that resulted in a substantial expansion of my intellectual and human interests.

The selection of writers presented in this book was affected to a certain extent by external circumstances. It had to do, first, with my having encountered the works of these writers and, second, with my having met some of them at academic meetings in the United States; these experiences facilitated the interview process. In 1983 a colloquium on Latin American women writers brought to Amherst, Massachusetts, many of the authors I had chosen to interview. There papers were read on the works of Rosario Ferré, Sylvia Molloy, Elvira Orphée, Marta Traba, and Elena Poniatowska. Also, each of these authors spoke about her experience as a writer. This colloquium was the most enticing threshold for my project of interviews.

Later I interviewed Sylvia Molloy, Elvira Orphée, and Luisa Valenzuela in New York and Rosario Ferré and Marta Traba in Washington, D.C. I interviewed Margo Glantz, Elena Poniatowska, and Ida Vitale in Mexico City. Besides those previously mentioned I also interviewed Albalucía Angel and Isabel Allende in New York. I am indebted to María Luisa Bastos for generously inviting me to be a guest in her home, where Albalucía Angel and I met and were able to talk for three full days and part of the nights about her work, her life, and her interests. Isabel Allende came to New York to do a video interview with me filmed by Ediciones del Norte, the publishers of the Spanish edition of this book.

I was able to carry this project through only because of the generosity of the writers interviewed and the support and the agency of several people to whom I would like to express my gratitude. Although I am deeply grateful to each of these writers for their warmth and hospitality, for their time, and for their candid responses to my intrusive questions, I am grateful most of all for their work, which will continue to enrich the literary production of Latin America as well as the experience and lives of many other women.

My colleague and friend Margaret "Petch" Sayers Peden was instrumental in helping me get started with this translation and by introducing me to one of her students, Trudy Balch, who translated the text, which I then edited to sharpen some contextual and cultural details. Petch Peden's comments on the introductory essay were also very helpful.

My friends Maurita and Michael Ugarte gave me the necessary spiritual encouragement to see this project through in spite of occasional turmoil. Special additional thanks go to Maurita for her help in editing the translation.

I am very grateful to Theresa May, executive editor, and Barbara Spielman, managing editor, from the University of Texas Press for their assistance, support, and patience in the publication of this book.

Finally, I want to thank the Graduate School Research Council of the University of Missouri–Columbia for its financial support in preparing the manuscript for publication.

Women Writers of Latin America

Yo quisiera que hubiese entre las mujeres de toda la tierra
una solidaridad no sólo objetiva sino subjetiva.

VICTORIA OCAMPO

Women's Writing in Contemporary Latin American Literature

A Bit of History

VICTORIA OCAMPO once remarked that typical male discourse tends to be monological and self-centered and does not accept interruptions, whereas female discursive preference is dialogical. Even conversation between men is but a dialogical form of a monologue. Because this indifference toward communication has prevailed among men, women have been confined to repeating bits and pieces of masculine dialogue while surreptitiously inserting some fragments of their own discourse.[1]

Thus, self-centeredness and monology are two characteristics that in defining male discourse have, in turn, contributed to silencing women, creating a surrogate voice that speaks for them: "Women have spoken only a little about themselves, and men have spoken at great length about them, the filters in male writing being either gratefulness or deception, enthusiasm or bitterness, which an angel or a demon left in their heart and spirit."[2] Having understood the situation in which women found themselves at the first half of the twentieth century, Ocampo projected a vision of the future for women, which would only be altered when "the miracle of a work of art" became the result of a long preparation: "I believe our generation, the one that follows, and even those yet to be born, are destined not to realize this miracle, but rather to prepare it and make it imminent."[3]

Ocampo shows a deep awareness of the inequalities of the sexes and of the subordinate role of women in all spheres, art notwithstanding. Since 1935—the date of the essay discussed here—women have made some progress toward advancing their intellectual and creative independence. Although the task ahead is of considerable scope and magnitude, Ocampo's prediction about preparing the way and the moment for women to achieve "the miracle of a work of art" has arrived sooner than she seems to have anticipated. And it has arrived with flying colors in the Latin American literary scene. Latin American women of letters can now not only look back at the considerable textual space created by their female predecessors, whose works have been both uncovered and recovered, but also reject the segregationist notion that some women must be listed in Latin American literary histories under the separate heading of "Feminine Literature," as if women's literary works were oddities or idle pastimes that must be dealt with separately. I am thinking of writers of the stature of Sor Juana Inés de la Cruz, Gertrudis Gómez de Avellaneda, Clorinda Matto de Turner, Juana Manuela Gorriti, María Luisa Bombal, Clarice Lispector, Teresa de la Parra, Delmira Agustini, Marta Brunet, Victoria Ocampo, Silvina Ocampo, Blanca Varela, Antonia Palacios, Armonía Somers, Alejandra Pizarnik, Olga Orozco, Elena Garro, Rosario Castellanos, Julieta Campos, Julia de Burgos, Fanny Buitrago, Luisa Mercedes Levinson, and Mercedes Valdivieso, among many others, whose works are today the subject of study and reflection by students of Latin American literature.[4]

In reflecting on the textual strategies that women writers have developed, the Mexican writer Rosario Castellanos, adding to Ocampo's vision, makes an incisive observation with regard to the female writing scene:

> Woman, by definition of the classics, is a mutilated male. In spite of both its intrinsic and extrinsic ugliness, and of the paralysis in her development that this concept of mutilation and of violent spoliation implies, there has not been a woman who did not take the opportunity to contemplate her image reflected in the mirrors that fate has put before her. When the crystal of the waters becomes turbid and the eyes of the man in love close and the litany of the poets is exhausted and their lyre is silenced, there is still another recourse: to construct her self-image, a self-portrait, to draft her defense, to exhibit the proof of discharge, to draft her will for posterity (in order to give it what she had, but, most of all, to certify what she lacked), to evoke her life.[5]

Thus, it becomes clearer why female writing not only developed textual strategies to circumvent exclusion, but, in addition, it also explored the possibilities of meaning-generating zones of reality generally considered to be in the realm of the irrational and the emotional. This situation is perceptively described by Nelly Martínez:

> Traditionally exiled from the culture-making processes, Woman has consistently been dispossessed of a participatory role in the task of naming and thus of signifying the world—of rendering it "meaningful." Ostensibly, this dispossession has, to a degree, preserved her from control by the Logos. Thus Woman appears to be more attuned to the aspects of reality which can neither

> be named nor made to signify, and which man has repeatedly struggled to subdue: passion and instinct, irrationality and madness, and also inspiration, intuition and ecstasy. The primary "possessor" of the Logos, man, has been regarded as essentially beyond these realms.[6]

On the other hand, Martínez contends, female power relies on interconnection and cooperation and on female power struggles to remake the world by focusing on the formless "now."

Martínez proposes a reading that marks a transition from a mimetic to a holographic paradigm in fiction, in which, while the former "affirms the one-to-one correspondence between the objective world and the universe of discourse (and between the signifier and the signified), and regards the mind as transcending both realms, the holographic paradigm views the objective world, the realm of discourse and the mind as intrinsically woven into a dynamic whole." In this view, the world is governed by imminent forces that endlessly recreate it in the "always already now." This shift (from the mimetic to a holographic paradigm in fiction) is "the emergence of the feminine."[7]

Within this proposed paradigm, we can read and decipher feminine fiction as fiction that claims attention to itself for its own sake, rather than for the value system placed obliquely in the critical practice, whose presupposition is a comparative and differential stance with the masculine writing practice.

Feminine fiction and women's relationship with language, considered within a holographic paradigm, can be further enlightened with illumination provided by one of its practitioners, the Brazilian writer Clarice Lispector: "I am in the realm of speech. To write is to struggle with absolute distrust. I write like one adds 3 algorithms. A mathematics of existence. What I write is as simple as a flight. A vortical flight. Is it ecstasy?"[8] The words of Ocampo, Castellanos, and Lispector provide fertile ground in which approaches to the Latin American feminine practice of fiction and poetry may take root. The works by the ten writers interviewed in this volume could then be considered fragments of the holographic paradigm through which feminine experience is given a distinctive voice and design.

The Authors

Victoria Ocampo's and Rosario Castellanos' vision of women's writing, together with the women's literary tradition represented by the authors mentioned earlier, places the contemporary writing scene within a larger perspective in which the writers presented in this volume are a vital presence: Isabel Allende from Chile; Albalucía Angel from Colombia; Rosario Ferré from Puerto Rico; Margo Glantz and Elena Poniatowska from Mexico; Sylvia Molloy, Elvira Orphée, and Luisa Valenzuela from Argentina; Ida Vitale from Uruguay; and Marta Traba from Argentina and Colombia. Each has contributed an original voice to the development of feminine Hispanic literature, supported by an ever-growing readership that has widened the appreciation of their work.

This project's intention has been to capture the inner voices of these women and the drive and desire that move them to write. Because of the open and candid responses to my questions, these conversations are a history of each writer and a history of their writing experiences. From the conversations came the title and the main theme of these interviews, which is the personal history of each author that began in early childhood and was molded during the learning process of the formative years. Notably, I was surprised to discover that in each case, there is added emphasis and enthusiasm in remembering remarkable friendships, which are considered equal in importance to extensive readings of the classics. They also recollect illuminating epiphanies that gave way to the pursuit of a literary career. Perhaps it is not entirely coincidental that these women share a number of experiential circumstances. As children, for example, they tended to be somewhat aloof from the external world and frequently found themselves absorbed in copious reading of Western literature. They grew up under somewhat strict parental control, and this upbringing triggered an enriching private intellectual activity in which writing slowly became vital.

An intimate history of personal and literary development has been forged through the exercise of recollection in practicing creative writing. For most of these women writing is a multi-faceted activity: they are active practitioners in literary criticism, journalism, and/or translation. Margo Glantz explains this primary yearning: "I wanted to devote myself to literature ever since I was very young, but I wasn't sure I could do it." She said in her interview that she understands writing as an intertextual dialogue of certain works by authors whose common and overriding concern is the writing process itself: "Roland Barthes has become a very important author lately. I've read all his books and applied his work to my own ideas. He's a truly fascinating writer. His concept of the fragment, along with his relationship with erudition and creation, nourishes me a great deal and delights me."

Extensive reading of literary works and recording of fragments mark some of these writers' first writing exercises. Sylvia Molloy recalls her first incursions into creative writing:

> I began to write fragments and to write down my dreams. . . . I wrote a few prose poems, but they were all small fragments oriented toward something I didn't understand very clearly then. . . . From that time on I didn't stop writing, and I even began working on what would become the book on Borges in 1972. . . . The Borges book came out of my preoccupation with Borges' characters. . . . One discovery I made was that Borges didn't compose characters but fragmented them, decomposed them. And through that idea of decomposition, I began to get interested in the idea of writing fiction.

Isabel Allende, Elena Poniatowska, and Luisa Valenzuela began their writing careers in journalism before dedicating themselves to full-time fiction writing. Poniatowska has remained very active in journalism. Albalucía Angel has written on art history, and Marta Traba was a renowned art historian of Latin American plastic arts. Sylvia Molloy is possibly one of the most brilliant literary critics in the field of Latin American literature today, and there is a remarkable correspondence between her critical and creative discourse. This is also true for Rosario Ferré, Margo Glantz, and Elena Poniatowska, who are also influential literary critics. Ida Vitale is both a literary critic and translator of European literary works. Thus, the centrality of writing is crucial to understanding these authors' works. In this sense, they are representative of an ever-growing group of contemporary women writers for whom full-time dedication to the practice of writing is now possible, a personal circumstance which until recently was almost unthinkable.

The Interviews

The act of interviewing generates an oral narrative whose texture is at times discontinuous, fragmentary, with gaps and holes that are commonplace in conversational discourse. My responsibility as the writer of these conversations has been to best represent these exchanges, at times very open and intimate, by keeping as close to the original dialogue as possible. Although some details such as dates, titles, and a few names were adjusted for the sake of providing accurate information, for the most part, what was recorded in conversation with each writer has been retained.

The interviews offered in this volume are intended as an introduction of ten distinguished Spanish American women writers to the English-speaking public, because as a group, their life experiences and literary achievements are representative of the vitality and multi-faceted picture of feminine literature in Latin America today. Although only recently acknowledged by a larger sector of the reading public, feminine literature has had a long and important tradition, generally acknowledged to have begun in the seventeenth century with the Mexican Sor Juana Inés de la Cruz, a writer whose work has only in the last decades been reread, reassessed, and translated in earnest.

The impulse, initiative, and interest in women's writing today were generated by the rise of the feminist movement in selected sectors of society, and its impact has produced significant results in terms of numbers of works studied. Literary women in Latin America are no longer "orphans" of a tradition, as Victoria Ocampo suggested in 1935. The foremothers are now a part of the intertextual dialogue that illuminates the contemporary textual scene. Women writers in all the Spanish-speaking countries have produced and are currently producing works in all genres—poetry, fiction, and drama—with a marked preference for the first two. In fact, it is not uncommon for the same author to cultivate two genres. On one hand, there are poets and fiction writers of the stature of Claribel Alegría, Olga Orozco, or Silvina Ocampo; on the other, there are authors who explore all genres: Sor Juana in the seventeenth century and Rosario Castellanos in the twentieth.

Women's experience, their world, their identity, their role in society, and the voicing of their concerns with regard to their private lives, their intimate desires, and dreams are the stuff of which these works are made, and they are the focus of these conversations. These dialogues thus become an extended conversation among themselves through the interviewer—the mediator-*voyeuresse*—and the reader, in particular, the female reader.

Their Works

The fiction of these writers is not a homogeneous body of literature. It can be best characterized as a kaleidoscope of modes and styles in fiction and in poetry that reflects the diversity and creativity of women's fiction in Latin America, a creation parallel to that of their male counterparts. So rich is the scope of their vision and the skills with which they have enriched Hispanic literature that it could be said we are witness to a female literary boom similar to the famous male boom of Latin American narrative of the sixties. To provide some background to the scope and diversity of these authors' writings, I present below a brief critical profile of each writer, in terms of her most significant works, in the order that the interviews appear in the book.

Chilean author Isabel Allende has rapidly captured large audiences around the world with her first three novels: *La casa de los espíritus* [*The House of the Spirits*], *De amor y de sombra* [*Of Love and Shadows*], and *Eva Luna* [*Eva Luna*]. She is the first woman writer to share the popularity of large audiences with the major male authors of the boom, both in Spanish-speaking countries and in other languages. Her novels have been translated into most languages spoken in the Western world, and they continue to be on best-seller lists in many countries. Her enormous appeal rests partly in the nature of her narrative style: a story told through a dynamic concatenation of events and characters, and structured around a fast-paced narrative plot. She is a natural storyteller whose reader immediately gets caught up in the fascinating web of the story, in the most canonical sense of the term. Her first work, probably the most skillfully conceived, is a family saga of several generations who are active participants in the life of their unnamed country. Intertwined with the main story is the modern history of Chile. She thus posits a contemporary concern in fiction and acknowledges the problem of the writing of history. Allende has successfully incorporated several innovations of her literary predecessors, most notably those of the marvelous and the fantastic, as developed by the Colombian writer Gabriel García Márquez in *Cien años de soledad* [*One Hundred Years of Solitude*]. Although she does not acknowledge this debt in our interview, it has been pointed out by many critics in Latin American literature: "The 'spirit' of *Cien años de soledad* floats constantly not only in Isabel Allende's imaginary world but also in her writing style. There are patent affinities and correspondences in her novels that will attract more than one critic inclined to infinite intertextual reflections."[9] The unusual, the mysterious, and the magic aura of the Trueba household, the features of the female characters such as Rosa's and Alba's green hair or Clara's gift of clairvoyance disappear in her second novel, *De amor y de sombra,* which differs in a number of ways from her first book. A realistic account of the political and social conditions of post-Allende, gloomy Chile ruled by Gen. Pinochet is at the center of her preoccupation, a situation that is skillfully intertwined with a melodramatic love affair between the female protagonist and an extraordinarily handsome army captain, Gustavo Morante, a type of character more typically found in Corín Tellado's romance novels rather than in contemporary fiction, which is noted for its critical and ironic gesture toward the world it creates. *Eva Luna,* Allende's third novel, was not yet published when this interview took place, so discussion of it is absent from our conversation.

Eva Luna does not reveal the skillful writer apparent in Allende's previous works. Perhaps hastily written, it does not share the preoccupation with language evident in her first two novels, most particularly in *La casa de los espíritus.* Eva Luna is the name of the protagonist-narrator of this contemporary twist of the picaresque genre. Consuelo, Eva's mother, leaves the convent to serve her only "master," a foreign doctor, Professor Jones, thus prefiguring the plot structure. This male character is "beautiful as a picture of Jesus, all in gold, with the princely blond beard and eyes of an impossible color,"[10] elements of kitsch that are part of Allende's fiction. Consuelo saves the life of an Indian dying of a snake bite by curing him with affection and sex. The child of this soap-operatic encounter is Eva Luna.

A narrative device privileged by Allende in her previous novels, the female gifted with an imaginative mind for telling fantastic stories, is once again developed here and is used to shape Eva's future. This embodiment of Scheherazade, an echo of the epigraph that appears at the threshold of the novel, could be considered the narrative paradigm of Allende's work. Her most recent book is *Cuentos de Eva Luna,* which underscores the Scheherazadian role of the main character.

Isabel Allende's fiction is a female-centered narrative. Her main characters are attracted to handsome males whose descriptions follow the convention of the popular romance, another element of her fiction. In her works, Allende has consistently empowered the main female characters with the gift of writing and telling in order to preserve the past and organize the future. These characters are narrators-writers; they record their version of the story told: in *La casa de los espíritus* she tells the story of the Trueba family through Alba's use of Clara's and Esteban's journals; in *De amor y de sombra,* Irene, the journalist, uncovers a story of cruelty and governmental excess; in *Eva Luna,* Eva Luna writes her own story.

The second writer interviewed in this series is the Colombian author Albalucía Angel, who began to write fiction in her twenties when she was living meagerly in Paris, supporting herself as a nightclub singer. She has written short stories, poems, plays, and novels. Her most notable works are novels, particularly *Estaba la pájara pinta sentada en el verde limón* (The petite colored bird perched in a green lemon tree), *Misiá señora* (Madam lady), and the parable *Las andariegas* (The wayfarers). Angel's meticulous elaboration of language in these three works is part of the task she has set for herself as a feminist writer: to develop a language endowed with the empowering attributes of representing women's culture, world, and experience. These three works mark successive stages in Angel's trajectory, beginning with *Estaba la pájara pinta sentada en el verde limón,* considered by some critics as an example of a feminine bildungsroman, or novel of formative education or character development.[11]

The fictional treatment of the historical material woven into the narrative of this novel is a good example of the new historical novel, a genre in which Latin American women writers have made important contributions as they posit new readings of historical reality and reinterpret historical accounts of that reality.[12] The novel's representation of one of Colombia's most difficult historical periods, the period known in Colombia's history as "La Violencia" (The violence) between 1946 and 1965, is dramatically developed through a female character's point of view in her imaginary dialogue with her nanny, Sabina. This rhetorical device allows Angel to recover fragments of the story of Ana's family and the history of her country. This is a powerful, ambitious work that Angel carries out successfully, and it is representative of a number of works of feminine fiction that deal with the most intricate and exacting realities in Latin American contemporary life. These works not only attempt to develop an understanding of society and its complex problems, but they also integrate a meticulous depiction of the psychological movements of the female mind. These characteristics are typical of Angel's other major undertaking, her difficult and challenging second novel, *Misiá señora*. Using as literary material the history of four women of the same family who represent four generations, the narrator weaves the memories and the lives of these characters in constantly intertwined levels. In *Las andariegas* there is a substantial change of narrative mode and voice that follows the narrative conventions established in Monique Wittig's *Les Guérrillères*. This new narrative is a sort of mirror image of the French text, conceived as a parable of women in search of their true destiny while they defy the dictates of the patriarchy. At the opening of the text, the epigraph frames the fiction by stating the intertextual principle sustaining this book: "Illuminated by Wittig's warriors, I too decided to undertake this voyage with female travelers coming from a nowhere region toward history."[13] A strong feminist, Angel's main motivation for writing is a continuing search for a feminist literary language with which to recover and reconstruct the underground history female courage founded in the collective experience of all the women of her culture.

Rosario Ferré, the third author presented here, is considered one of the most important writers in the literature of Puerto Rico, whose aspiration to become an independent state is in constant conflict with the culture of its protector, the United States. Ferré's work is partly concerned with that problem. As did Allende and other women, she began to write relatively late in life; it was after she divorced her first husband that she decided to become a writer. She has written short stories, poems, children's stories, and critical essays, and most recently the novella *Maldito amor.*

Her themes are all linked to many aspects of upper- and middle-class life in Puerto Rico. Her family, originally from Ponce, is from the class of wealthy landowners who enjoyed a very comfortable life but whose world is rapidly fading today because of the demise of the island's agricultural economy and the advancement of North American economic and cultural influence on Puerto Rican society. Their world is the subject of Ferré's fiction; she both questions it and destroys it and in the process nostalgically recovers it for all time. Her best fiction is found in her collection of short stories and poems entitled *Papeles de Pandora* (Pandora's papers), considered by critics to be one of three fundamental texts in Puerto Rican contemporary literature together with *La guaracha del Macho Camacho* by Luis Rafael Sánchez and *La novelabingo* by Manuel Ramos Otero. All three were published in 1976.[14] In these stories Ferré elaborates conflicts from a woman-centered point of view, made critical by character types presented, such as a young woman-doll, a faithfully married woman, a black mistress, and other types of Puerto Rico's bourgeois society in transition, focusing on superficial and hypocritical values that undermine, curtail, and victimize women by keeping them within traditional and patriarchally determined roles. Another aspect of Ferré's fiction is her literary language, in which humor and irony are the dominant rhetorical devices for subversion of the assumed meaning. Her language incorporates Puerto Rican Spanish, as is the case of other writers, to create a new system of expression that could best identify with the spirit of liberation of Puerto Rico in the largest sense of the term. She explores the relationship between women, eroticism, sexuality, and language, upsetting the social referent by disseminating doubt of established values.

Ferré has also written a collection of long poems and lyrical prose fragments entitled *Fábulas de la garza desangrada* (Fables of the bleeding heron, 1982), also the title of one of the poems, all texts of remarkable beauty of expression. The title makes reference to and deconstructs the notion of fable and the fictitious or invented re-creation of classical myths that molded the beliefs about women in Western societies. These fables are intended to turn well-established beliefs and myths upside down by rewriting them as different stories with new and unexpected endings. The heron-woman symbol integrates both the assigned classic meaning of indiscretion and alertness, as well as vigilance, with that of immortality. With these three significations embedded in the literary and cultural tradition, Ferré envisions the heron as the embodiment of woman's fate, jumping from branch to branch, dispossessed of her own destiny:

¿cómo llamarla vencedora
si la muerte la habita y la define?
¿cómo sacerdotisa del misterio,
si ignora a dónde va, de dónde viene,
saltando de rama en rama como garza
desangrada de la propia vida,
sin caminar jamás del propio brazo?
. . . .
terminada su historia se levanta.
. . . .
yace su doble entre los espejos estallados
con todas las venas abiertas
. . . .
se desangra por sus mil heridas;
fluye su sangre blanca en éster nítrico
y escribe con ella su nombre al pie de los
fragmentos del poema
para mejor después desvanecerse.[15]

Margo Glantz is the author of nearly fifteen books ranging from fiction to critical fiction to literary criticism. Her writing is atypical in women's Latin American literary work in that she has not written works that fall within traditional genres. As a fiction writer, she has been markedly influenced by French literary critics and writers, most notably by Roland Barthes and Georges Bataille, but also by Walter Benjamin and Jorge Luis Borges. Her fiction and critical fiction stem from a single deliberate intertextual exercise, having texts that are the very motivating factor, the pretext, in both senses of the term, of their reflexivity. Her fictional work is grounded in a surrealistic vision of the world, in which mythical, biblical, and literary characters wander and wonder in the midst of beautiful animals. These include whales, as in *Doscientas ballenas azules . . . y . . . cuatro caballos . . .*, creatures with whom Glantz claims some affinities. She also acknowledges her indebtedness to Melville's *Moby Dick,* a presence in more than one of her fragmented fictions.

Margo Glantz is an experimental writer who constantly elaborates on a game of textual interactions that function at several levels, including graphic thematic relations on the page, as is the case for one of her most recent works, *De la amorosa inclinación a enredarse en cabellos*

(1984). In our conversation she describes the underlying project of this book: "There's a very long chapter called 'Beauty Salons and Laboratories' that puts together in two columns—with white space and different typefaces—two ways of looking at the world: that of vanity and frivolity and that of death, because hair is frivolity and death."

The book that has received most attention from the public and the critics is her autobiographical work *Las genealogías,* now in its second edition. This book is quite different from her other books in terms of language, tone, style, and theme. Her motivation was to record the family history before it was erased from the memory of its protagonists. She had long conversations with both of her parents, Ukrainian Jews who immigrated to Mexico in 1925. She recorded these conversations to preserve the details, and with that material she created *Las genealogías,* which can be read not only as an autobiography, but also as a documentary work on the life of European immigrants in early and mid-twentieth-century Mexico. E. Otero Krauthammer, one of the critics who studied this work, defines it as a double voyage in space and time: "One of the journeys takes place on an objective level, external, historical, cultural, documentary, biographical, and illustrative. This journey becomes reality through family stories and conversations, telephone calls, photographs, and historical-cultural anecdotes as much national as international. The other journey is subjective, internal, self-searching, emotional, and tender. This second journey, verbalized through commentaries, questions, reflections and interior monologues is perhaps born of an interior need of the author to become *one.*"[16]

Glantz remains an influential intellectual figure in Mexico today, and following in the steps of compatriot Rosario Castellanos, she served as a member of the Mexican diplomatic corps in England.

Sylvia Molloy best represents the centrality of writing in an author's career in having blended her critical and fictional work into one major project. She said in her interview, "I like to write about authors I enjoy and in whose work I recognize something of myself. For example, when I write about Onetti, I'm interested in gossip, in voyeurism, because I use both in my fiction. The practice of criticism strengthens my fiction, and my fiction is made of the threads of all the writers' voices that come together in my own."

Molloy possesses one of the finest literary minds I have encountered in contemporary criticism or creative writing. She first wrote short stories, but it was with her first novel, *En breve cárcel,* published in 1984, that she attracted the attention of the reading public. This novel was recently translated as *Certificate of Absence.*[17] Molloy belongs to the "tradition" of the novel of language and introspection; her writing is also characterized by an unrelenting quest for the construction of a language empowered with an expressive puissance to reveal women's lives, their world, and their experience from their viewpoint. The fictional worlds proposed by Virginia Woolf, Clarice Lispector in Portuguese, and María Luisa Bombal in Spanish are predecessors to Molloy's fictional world, even though she says of Woolf, "I'm a little afraid at times of certain lyrical aspects of her fiction that seem somewhat overdone."

In *En breve cárcel,* Molloy's fiction breaks new ground in terms of the concept of how the story is told, which discloses the mental and emotional movements of self-discovery of the narrator-protagonist while she seeks to understand her sexual and sentimental relationship with two women. As pointed out by Oscar Montero, Sylvia Molloy's novel incorporates a narrative model of two intersecting textual levels that display the crossing of that which is told with that which is the mark of the act of telling.[18]

Elvira Orphée is the author of four novels and three collections of short stories. Perhaps the most striking feature of her prose is its lyrical quality: all elements are centered around a narrator's intimate point of view. This narrative quality defies the demands of a chronological sequence; instead, the series of events, the information about the characters in the story, the psychological construction of the characters, the temporal and spatial structuring principles—all are governed by the lyricism permeating the narrative, which is presented in a fragmented prose form. The novel that is probably Orphée's best known work, *Aire tan dulce,* exemplifies this lyrical trait of her fiction.

Orphée has shown a particular interest in exploring and experimenting with cruelty as an ever-present trait of the human character, especially when connected to childhood.[19] Most of Orphée's characters are cruel, wicked, ugly, lonely, and/or dispossessed, as in the case of *Aire tan dulce, Dos veranos,* and *La última conquista de El Angel.* In this last collection of short stories, the cruelty theme is taken a step further in creating the psychological construct: there is a man whose main task is to supervise torture of political prisoners in an unnamed country.

The limits of suffering from an unknown or unnamed disease are part of the reality of the human condition and are another element of Orphée's fiction. They are skillfully explored in *Aire tan dulce* and *En el fondo.* Her narrative reflects her obsession with uncovering the many layers that make up reality by exposing their strange and odd relationships, as expressed by one of the characters in "Los aprendices aprenderán": "The apprentices made fun of something that they are incapable of possessing: my ability to pierce reality and see its strange associations."[20]

A voice quite different from the voices of authors previously discussed is that of the Mexican writer and journalist Elena Poniatowska, author of nearly twenty works, encompassing the short story, novel, testimonial literature, and literary criticism. Some of her books continue to be read by a large audience, as is the case of *Hasta no verte, Jesús mío,* first published in 1969 and recently translated into English as *Until We Meet Again,* and *La noche de Tlatelolco,* translated into English in 1976 under the title *Massacre in Mexico.* Both books have had multiple editions in Mexico, a fact that underscores the number and diversity of her readership.

Perhaps her two most memorable fictional literary creations are *Hasta no verte, Jesús mío* and *Querido Diego, te abraza Quiela* (1978). The first is a realistic representation of life of the underclass from the time of the Mexican Revolution of 1910. The protagonist, Jesusa Palancares, after participating in the civil war, returns to Mexico City, where she tries to make a living. She is never able to break through the social and economic barriers that keep her locked in the deprived underclass of Mexican society. This novel, re-created from recorded conversations with a Mexican woman Poniatowska met in Mexico City, has been considered by some critics as testimony rather than fiction. We talk about this issue in our interview.

In general, it seems that Poniatowska's work in Mexico is perceived as controversial because she represents a voice critical of the economic and social policies of the Mexican political establishment. In my view, it also helps explain the enormous success and popularity of her works in her country. Literary critics in the United States and in Mexico have studied *Hasta no verte, Jesús mío* extensively, and it remains one of the major works of fiction of the sixties.

The second work, *Querido Diego,* is a novella written in a much different register. The pretext of this book is a moment in the life of Russian émigré painter Angelina Beloff, who lived in Paris early in the century. There she met the Mexican painter Diego Rivera, with whom she lived for ten years. In 1921, Rivera was invited to return to Mexico, and Angelina remained in Paris. The letters that make up this book are the love letters that she wrote to the artist, as imagined by Poniatowska, in a lyrical tone and language of striking beauty and sensitivity. It exposes the unfortunate and not uncommon experience of women in love with an illusion.

Poniatowska has published three additional books. The first one—*¡Ay vida, no me mereces!*—consists of four essays on contemporary Mexican writers: Carlos Fuentes, Rosario Castellanos, Juan Rulfo, and the *literatura de la onda* authors. The second is the novel *La "flor de lis,"* which contains autobiographical elements discussed in the interview in this volume woven into fictional material. The third work, a new testimonial work in the model established by *La noche de Tlatelolco* and *Fuerte es el silencio,* is *Nada, nadie: Las voces del temblor,* which records the collective voice of the Mexican people in the aftermath of the tragic Mexico City earthquake of 1986. As her prolific writing endeavor continues, Poniatowska never ceases to amaze her readers with her constant denunciation of the social and economic injustice that goes hand-in-hand with abuse of political power in her country: "In the fourth delegation, located at 100 Chimalpopoca Street, Colonia Obrera, the agent from the Public Health Ministry demanded various quantities of money from the relatives of the earthquake's victims in order 'to speed up the delivery of the bodies.' In front of the chief of the Cuauhtemoc delegation, known only to us as 'Zorro 1,' officials from the Secretary of Protection and Roads were looting the offices that were still standing in Tlatelolco after the earthquake."[21]

Once more, Poniatowska, consistent with her stance on social issues stated some years ago, has given a voice to those who do not have one and engaged in a writing practice committed to working against official discourse.[22]

Marta Traba was another powerful, polemic, and passionate female voice, both in art criticism and in creative writing. Although she was born in Buenos Aires, she developed her professional career in other countries in Latin America, most notably in Colombia, where she founded the Museum of Modern Art of Bogotá. She was a pioneer in the revitalization and dissemination of contemporary Colombian and Latin American plastic arts. She taught in several Latin American universities and wrote extensively on young painters and sculptors such as Edgar Negret, Eduardo Ramírez Villamizar, Feliza Bursztyn, Luis Caballero, and Fernando Botero, among many others. Her work on the plastic arts comprises twenty-three books plus numerous articles in journals and weekly and daily newspapers published throughout Latin America.[23]

Although she published a book of poems in 1951, she was primarily a prose stylist. Her work as a fiction writer began in earnest in the sixties with *Ceremonias del verano,* which received the distinguished Premio Casa de las Américas literary award in 1966 from a jury consisting of three major writers, Alejo Carpentier, Manuel Rojas, and

Juan García Ponce. This excellent first novel was followed by two collections of short stories and five works of fiction. Her untimely death in November 1983 put an end to the writing career of an indefatigable spirit.

Two of the last three novels she wrote—*Conversación al sur* (1981), *En cualquier lugar* (1984), and *Casa sin fin* (1988)—and "Veinte años no es nada," which she had not begun by the time of her death, were conceived as a trilogy. *En cualquier lugar* and *Casa sin fin* were published posthumously and contain introductory articles by Elena Poniatowska and the Colombian poet and critic Juan Gustavo Cobo Borda. Another collection of short stories entitled *De la mañana a la noche (Cuentos norteamericanos)* was also published posthumously in Uruguay with an introduction by her friend Juan Gustavo Cobo Borda.

Traba was a talented intellectual whose work will endure as an example of an extraordinarily lucid mind and spirit devoted to understanding Latin American reality through its cultural and artistic expression.

Luisa Valenzuela is another prolific writer whose career began in journalism. She wrote *Hay que sonreír,* her first novel, in Paris, a city considered a necessary stopover, or perhaps rite of passage, for Latin American artists. Since then she has written six novels and three collections of short stories, most of which have been translated into English. She is well known in the United States, where she has lived for extensive periods, and her exposure in cultural and literary circles has contributed to a greater dissemination of her work. Her fictions explore the literary possibilities of experimenting with language and narrative devices in the tradition of the vanguard Latin American writers. The narrative form in which she seems most at home is the short story. From her early collection entitled *Los heréticos,* Valenzuela showed a remarkable ability in this genre. It was with the publication of *Cambio de armas* in 1982 and *Donde viven las águilas* in 1983 that she has achieved the highest degree of tension and quality in her fiction. The first of these two collections centers around characters whose lives become entangled in the complex and exacting political developments of recent Argentine history. Her most recent novel, *Cola de lagartija,* translated into English by Gregory Rabassa, presents a protagonist based on the colorful and quasi-fictional politician José López Rega, minister of social welfare during the Isabel Perón administration (1974–1976). The period chosen by Valenzuela is propitious for satire, because it is a moment when Argentine history is both carnivalized and cannibalized. In this sense, Valenzuela's novel is a fiction that portrays this eschewed reality by focusing on the kaleidoscopic absurdities of the political process.

Ida Vitale is one of Uruguay's most important poetic voices in the last several decades. She is the only one in this group of writers whose work is almost entirely dedicated to lyric poetry, although she has also written prose fragments entitled *Léxico de afinidades,* a sort of dictionary or thesaurus of semantic affinities. Her poetic pursuit has been developed in the lyrical space of seven books that are, in fact, seven stages of an extended book of poems, whose centerpiece may be *Jardín de sílice* (1980), carefully constructed with extreme rigor and austerity of language and form. Vitale's profound respect for the poetic word—her search for *le mot juste*—is best understood if we connect it to her discussion in our interview of the poetry of Juan Ramón Jiménez, the Spaniard whose life was devoted to the writing of poetry. Since I talked with Vitale, she has published two more books, and the Mexican publishing house Fondo de Cultura Económica has published the first edition of her complete works under the title *Sueños de la constancia* in 1988. This is an important event because the early editions of Vitale's books of poems are not available, a fact that is too often the sad fate of poetry. For this reason, among others, I have included several poems in the text of her interview. She has also translated many works into Spanish and is an active contributor of articles, book reviews, and other texts in major Latin American literary journals and daily newspapers.

Notes

1. Victoria Ocampo, *La mujer y su expresión* (Buenos Aires: Ediciones Sur, 1936).
2. Ibid., 12–13. All translations from this essay are mine.
3. Ibid., 24.
4. For a partial listing, see *Women Writers of Spanish America: An Annotated Bio-biographical Guide,* ed. Diane E. Marting (New York: Greenwood Press, 1987).
5. "La mujer, segun definición de los clásicos, es un varón mutilado. Pero no obstante lo que este concepto indica de fealdad intrínseca y extrínseca, de parálisis en el desarrollo, de despojo violento, no ha habido mujer que haya desperdiciado la oportunidad de contemplar su imagen reflejada en cuantos espejos le depara la suerte. Y cuando el cristal de las aguas se enturbia y los ojos del hombre enamorado se cierran y las letanías de los poetas se agotan y la lira enmudece, aún queda un recurso: construir la imagen propia, autoretratarse, redactar el alegato de la defensa, exhibir la prueba de descargo,

hacer un testamento a la posteridad (para darle lo que se tuvo pero ante todo para hacer constar aquello de lo que se careció), evocar su vida" (Rosario Castellanos, *Mujer que sabe latín* [Mexico City: Fondo de Cultura Económica, 1984], 41). The translation is mine.

6. Zulma Nelly Martínez, "From a Mimetic to a Holographic Paradigm in Fiction: Toward a Definition of Feminist Writing," *Women's Studies* 14 (1988): 234.

7. Ibid., pp. 234, 238.

8. "Estou no reino da fala. Escrever é lidar com a absoluta desconfiança. Escrevo como se somam 3 algarismos. A matemática da existência. O que escrevo é simples como um vôo. Um vôo vertiginoso. ¿Extase?" Olga Borelli, Clarice Lispector, *Esboço para um Possível Retrato* (Rio de Janeiro: Nova Fronteira, 1981), 65.

9. "El 'espíritu' de *Cien años de soledad* flota constantemente tanto en el mundo imaginario como en la escritura de Isabel Allende. Hay en las dos novelas patentes afinidades y correspondencias que atraerán a más de un crítico amante de los infinitos reflejos intertextuales" (Mario Rojas, "Un caleidoscopio de espejos desordenados," *Revista Iberoamericana* 51 [July–December 1985]: 917). The translation is mine.

10. "Hermoso como una estampa de Jesús, todo de oro, con la misma barba rubia de príncipe y los ojos de un color imposible" (*Eva Luna* [Buenos Aires: Editorial Sudamericana, 1987], 14). The translation is mine.

11. "En oposición al predominio absoluto de un narrador en primera persona del formato general, *La pájara pinta* presenta una especie de *collage* de voces en el que domina la de Ana adulta, en imaginario diálogo con la criada Sabina, pero alternado con otras voces que ocupan a veces muchas páginas. . . . Es decir, que a diferencia del formato prototípico que siempre tiene al protagonista como columna vertebral, la autora le dio gran atención a otros personajes, y dedicó mucho espacio para insertar sucesos históricos que afectan a toda la sociedad" (Gabriela Mora, "El bildungsroman y la experiencia latinoamericana: *Estaba la pájara pinta sentada en el verde limón* de Albalucía Angel," in *La sartén por el mango,* ed. Patricia Elena González and Eliana Ortega [San Juan, P.R.: Ediciones Huracán, 1984], 73).

12. Two examples are *El río de las congojas* and *La flor de Hierro* by the Argentine writer Libertad Demitrópulos and *Borrasca en la clepsidra* by the Argentine Laura del Castillo.

13. "Iluminada por la presencia de 'les guérrillères' de Monique Wittig, decidí también emprender este periplo con viajeras, desde ninguna región hacia la historia" (Albalucía Angel, *Las andariegas* [Barcelona: Biblioteca del Fénice, Argos Vergara, 1984], 11). The translation is mine.

14. See Juan Gelpí, "Apuntes al margen de un texto de Rosario Ferré," in *La sartén por el mango,* ed. Patricia Elena González and Eliana Ortega (San Juan, P.R.: Ediciones Huracán, 1984), 133–135.

15. "Can I call her conqueror / if she is inhabited and defined by death? / call her priestess of mystery / if she knows not where she goes or where she comes from, / jumping from branch to branch like a heron / bleeding by her own life, / without ever walking by her own arm? / . . . her story now over,

she gets up. / . . . her double lies among shattered mirrors / with her veins opened / . . . she bleeds from her thousand wounds; / her white blood flows in nitric ester, / and with it she writes her name at the bottom of the / fragments of the poem / the better to faint afterward" (Rosario Ferré, *Fábulas de la garza desangrada* [Mexico City: Joaquín Mortiz, 1982], 19, 21, 22). The translation is mine.

16. "Uno de los viajes sucede en un plano objetivo, exterior, histórico, cultural, documental, biográfico y ilustrativo. Este viaje se hace realidad por medio de relatos y diálogos familiares, conversaciones telefónicas, fotografías y anécdotas de carácter histórico-cultural tanto nacionales como internacionales. El otro viaje es de carácter subjetivo, interior, autoanalítico, sentimental, afectivo y tierno. Este segundo viaje, que se exterioriza por medio de comentarios, preguntas, reflexiones y monólogos interiores nace quizás de una necesidad interior de la autora de ser una" (Elizabeth Otero Krauthammer, "Integración de la identidad judía en *Las genealogías*, de Margo Glantz," *Revista Iberoamericana* 51 [July–December 1985]: 868). The translation is mine.

17. Sylvia Molloy, *Certificate of Absence*, tr. Daniel Balderston and the author (Austin: University of Texas Press, 1989).

18. "Ha sido marca de nuestra modernidad narrativa el cruce en el relato de lo que se cuenta con la marca del contar. En ese cruce se define la fuga de un sujeto huidizo, 'en un tránsito sin reposo.' En la novela de Molloy se adopta ese modelo de la producción sin desdén resentido, sin apropiación aparatosa en un gesto seguro donde se marca a la vez la intimidad y la distancia" (Oscar Montero, "*En breve cárcel:* La Diana, la violencia y la mujer que escribe," in *La sartén por el mango*, ed. Patricia Elena González and Eliana Ortega [San Juan, P.R.: Ediciones Huracán, 1984], 118).

19. Cruelty is a theme explored by several Argentine writers, including Roberto Arlt, Silvina Ocampo, and Juan Rodolfo Wilcock, among others.

20. "Los aprendices se burlaron de algo que son incapaces de tener: mi capacidad para taladrar la realidad y verle sus asociaciones extrañas" (Elvira Orphée, "Los aprendices aprenderán," in *Su demonio preferido* [Buenos Aires: Emecé Editores, 1973], 12). The translation is mine.

21. Elena Poniatowska, *Nada, nadie: Las voces del temblor* (Mexico City: Biblioteca Era, 1988), 64. The translation is mine.

22. "La actual literatura de las mujeres ha de venir como parte del gran flujo de la literatura de los oprimidos: la de los sin tierra, la de los pobres, los que aún no tienen voz, los que no saben leer ni escribir" (Elena Poniatowska, "La literatura de las mujeres es parte de la de los oprimidos," *Fem* 6 [February–March 1982]: 27).

23. See the list of works published at the end of this volume and *Marta Traba* (Bogotá: Museo de Arte Moderno de Bogotá, Planeta Colombiana Editorial, 1984) for additional bibliographical information.

The Interviews

I speak not with one voice
but with many.

ALEJANDRA PIZARNIK

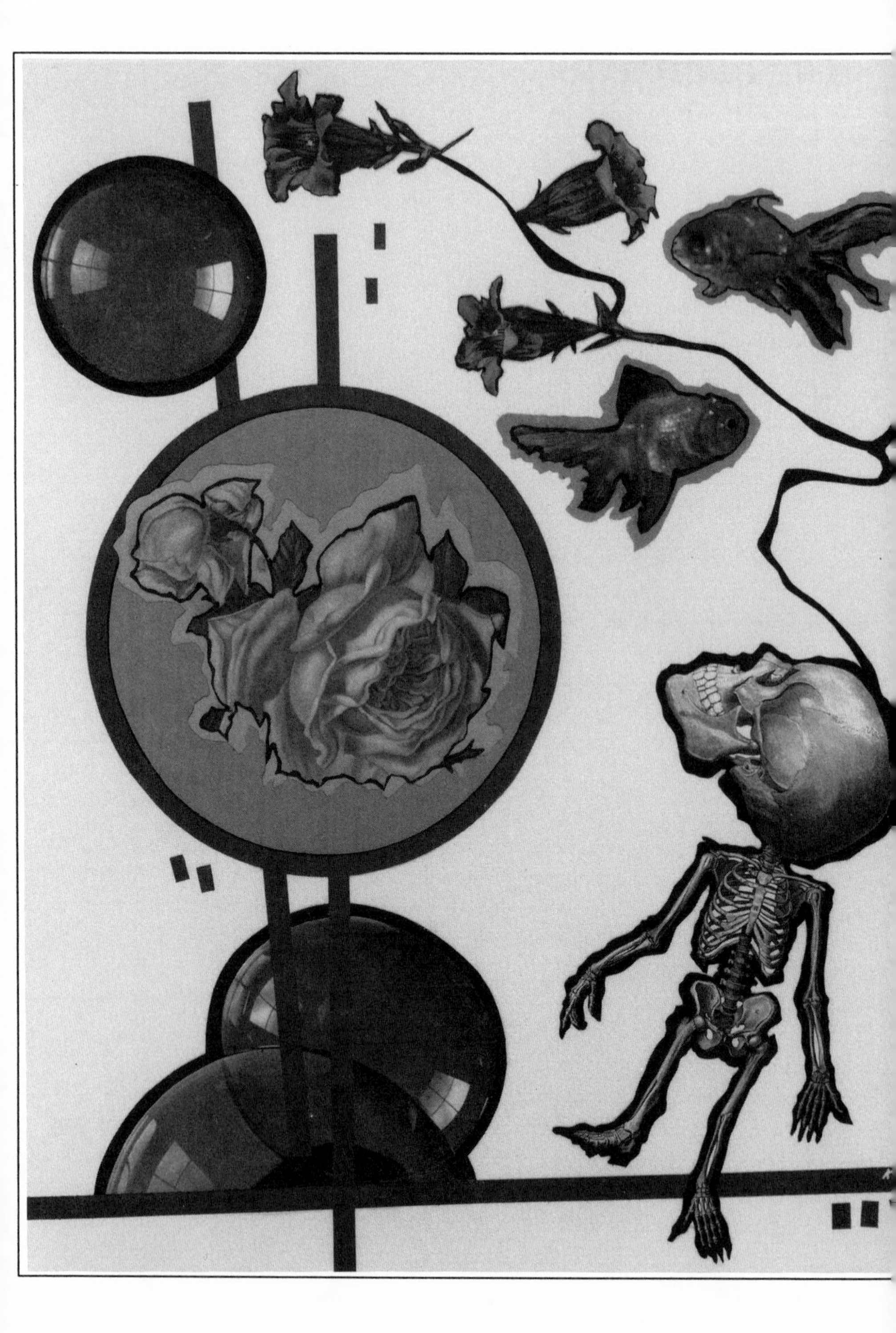

✣ ✣ ✣

Isabel Allende

✣ ✣ ✣

MGP: Where does your personal chronology begin, Isabel Allende?

IA: I was born in Lima (because my parents were diplomats), but by nationality I'm Chilean. I was so young when my parents separated that I have no memory of my father, and when it came time for me to identify his body in the morgue, twenty-five years later, I couldn't do it because I'd never seen him. I grew up in my grandparents' house—a somber place—huge, drafty, marvelous. I grew up surrounded by eccentric adults. I wasn't what we could call a happy child, but I did have my mother's unconditional love, and vast intellectual freedom. I learned to read when I was very young, and books were my companions throughout my childhood. There were so many in that house that you couldn't count them, organize them, or keep them clean. And I had access to them all, so I can't say which ones influenced me the most. My head is full of written words, authors, stories, characters, everything all mixed up together.

MGP: What kind of relationship do you have with your family now, particularly with your mother?

IA: My mother was the most important person in my childhood, and she has been the most important person in my life. She's my friend, my sister, my companion. We laugh at the same things; we cry together; we tell each other secrets and share the fun of writing novels. She made a very strong impression on me. Her love has always nourished me, and I'm sure I wouldn't be who I am now without having had such an extraordinary relationship with her.

MGP: Was your grandmother very special to you?

IA: Yes. My grandmother also occupies a special place. She was the guardian angel of my childhood and still watches over me, even though she died thirty-five years ago. She was adorable, a refined spirit, a complete stranger to anything vulgar; she was delightful, with a wonderful sense of humor and a love of truth and justice that turned her into a hurricane when it came time to defend those principles. She died when I was very young, but she stayed with me. She never abandoned me. She is Clara del Valle in *La casa de los espíritus* [*The House of the Spirits*].

MGP: Are there certain childhood memories that have stayed with you and have colored your life in some special way?

IA: One of my most vivid memories is of my grandparents' cellar, where I used to read by candlelight, dream of magic castles, dress up like a ghost, invent black masses, build forts out of an entire series of books that one of my uncles wrote about India, and then fall asleep among the spiders and mice. That dark, damp cellar was full of discarded objects, broken furniture, worn-out things, and ghosts. Time was suspended down there, trapped in a bubble. A cavernous silence reigned, and even my most tentative sigh sounded as strong as a gale. It was a beautiful world where the imagination knew no limits.

MGP: What part do your husband and children play in your life?

IA: My husband's name is Miguel Frías. We met when he was nineteen and I was fifteen; we were complete children, absolutely truthful, with no secrets. We swore eternal love to each other with the certainty of those who know nothing of life. We've always been together, and it hasn't always been easy. We've fought and made up, we've destroyed and rebuilt, we've killed illusions and given life to children. We're growing old together. He gives me support, loyalty, love, confidence, tenderness, and freedom. I make him laugh.

MGP: By 1985, you had published two titles. The first, *La casa de los espíritus,* has been through seventeen printings in Spanish and has been translated into almost every language in Western Europe. The second, *De amor y de sombra* [*Of Love and Shadows*], has already had five printings in Spanish. So the name of Isabel Allende has become synonymous with tremendous success in Latin American literature. Also, you probably are the first Latin American woman writer who has become a best-selling author overnight. These two facts lead me to inquire about the beginning of your literary vocation. At what point did you start thinking about becoming a writer?

IA: The truth is that I'm a journalist and I've always worked as a journalist. I never had a literary vocation until I left Chile, my country. I think that the desire to write flares up inside me when I feel very strongly about something. There are people who say they need an image or an event before they can start writing. I need to feel a very deep emotion. In the case of *La casa de los espíritus,* it was knowing that my grandfather was going to die. For many long years after I left my country, I felt a tremendous paralysis. I felt I'd lost roots, that I'd lost my native land, that I'd lost my whole world. My friends were scattered: many had disappeared, many others were dead. One day I got a phone call from Chile saying that my grandfather, who was going to be a hundred, was very tired and had decided to die. He had stopped eating and drinking, and he sat in his chair to wait for death. At that moment I wanted so badly to write and tell him that he was never going to die, that somehow he would always be present in my life, because he had a theory that death didn't exist, only forgetfulness did. He believed that if you can keep people in your memory, they will live forever. That's what he did with my grandmother. So I began to write him a long letter, elaborated from the awful thought that he was going to die.

MGP: Do you see a close relationship between your journalism and your literary creativity? Do you think that being a journalist helped prepare you to write these two novels?

IA: People say that all journalists want to be writers and all writers have been journalists. I think journalism is important, because, first of all, it teaches you to control language, which is your basic tool, and second, because it is a form of communication. I think communicating is terribly important for a writer, because a book begins to exist only when another person picks it up. Before that it's only an object, some pieces of paper glued together that become a book only after someone else picks it up. That's why journalism is so important—because it forces you, in very little time and usually in very little space, to grab your reader and not let her go, so that she becomes involved with whatever news you have to offer. It's good training for writing literature. I think theater helped me a lot, too. I'd worked on four shows in Chile. I don't like to claim I'm a playwright, because it seems an exercise in vanity. Theater is really something you create as a team. At least that's how I did it, and it was a fantastic learning experience that later helped me with character development.

MGP: When were you involved in theater?

IA: From 1970 to 1975.

MGP: In other words, you were doing journalism and theater at the same time. What kind of journalism were you involved with?

IA: Every kind, except politics and sports. From horoscopes to advice to the lovelorn, features, interviews, even recipes.

MGP: Working in both journalism and literature is very common, especially among Latin American writers, not only in order to communicate, but also as a way of earning a living. In what way, specifically regarding the use of language, do you consider that your journalistic career has contributed to your literary formation?

IA: Well, as far as language goes, it didn't teach me much of anything, except that it refined my capacity for observation, my powers of synthesis. I think that's more important.

MGP: And when did you start out as a journalist?

IA: The truth is that I almost don't remember, because I graduated from high school when I was sixteen and started working as a journalist right away. I've always worked in journalism, so it was almost like a continuation of schoolwork. That's why I don't feel as if my work in journalism began one moment and ended the next, but rather that it's like marriage, a natural state—at least for me—because I married very young.

MGP: In spite of the fact that you're not interested in politics, politics has played a fundamental role in your life. I'm referring to the 1973 military coup that interrupted Chile's constitutional history, and, as with many others, interrupted your life in Chile as well. And you had to leave, didn't you? How and when did you leave Chile?

IA: Well, I feel that the military coup split my life in half with the blow of a hatchet, just as it split the lives of so many thousands and thousands of Chileans. In my case, I was deeply affected because my family was particularly involved. Nevertheless, I didn't leave Chile immediately after the coup, partly because I didn't understand what was going on and partly because I didn't have enough information. Even though I was a reporter and I did have access to information, at least more than other people had, we Chileans weren't used to governmental repression. We hadn't been trained for terror. We didn't know what a military coup was. We had had many years, many generations, of democracy in Chile, and it always seemed to us that these things happened in other countries, not in ours. We were very proud of that. There was a very strong civic sensibility in Chile. I, for example, had never heard the word *torture* in connection with any familiar or contemporary situation. For me, torture was part of the Inquisition, the Middle Ages—a part of history. I couldn't imagine that it could exist within our reality or could touch us; nevertheless, hours after the military coup, all the repressive apparatus was in place. They were already torturing people, already killing people. Everything was organized, and we didn't even realize it. We were waiting to hear that it had been a historical accident and that at any moment the soldiers were going to go back to their barracks and that the democratic process was going to be reinstated. Then we kept on waiting, like a lot of people, for this to happen, and meanwhile there was tremendous, tremendous poverty. Many people were persecuted, and there was a tremendous need for solidarity and mutual support. A few months went by, and then I realized that there wasn't much any single person could do. I'm not very brave, and after a few months I came to believe that any direct action would mean an enormous risk for me and for my family. I was so terrified that I began to break out in rashes. I couldn't sleep. I had asthma and a whole series of physical symptoms. One day, my husband and I finally made the decision to leave. We spread out a map of the world on the dining room table and looked at where we could go. We looked for a country that would be a democracy, where Spanish was spoken—because I'm a journalist and I needed to work in my language—and where there was work. At that time, half of Latin America was living under fascist dictatorships, so we discarded those countries. In other places it was hard to get a visa, or else it was impossible to work because of the country's economic situation. That's how we ended up in Venezuela, without knowing anything about the country, with tourist visas and twenty kilos of luggage. We left everything behind—the past, our entire lives, grandparents, friends, my country's landscape, everything. Nevertheless, we've been very lucky in Venezuela, much luckier than other exiles in other parts of the world. We were welcomed with generosity and hospitality in that warm, green country, where you can put down roots and make another home.

MGP: How do you think being in exile has affected your writing? Also, how do you see your relationship with Venezuela?

IA: Exile has had an effect on hundreds of thousands of human beings. We live in an era where masses of people come and go across a hostile planet, desolate and violent. Refugees, emigrants, exiles, deportees. We are a tragic contingent. This situation, which we became involved in through a fluke of fate, has changed our lives, but I don't have any complaints. We've been very fortunate, because we've stayed together and we were able to choose what country to go to. We live in a democracy, in a warm, green land where we feel free, where we belong, which we love like a homeland.

MGP: Did the name Allende help you when you left, or rather was it a burden?

IA: Well, my name is always a problem, in Chile as well as in airports. When I have to cross a border and show my passport, there are always some officials who call others over and look through some thick books to see if I'm in any of them. On the other hand, I'm very proud of the name I bear, and I think it's helped open the hearts of many people to me. I think of the name of Salvador Allende as a banner and not a stigma.

MGP: Then, as you said earlier, your literary vocation, triggered by politics, has come alive in exile. You mentioned earlier that your literary vocation was triggered by a family situation. You said that it started in the form of a letter addressed to your grandfather. How does a letter grow into a five hundred–page novel? Is there anything else you can tell me about this phase in the evolution of your writing career?

IA: I've always needed to write because I've always been writing—journalism or theater or something. I've always been connected to the written word. When I began to write *La casa de los espíritus,* I wasn't thinking about composing a novel, just a letter, and when the letter got to be five hundred pages long, my husband suggested it would be better to think of it as a novel. That's how the idea gradually came to be a book, but I had had no experience with literature. I didn't have any publishing contacts. I didn't know anything about it, and the only thing I could think of was to take those five hundred pages, tie them together with a string, and take them to publishers whose addresses I found in the yellow pages. But no one wanted to read it. No one was interested. They told me it was too long, and they suggested a lot of cuts—in some cases, about two hundred pages' worth. It seemed a pity to me to cut it, because I thought if it hadn't all been important I wouldn't have written all those pages in the first place. Coincidentally, I was reading José Donoso's *El jardín de al lado* [The garden next door], in which one of the evil characters in the novel is a literary agent. Someone told me that such a character really existed: her name was Carmen Balcells, she worked in Barcelona, and she was responsible for getting the Latin American literary boom off the ground. I, who have always been daring, thought, why shouldn't I get lucky? I went to the post office to mail my manuscript to Carmen Balcells. Curiously enough, the postal officials told me that same thing the publishing houses had: "This is very thick. Cut it in half, and we'll put it in two envelopes because you can't send more than one kilo by air mail." So I put it in two separate envelopes and sent it to Spain. Of course, my cover letter was in the first envelope, and the first envelope got lost. The second envelope got there. And in spite of that mix-up, or maybe because of it, Carmen Balcells agreed to be my agent. Six months later, the book was published in Spain. And from then on, it has been like the Star of Bethlehem was shining on the book. I've been extremely lucky.

MGP: Truly. You say it was a letter to your grandfather, but it's a five hundred–page novel, so you must have spent some time planning that letter. How did that letter become the magnificent narrative of *La casa de los espíritus*?

IA: It began like a letter, but along the way I began to forget it was a letter. My passions, my obsessions, my dreams, and all those other characters I stole from other families, other lives, started getting into it. I think that somehow I wanted to tell the story of my country. I wanted to describe what had happened. It was a kind of therapy for me, a way of drawing out all the sadness that had built up inside, of trying to share the painful experience that I didn't go through but so many other Chileans did: the experience of a military coup, of all those years of repression. When I began to feel it as a book, I also visualized it as a mural, an enormous tapestry, a canvas on which I was going to embroider a very complicated story with many characters, a story that shifts through time and begins to change color as it gets closer to the present. It's a tapestry that, in a far-off time, say at the turn of the century, has that smoky sepia color of antiques, of old things, of things told. And as we get closer to the present, the colors grow brighter and brighter, until they acquire the almost brutal colors of the reality of Alba, the present-day narrator of the story. That's the way I saw it, like a very complex mural where I knew the order but had a hard time explaining it.

✣ ✣ ✣

Around the age of eighteen, Alba left childhood behind for good. At the exact moment when she felt like a woman, she locked herself in her old room, which still held the mural she had started so many years before. Next she rummaged through her paint jars until she found a little red and a little white that were still fresh. Then she carefully mixed them together and painted a large pink heart in the last empty space on the wall. She was in love. Afterward she threw her paints and brushes into the trash and sat down to contemplate her drawings, which is to say, the history of her joys and sorrows. She decided that the balance had been happy and with a sigh said goodbye to the first stage of her life [*From* La casa de los espíritus].

✣ ✣ ✣

Sometimes some student will tell me that the novel has a spiral structure, because it moves forward in a series of circles, one always a little ahead of the other. I think that's a nice way to read the novel, but I don't see it that way. I see it as a gigantic tapestry in which everything is all mixed together and some things are topsy-turvy. On the other hand, the second book, *De amor y de sombra*, reminds me of a bicycle wheel, and that's how I saw it from the beginning. There is a central event, which is the hub, and all the spokes converging on it are the characters, the situations, all the parts of the narrative.

MGP: In *La casa de los espíritus* you use the letter-chronicle whose writers are all female. As each one of the women writes in those continuing diaries, each starts to redeem herself, each begins to give a perspective of history and of life at the same time, of fiction and of reality. Besides, the novel begins and ends in the same way, with the same words, right? That's why some people say it has a spiral structure.

IA: Or that it's a circle.

MGP: What led you to choose the color white as a link in a chain of the name of all the women in the Trueba family: Nivea, Clara, Blanca, and Alba?

IA: I wanted to symbolize a state of purity. Not the purity that means virginity, normally assigned to women, but the purity of facing the world with new eyes, free from contamination, without prejudice, open and tolerant, having a soul capable of being moved by the world's colors. That's why the women's names are colorless, because the color white includes all the other colors. And that's what I wanted to symbolize. On the other hand, every one of those names, even though they're synonyms, still has its own meaning, the significance it's built up and shared, all that it has lived, and it stands out in a new world, in a new dawn.

MGP: Keeping diaries has been a very traditional way for women to express themselves. Did you choose that writing technique because this was a novel about women?

IA: No. And if I'd known it was a feminine technique, I wouldn't have used it.

MGP: Why not?

IA: Because I don't think literature has any gender, and I don't think it's necessary to come up with a plan to write like a woman, because that seems like a kind of awkward self-segregation to me. I think you have to write as well as possible, and you have to write like an authentic person as much as possible, like an open human being, tolerant and educated. And those qualities are independent of gender. If people pick up any one of my books and don't see my name on the cover, they have no reason to assume that a woman or a man wrote that book. They could say whether or not they liked it, but they don't necessarily have to guess my sex.

MGP: Would you agree that *La casa de los espíritus* is about women and that it is, in many aspects, a feminine novel?

IA: It's a novel where the main character, the spinal column of the novel, is a man, a patriarch, and throughout the narrative frame of the story he's surrounded by a succession of women. In some way, the women narrators are the voice of emotion, the voice of the subjective, the voice of the most human, the voice of the soul, that is telling the underlying story, not the story everyone can see. Esteban Trueba speaks of life and the world, and he tells the story from an intellectual, rational point of view; he represents the voice from the outside, always trying to construct the world. The women, on the contrary, are trying to understand the world. They're trying to seize it and participate in it, and they have another vision of the world. And, yes, they're the narrators, all right, but I don't feel that means I write like a woman. Rather it may mean that I express a feminine point of view about life. To be sure, I'm a woman and I have to have a feminine point of view.

MGP: There is an important debate over whether it is possible to claim that there's a feminine way of writing that is different from a masculine way of writing. Do you think it's possible to distinguish these two types of creative writing?

IA: I think there's a feminine way of feeling and a masculine way of feeling, but these differences fade more and more as time goes by. Perhaps at the turn of the century, when Esteban Trueba came to life, along with Clara del Valle, the roles were very clearly defined. It's not like that today, fortunately, and my children and my nieces and future grandchildren will be less and less aware of that barrier. And each one of us will feel more like a human being and less in agreement with a role previously established by gender.

MGP: It's precisely the distinction you've just made, in discussing the character of Esteban Trueba, where you've outlined the man of action, the man-builder of the world, a world of his particular design. He's the doer. He turns nothing into something. He puts the world together and starts to populate it. He builds a farm, he builds a town, and he builds a world emanating from that huge house in the city. But, as you said, it's the women who besides recording the intimate history of the family (precisely the mark of a feminine world) also begin to provide a vision of inner space, to furnish that world with particular forms that stem from the masculine ambition to shape the universe. Women try to fill in the gaps in the world. They furnish it with details, with intimacy, with family love. That is, as they leave their own particular mark, they humanize it. In that sense, we could say that *La casa de los espíritus* is a feminine novel insofar as it gives a voice to that part of the world that doesn't have a voice.

IA: But many people do that, not only women. Men do it too. Just recently, a critic said I would never truly become a writer of worth until I was capable of creating a masculine character with as much strength as the feminine characters I created, until then I wouldn't have demonstrated that much craftsmanship. I wonder how many male writers have good female characters. Very few. And that doesn't mean that they write badly or that they aren't recognized as writers. Perhaps their masculine characters are much stronger because they're men themselves and that's how they feel. But that doesn't count for or against their quality as writers, their literary quality. That's what I'm trying to say: I don't want my worth as a writer to be decided from a female point of view or a male point of view. It's possible that my female characters are stronger or that I have a feminine point of view. But literature, language, structure, and the final product that a book is, should be accepted for its intrinsic value, for its literary quality. I'm not asking for any concessions because I'm a woman, nor do I permit superfluous demands to be made of me because I'm a woman.

MGP: Precisely. I don't think it's about making or not making concessions; rather, it's about differentiating a way of being and existing in a woman's world that until recently had not been taken into account or, better yet, acknowledged. Now, with women writers of your caliber who are imagining and creating worlds from the female perspective, who elaborate fictional worlds from another point of view, readers will discover worlds that speak to the feminine experience. That's an important distinction that engenders different ways of working with language. The comment that critic—a man—made to you comes from a phallocentric way of looking at the world that is rejected within a feminist perspective. In any case, feminine literature seems to be engaged in restructuring, revising, rethinking all these ideas. How did you develop the dominating theme of your second novel?

IA: The origin of *De amor y de sombra* goes back to a newspaper story that moved me very deeply. I extracted from it a case, exemplary of so many that have happened and keep happening in Latin America: people who disappear and die, graves that, when opened, are found to contain dozens of corpses. This story wasn't very different from the others, but it made a big impact on me. In an abandoned mine, they found five corpses from the same family: a father and his four children. When I read that, I immediately put myself in the mother's place and felt an emotion so intense, so strong, that it haunted me for a long time. For two years I tried to exorcise that image, that sorrow, through writing. Although Chile is never mentioned, the story comes from a highly publicized incident that occurred in 1978 in the Lonquén mine, an abandoned mine shaft fifty kilometers outside of Santiago. And it happened just as my book describes it. Although segments of the story have been fictionalized, it really happened in just that way. There are even parts in the book that are almost exact copies of the court records or taken from testimony presented at the trial. That's how the novel grew, out of a newspaper story and some strong emotions I felt. Afterward came the literary elaboration, shall we say, when I combined characters and actions together in time. *De amor y de sombra* is an example of the way I always work: I take something from real life, something from the papers, things I know, interviews I do, and I add fiction to it. I put things together that aren't usually related. In this case, Evangelina Ranquileo is a real person I wrote about when I was a journalist a long time ago in Chile, but she doesn't have anything to do with what happened in Lonquén. I simply put these elements together, though they don't go together in real life.

✣ ✣ ✣

Isolated from the Leals' grief, Irene Beltrán borrowed her mother's automobile and set out alone for Los Riscos, determined to find Evangelina on her own. She had promised Digna that she would help her in her search, and she did not want to give the impression that she had spoken lightly. Her first stop was the Ranquileo home.

"Don't keep looking, señorita. The earth has swallowed them up," the mother said, with the resignation of one who has endured many afflictions. But Irene was prepared, if necessary, to move heaven and earth to find the girl. Later, looking back on those days, she asked herself what had propelled her into the world of shadows. She had suspected from the beginning that she held the end of a long thread in her hands that when tugged would unravel an unending snarl of horrors. Intuitively, she knew that Evangelina, the Saint of the Dubious Miracles, was the borderline between her orderly world and the dark region never explored until now. Irene concluded that it was not only her natural and professional curiosity that had driven her forward, but something akin to vertigo. She had peered into a bottomless well and had not been able to resist the temptation of the abyss [*From* De amor y de sombra].

✣ ✣ ✣

MGP: We could think of *De amor y de sombra* as a political novel, but to call a novel "political" is to run the risk of turning it into a pamphlet, an accusation. It seems to me that one of the successes of *De amor y de sombra* is that you work through—and maintain—that tone we referred to a moment ago. You succeed very well in creating a structured fiction; it may even be better structured and more elaborate than *La casa de los espíritus.* It's a world, the current world, of Chile in which all the characters—with their individual stories—eventually become united in the narrative's core. I particularly wanted to ask you about the group of characters who are members of the military: there's a sergeant, there's a lieutenant, there's a foot soldier, and there's a captain. They are sympathetically and humanely represented. The captain is developed according to the canon of the romantic hero. He's right out of a Hollywood movie, very strong and tough, very idealistic, and physically perfect. He's treated with great gentleness. How did you decide to give the military element, which is precisely what is creating the problem of oppression in Chile, such benevolent literary treatment?

IA: Well, it's very hard for me to see the world in black and white. I think there is always some shading. There are many colors in between. And every person has good points and points we could call bad, if we wanted to put an adjective to them. I'm sure Pinochet is a charming grandfather and his grandchildren adore him and maybe his friends do too. The fact that he is what he is in the eyes of most Chileans and of the world—that he represents tyranny, torture and death, and exile and prison for so many people—doesn't mean he's not a human being. And if I had to describe him in writing, I'd have to capture all the aspects of his personality. I think that people come in many different shades, and I try to see all of them. For me, it's very hard to make a character black or white, totally good or totally evil, perhaps because in real life I've never found anyone who's completely one thing. I can have more or less sympathy for one or the other, but in the end, I love them all. And after living with these characters for two years, after you begin by pulling them out of the air, when they're like ghosts haunting your brain, all out of proportion, they start taking shape as you work with them, so much so that by the end you know the sound of their voices, you know how they smell, how they look. You know everything about them. They may be closer to me than my own children. Then I have to love them. Whoever they are, I end up loving them. In *La casa de los espíritus,* I worked a lot on the character of the torturer, and, of course, I felt all the horror that any person facing someone with those characteristics would feel. But I ended up loving him because he was one of my characters. It's like a mother with a retarded child who has to love that child more than the others at times.

MGP: Irene is a character that evolves through the narrative. She seems to share some features with you, with Isabel Allende. She's a journalist, she's very decisive and clear in her activities and intentions, and she finally commits herself to her political reality and suffers the consequences of that critical position, which forces her to leave her country. Are there some autobiographical elements in Irene?

IA: No. I would like to be like Irene. You always want to be like your favorite character. I'd wanted to be like Clara and to be like Irene, but I'm not. Irene is like many, many Chilean women journalists I knew and still know, who have lived a similar destiny, and, deep down, that character is an homage to all of them. At no time am I there. The only thing that could be autobiographical in Irene is her life at the magazine where she works, which was a lot like my life at *Paula,* the magazine I worked on in Chile, but besides that, Irene is not me. Rather she's a kind of homage to my friends.

MGP: You seem to be making the same point you already made about *La casa de los espíritus,* that the autobiographical material isn't there.

IA: The only autobiographical element in *La casa de los espíritus* is the whole household: that family, those people, are like mine, but I'm not there. I'm not Alba, though many people think I am. So many people think I'm Alba that when I was invited to the Frankfurt book fair in Germany, people looked at my hair to see if it was green, and they looked at my hands to see if there was a finger missing because they wanted me to be the character, but, unfortunately, I'm not.

MGP: What relationship is there between your work and García Márquez's narratives, especially *Cien años de soledad* [*One Hundred Years of Solitude*]? It's frequently been pointed out that *La casa de los espíritus* is strongly resonant of *Cien años.*

IA: If you're talking about the family saga, I really wasn't thinking of García Márquez when I wrote *La casa de los espíritus.* Or when I turned that letter into a novel. García Márquez is very important to Latin American literature, and I think he's a very powerful influence on me. Nevertheless, I wasn't thinking about him, but rather about Henri Troyat, the French writer who left Russia after the revolution and wrote the story of the many Russian families who lived that exile in Europe, especially in France. I was thinking of Stendhal. I was thinking of our very own Latin American families. I live in a continent where the family is very important, so it seemed natural to tell the story of a country and a continent through the eyes of a family. My theory is that in my continent the state is generally my enemy. It's every single citizen's enemy. You can't hope for anything from the state. You can only hope for repression, taxes, corruption, inefficiency. Where is your protection, your security? In your family, and to the extent that you have your tribe around you, you're safe. That's why the family is so important, and that's why it's constantly present in Latin American literature, not only in *Cien años de soledad*. It's always there.

MGP: Is your intention to tell the truth through fiction?

IA: Yes. I'm not trying to get across a specific message or accuse anyone or give testimony or capture the world with what I write, but I do want to tell the truth. It seems to me that truth is important because—that's what I learned in journalism, I think, with the first story I wrote—only the truth touches people's hearts. People instinctively know the truth, and it's impossible to fool them forever. They immediately recognize truth, and so for me it's very important to touch readers, move them, bring them over to my side. And for that I can only use the truth, because tricks don't work.

MGP: Then your connection with García Márquez would be related to the narrative techniques used, together with the attempt to develop a saga that could be interpreted as a representation of the Latin American world. But I think you're different in that you adopt the position, perspective, and tone of an involved chronicler. The vision you articulate seems to start out with a very personal view of Chile, of a Chile you never name in either of the two novels but that we can see on the skin of the female narrator, the one I call the chronicler, which is very much like the tone of Neruda in *Canto general* [Canto general] or *Memorial* or *Las piedras de Chile* [The stones of Chile]. Would you say you consciously intended to create this tone in order to get closer to or, rather, not to get farther away from Chile?

IA: There I do accept direct influence. The only book on my nightstand is always a book by Neruda, and Neruda has been present in my life since I was very young. He was a friend of my grandfather's, and he visited our house many times. I saw him a few days before he died, a few days before the military coup. His funeral is in *La casa de los espíritus*, and it's a very powerful influence. Neruda taught me, I think, to value small things, to find poetry in an onion, a carrot, in conger stew [a typical Chilean soup]. It's very important in my life, that feeling of "I am." It's the relationship with the world of small things that inspires a vision of big things. It's a sensory and sensuous link with reality. That's what's most important in my writing. Whenever I get ready to write about a situation, a love scene, a scene of violence, or simply a description of a landscape, Neruda comes into my heart, and I think of the aroma, I think of the murmur, I think of the flavor—not just of what we can see, because we have a tendency to relate to the world through our eyes and forget the rest. Neruda, I think, constantly reminds me of that.

✣ ✣ ✣

The Poet was dying in his house by the sea. He had been ailing, and the recent events had exhausted his desire to go on living. Soldiers broke into his house, ransacked his snail collection, his shells, his butterflies, his bottles, the ship figureheads he has rescued from so many seas, his books, his paintings, and his unfinished poems, looking for subversive weapons and hidden Communists, until his old poet's heart began to falter. They took him to the capital, where he died four days later. The last words of this man who had sung to life were: "They're going to shoot them! They're going to shoot them!" Not one of his friends could be with him at the hour of his death; they were all outlaws, fugitives, exiles, or dead. His blue house on the hill lay half in ruins, its floor burnt and its windows broken. No one knew if it was the work of the military, as the neighbors said, or of the neighbors, as the military said. A wake was held by those few who were brave enough to attend, along with journalists from all over the world who came to cover his funeral. Senator Trueba was his ideological enemy, but he had often had him in his house and knew his poetry by heart. He appeared at the wake dressed in rigorous black, with his granddaughter Alba. Both stood watch beside the simple wooden coffin and accompanied it to the cemetery on that unfortunate morning. Alba was holding a bouquet of the first carnations of the season, as red as blood. The small cortege walked on foot, slowly, all the way to the cemetery, between two rows of soldiers who had cordoned off the streets.

People went in silence. Suddenly, someone hoarsely called out the Poet's name and in a single voice everyone replied, "Here! Now and forever!" It was as if they had opened a valve and all the pain, fear, and anger of those days had issued from their chests and rolled onto the street, rising in a terrible shout to the thick black clouds above. Another shouted, "Compañero President!" and everyone answered in a single wail, the way men grieve: "Here! Now and forever!" The Poet's funeral had turned into the symbolic burial of freedom [From La casa de los espíritus].

✣ ✣ ✣

MGP: How did you react to the tremendous success of *La casa de los espíritus*?

IA: No one thought that *La casa de los espíritus* would be as successful as it was: not my family, not my editors, not even me. The manuscript was appalling: a book by an unknown journalist, too long and with a complex theme. It's not at all strange that it got rejected several times. When I finished writing it, my children joked that we'd have to publish it ourselves and sell every copy in bus stations and coffee shops. What made readers receive it with such generosity? It's really a mystery. Maybe a guardian angel is watching over me, or else certain books have a life of their own.

MGP: How did you learn to handle the tremendous popularity this book has brought you?

IA: I don't handle my "tremendous popularity." Instead, I'm isolated in a house high on a hill. I write in a tiny room full of books, photos, toys, and plants. I'm very selective about my friendships. I spend a lot of time with my family, and I only assume the role of writer when I travel.

MGP: How do you react when critics put you beside our best writers? What do you have to say to novelists of your generation and to the ones who'll come after you?

IA: When critics put me among good writers, I feel a great responsibility, which I assume with pleasure and pride. I can be the voice of the many who are silent. I can convey the truth of this magnificent, tortured Latin American continent. I have nothing to say to the women novelists of my generation. That would be unforgivably pretentious. I want to hear them and learn from them.

MGP: Do you realize you're the first woman who has succeeded in entering the publishing market on such a grand scale?

IA: Maybe I'm one of the first Latin American women to do it, but in Europe and the United States women occupy almost the same place as men do in literature. For Third World women, it's difficult, but we're getting there. We need to overcome a lot of prejudice: critics ignore us; editors aren't interested in our work; college professors don't study us. Add to that cultural backwardness, social pressures, hard labor, poverty, bearing children, housework, and submission to men, and you can see it requires superhuman talent and assertiveness to stand out in any field, especially in the arts.

MGP: When and how did your first novel appear in Chile?

IA: My first novel appeared in Chile as soon as it was published, underground at first and then openly. At first, people photocopied it, and there were long lists of people interested in reading each photocopied edition. The books that crossed the border without covers or hidden in diaper bags went from hand to hand, from house to house. They served as a topic of discussion and told a generation of children the story that the dictatorship had tried to erase from memory. I received hundreds of letters from Chile, all of them very moving. I realized I'm not far away, that I live in my homeland still and no one can take it away from me. I have it with me. In the middle of 1983, book censorship was suspended in Chile because the dictatorship wanted to improve its image. Now you can buy—although they're very expensive—the books that were forbidden before, and they are, of course, very sought after. It's just like what happened with pornography—prohibiting it was enough to arouse everyone's curiosity.

MGP: How was your second novel, *De amor y de sombra,* received in Chile? Can you buy it there?

IA: My second novel got a terrific reception from the Chilean public, bad reviews from *El Mercurio,* silence from the official media, and excellent reviews from professors, intellectuals, and literary journals. They say it's more well written than the first one, better structured, a more mature book. The theme is painful in Chile, and no one is indifferent to it. Some people feel solidarity, and others deny it happened.

MGP: And the reception in general?

IA: They've told me that people remember me in Chile and hold me in high esteem. My name isn't completely unknown, but I haven't been able to find out for myself because I haven't gone back.

MGP: What has the reaction been in non-Spanish-speaking countries?

IA: I've been lucky with all my translations. The reaction has always been very good. In Norway, they sold forty thousand copies in a few weeks, and that's a country with four million people. In Germany I was at the top of the best-seller list for almost a year. In France the Club du Livre alone published 350,000 copies. It seems vain to talk about all this, but that's how it's been. And I don't look at it as a personal success but as more recognition for Latin American literature. Our continent has considerably more to say, we've hardly begun to talk, to write.

MGP: To what do you attribute the universal success of your two novels?

IA: I've thought a lot about why my novels have been so successful, without discovering the formula. Someone told me I write about feelings, values, and emotions that are common to all human beings at any point in history. Love, hate, justice, violence, the search for truth, for passions and obsessions concern everyone.

MGP: Taking up the theme of feminism again, what do you think of the feminist movement? Do you support it or oppose it?

IA: I'm a feminist, of course; no woman who stops for an instant to think about her future cannot be one. But I don't look at the women's liberation movement as a fight against men, a battle to replace machismo with feminism. Not at all. I believe it's a war both men and women are waging to build a more just and free society. That's how the world is conceived. We are all victims; we are all prisoners. Very few have the opportunity to grow, to love, and to develop creativity. We have mutilated each other, all of us. Machismo hasn't made men happy either, and though we women are the main victims, the man's role is also very hard—to be the provider, to be superior, to always be strong, not to cry. Poor creatures, living dissociated from their own nature, from their emotions, estranged from tenderness, relating to the world and to women through power, possessiveness, domination. What a bore! What a waste!

I'm not opposed to women organizing themselves in liberation movements. On the contrary, I believe it's the only way to get what we ask for. I don't belong to any such groups because I'm incapable of accepting group discipline. That's why I don't belong to any churches, political parties, or clubs.

MGP: Is feminism important in Venezuela? Are there feminist groups there?

IA: Laws in Venezuela favor women more than laws in other parts of the continent. Half of the students at the Universidad Central are women. Women hold important posts in the country's administration, in business, in science, and in the shaping of national culture. Of course, I'm talking about women who've had access to education. Working-class women, peasants, and poor women live in the same backward conditions as in any other Latin American country. Venezuelan women are strapping specimens, tremendous females. They stride like goddesses—their breasts and hips swaying like flags—proud of their bodies, ready to win any beauty contest. This is a very macho country, but I've seen the freest, most shrewd, most stable women here. It's as if deep down they make fun of those rules that men try to impose on them; they shake them off with a swish of the hips and a flick of the eyelashes. There are a few small feminist groups, and they publish a small feminist journal. Although I don't see a growing, important liberation movement, I perceive that women are gaining ground every day. At any rate, we're very far from equality.

MGP: What kind of journalism do you do in Caracas? Are you still working as a reporter or are you devoting yourself exclusively to creative writing?

IA: Until recently I was working at the Caracas daily *El Nacional*, but I had to leave because I travel too much and my new commitments won't let me keep it up. I only work in literature—if you can call that work.

MGP: How do you view your future as a writer?

IA: My future as a writer? I don't think about it. I keep putting one word after another, and so I do a little every day.

MGP: Do you know any Latin American writers personally? How have they reacted to your work? Have you met García Márquez?

IA: I know Ernesto Sábato, Mario Vargas Llosa, Pepe Donoso, and others. Antonio Skármeta is a friend of mine, a tremendous man, full of talent and generosity, who praises my work and stimulates me, which is rare in the world of literature where people are fairly egocentric. I don't know García Márquez. I think I'd be overcome if I could shake his hand someday.

MGP: Do you think it's important to integrate yourself into this group of writers?

IA: It's important for Latin American writers to be in contact with each other, to be involved with each other, to help each other, and also to help young writers who are struggling to write and get published. All of us have a very important task: we have to tell the story of our continent, be a common voice, put into words the tragedy and the dreams of our people who have been tortured and forced to submit. If we are united, if we work along the same lines, we can contribute to building a different world.

MGP: For whom do you write?

IA: I write for *a* reader. I always try to tell the story to *one* person. I don't imagine who the person is, but I always try to make the tone I'm going to use as intimate as possible. I feel like one of those African storytellers who go from village to village and sit in the middle of the village and the townspeople sit around him and he tells the stories and the news he brings from other places. And then the people give him a chicken or a tomato so he'll add the news of that village to his repertoire, and then he'll go to another village and will tell the same story plus the news he has of that last village. And that's how you find out that so-and-so died, that so-and-so got married. You find out that there was a war; you find out the news.

MGP: Like a troubadour?

IA: Like a troubadour . . . That's how I think of myself. That's how I feel. I want to go from village to village, from person to person, from town to town telling about my country, telling about my continent, getting across our truth—that accumulated suffering and that marvelous expression of life that is Latin America. And that's what I want to tell. To Latin Americans and everyone.

MGP: And do you have a particular purpose in your literary activity? Why do you write?

IA: Because it's like celebrating something! I love it. It's a lot of fun. I like it as much as making love—that's why I write. And if it weren't for that, I wouldn't do it because it's very hard work.

MGP: What kind of project are you working on now?

IA: Right now, my project is to go on writing. I'm immersed in another novel, but I have to put up with a lot of interruptions. And every day I find it more difficult to find the peace and quiet to do it. Sometimes I miss the cellar in my grandparents' house.

Note: Since the date of this interview, Isabel Allende has divorced and remarried. She is now living in the United States and has published a new novel, *Eva Luna,* and a collection of short stories, *The Stories of Eva Luna.*

KPL.

✣ ✣ ✣

Albalucía Angel

✣ ✣ ✣

MGP: To begin this conversation, I'd like to ask you about the place where you grew up. What part of Colombia are you from?

AA: I was born in Pereira, a small city my grandparents founded. It was small then, and it's still small, even though in Colombia it's considered the fifth-largest city. It's coffee country as well as the best place to grow marijuana, because coffee and marijuana require the same climate. It's also the best place for refining cocaine. Today they make it all seem mysterious and frightening, but when I was growing up, there was no mystery surrounding these weeds. That's Pereira.

MGP: Was there marijuana in Pereira when you were a little girl?

AA: Always. Ever since I can remember, people talked about *marihuaneros* [marijuana smokers].

MGP: Is it part of Pereira's tradition?

AA: Yes. Working-class people have always smoked marijuana in my country, but what's happening now is that it's all on a much larger scale. It's become something chic, and the middle class has picked it up. Before, there was no mafia or trafficking. It was just an everyday activity.

MGP: So it's part of the culture, as coca leaves are in Bolivia or Peru. How would you describe Pereira's character?

AA: It has a strong personality. For example, it has a nude statue of Bolívar in the center of Plaza de Bolívar.

MGP: How did that come about?

AA: The people of Pereira are very idiosyncratic. No city that had anything to do with Bolívar would take that statue, which was done by Rodrigo Arenas Betancur, a Colombian sculptor who lived in Mexico. He'd offered it to Bolivia, Peru, Venezuela, and Colombia, and they all turned it down. The people of Pereira thought it was wonderful.

MGP: When did he make it?

AA: Some twenty years ago. I'm telling you about this to give you an example of the desacralizing attitude people have in Pereira. Besides its idiosyncrasies, it seems symptomatic of Pereira that it happens to be a center for Black Masses. There are temples where very important Black Masses take place.

MGP: Where did the Black Masses come from?

AA: From sorcerers.

MGP: Is it an Indian practice connected to ancient rituals?

AA: No. It's neither indigenous nor voodoo. They're performed by some kind of secret Masonic society. The initiates tend to be very important people. It's a kind of Black Masonry in which the participants are high-level politicians; that is, it's not a game. And the context is Pereira, which has produced some of the most peculiar personalities in our political folklore.

MGP: You said before that someone in your family founded the city of Pereira. How did that happen?

AA: My grandfather founded it along with his four young sons and some other people. That makes ten people at the beginning, including him and his sons.

MGP: Where did they come from?

AA: From Sonsón, Antioquia. We call ourselves *paisas* [people from the Province of Antioquia]. Pereira hardly changed until twenty years ago. It can be considered a very concentrated place. My maternal uncle called it "Viboral," a sort of Peyton Place.

MGP: What kind of cultural life is there in Pereira? Is it very restricted and provincial?

AA: It's very classist, terribly provincial but bold at the same time. It was the first and only city in Colombia to have built its airport through a community effort. It also built an Olympic villa with the same kind of spirit of solidarity and civic pride, something unusual in Latin America.

MGP: Culturally, how would you characterize Pereira?

AA: Daring and headlong. The city built a university out of nothing, the Universidad Tecnológica. It also built the Casa de la Cultura y del Arte, in which I participated when I was young, although today it seems pretty run-down. I think it has deteriorated because artistic people are now categorized as either unemployed or Communists.

MGP: What was it like to grow up in Pereira? What do you remember of that world?

AA: I had a very complex childhood. I remember most vividly my childhood in the mountains, on my family's farm. I used to spend entire days taming wild horses. The rest of the time, I was in a Catholic school, but that was in another childhood, a bourgeois childhood, where I was cared for and controlled, the same way all girls in my generation were. That's why only my wild childhood interests me.

MGP: Did you live in a boarding school?

AA: No. My family lived very close to the school. Every morning at seven, we'd have classes taught by Swiss Franciscan nuns who spoke Spanish very badly. My mother had studied with them in a different city, so she had decided that I should go to their school, too.

MGP: Did you learn any French or German?

AA: No. In spite of how bad their Spanish was, they still taught in Spanish. That was my formal education in a very provincial Colombian village. I was educated with a Swiss view of the world. They taught us ways of doing things that were very strange for girls from Pereira. They were very rigid.

MGP: What kind of relationship did you have with your mother and with the rest of your family?

AA: Well, I turned out contrary to their expectations, but there was no way to remedy it. My mother died seven years ago, and my last novel, *Misiá señora* [Madam lady] was dedicated to her memory.

She aroused so many conflicts in me: love, disaffection, passions, problems that couldn't be solved. It wasn't my mother who raised me, but my father's mother, who lived across the street from us when I was small. I had a fierce admiration for this woman. She raised me until I was seven, together with a daughter who still wasn't married and six other unmarried sons. I was the first granddaughter, so I was pampered to death. My mother had a very hard time controlling me. At a time when she was trying to instill rigid principles in me—of course she wanted me to be well-behaved—I emerged utterly disheveled from my grandmother's house, a place that was all love and learning.

MGP: Why did your grandmother fascinate you?

AA: My grandmother was a very wise woman, as all grandmothers are. She was Catholic and conservative to the day she died, while my grandfather stayed morally liberal and politically conservative. They supported themselves by my grandfather's work as a lawyer, a profession that he practiced almost for free because his clients would pay in kind, with tomatoes or eggs and chickens. That's how my grandmother raised seven children.

MGP: I thought they were landowners.

AA: No, they weren't. The Angel family was relatively poor but strong. My grandmother was devoted to the Holy Virgin and the Sacred Heart. She constantly told me stories about them and gave me a copy of the Bible. To increase my enthusiasm, she'd give me ten *centavos* for every page I read.

MGP: Was there a conflict between your parents and your grandparents over how to raise you then?

AA: Yes, but they only realized it later, when there was no way to fix it, because I'd already grown up. My grandmother had told me her Bible stories and had given me, without really knowing what it was, a copy of the adult version of *Las mil y una noches* [*The Thousand and One Nights*]. As far as my mother was concerned, she didn't want me to read. During my childhood, we moved from house to house; we were always changing our surroundings. It was very disturbing to move from one street to another, because each move brought about a complete change. But that's how we lived until I was thirteen. Finally, after I'd prayed very hard to St. Jude, my mother got a house of her own, a magnificent house that is in the family to this day. Once we got the house, my grandmother was too far away for me to go see her as often, but my relationship with her never changed. She was a very tolerant woman. My mother called her Policarpa, which was the name of a great Colombian heroine. She never complained and always laughed at everything. She had a wonderful sense of humor. When she was eighty-four and it came time for her to die, she didn't care. She taught me that life was like a sharp-edged sword, good for clearing the underbrush without having to kill anyone. A woman of remarkable character, much the way I imagine St. Teresa of Avila was. I don't know if that quality was passed down to me, but I would like very much to be a reflection of her smile. Her wisdom expressed itself in her sayings, in her way of speaking, her verbal richness, which is perhaps where she remains with me, in my writing. Gabriel García Márquez says that he writes the way his grandmother used to talk, and I share the same view.

MGP: Where do you think the richness of language and metaphoric wit that so characterizes Colombian literature comes from?

AA: In my case, it's one of the traits of our region. Almost all of the wordplay comes from Antioquia. There we can't say a simple sentence, because we have to keep connecting one word, one metaphor, onto another.

MGP: What role did your maternal grandmother play in your life?

AA: She was like a Quimbaya princess. [Quimbaya Indians are one of the native Andean tribes known for their work in goldsmithing, sculpture, and ceramics.] She was a very beautiful and mysterious woman who always lived alone, a true Virgo. When I was much older, I discovered that she, unlike the rest of my family, enjoyed reading. I used to buy storybooks with my school allowance because my mother wouldn't buy them for me. She used to say my eyes would give out. I used my allowance to buy *Peneca, Billiken,* and *Leoplán* [children's magazines published in Argentina]. Then I discovered Emilio Salgari's novels, which I bought from a Turkish barber, who was the only bookseller in Pereira. There wasn't a bookstore in town until I was fifteen years old.

MGP: That's being considerably anti-intellectual.

AA: Absolutely. When I was fifteen or sixteen, I found out that my mother's mother read, a major discovery for me. She was a very distant woman, not really of this world. A very private person. When she was fourteen, her family married her off to a cousin who was much older than she was, who already had nine children from a previous marriage. Then the two of them had another nine, so when she became a widow, she was faced with having to raise eighteen children. She shut herself up in her house and refused to raise the stepchildren, who, besides being stepchildren, were older than she was. Her husband was the man who founded Pereira: Don Pacho Marulanda. She lived in her house by herself, and she was the first person I'd ever seen who had male servants. She never had female servants, because she said they would look out the windows all day and try to snare boyfriends. The servants waxed the floors, and we were forbidden to walk on them afterward. She was a very wealthy and powerful woman. This part of the family owned most of the property in town. When she was finally disinherited by her stepchildren, she lived off her investments, all alone with her servants, and managed the family money.

✣ ✣ ✣

Don Valeriano became the master. He had eighteen sons and built a two-story house with ten bedrooms, three parlors, a family room, a sewing room, two baths, a kitchen, and a huge stable and carriage house, where he kept Prince, Comet, and Mouse, his three favorite thoroughbreds. He ordered mirrors from Vienna and crystal from Bohemia; he had the bedrooms done in greenish gray. The carpets were brought from Persia, and he had two chandeliers made of Murano crystal for the parlor where he'd put a grand piano, which was opened only when the mayor or Don Tico Morales, the town musician, was invited. He was the owner of the Alsace and Lorraine, of the Quimbaya, and the Cofre and La Honda ranches, where they grew corn, coffee, sugar cane, plantains, bananas, rice, cacao, and all kinds of fruit, and could rely on some thirty thousand acres of land good for pasture. But never did he flaunt his wealth. He walked barefoot as he always had because those modern boots everyone wore always bothered him—They choke my feet! What more uncomfortable thing could be invented?—and as a good Christian, he distributed goods among the widows and the poor [*From* Estaba la pájara pinta sentada en el verde limón].

✣ ✣ ✣

MGP: She must have been a veritable matriarch.

AA: Her daughters had a tremendous amount of respect for her, and they wouldn't let us come visit. All we could do was say hello through the door. I got to know her little by little when she went to spend some time on my aunt's *finca,* which was near ours. She would discuss very serious topics, and she would talk politics with the men, something women didn't do in those days. She had an exquisite vocabulary and formidable ideas. She was the only intellectual in a family of anti-intellectuals. She had lived in Baltimore for a while and was considered a little eccentric when she came back because she spoke English and because her younger daughter drove a car (when there were only four cars in the whole town). When I was sixteen, I dared to show up at her house one day, and she gave me a book. That was when I saw her library for the first time. She gave me a biography of Marie Curie. I then discovered that there were women scientists, and the world began to open up for me. At that time, I was reading Rocambole, Salgari, Agatha Christie, Tarzan, and Delly.

MGP: You said there was no place in town to buy books. Where did the books you'd been reading come from?

AA: I used to go to the barber's shop where the barber let me exchange books. I would hoard books at the ranch, which was why it was so important for me to go there. It was where I could keep my secrets. When my father sold the ranch without telling anyone, my books got sold along with it. Later in Barranquilla, I read more important books like *Madame Bovary* and Freud's *Three Essays on the Theory of Sexuality. Wuthering Heights* was the only book I ever saw my mother read. I took it away from her while she was sleeping so I could read it, too.

MGP: Did you ever talk to your mother about what you were reading?

AA: No. We only talked about trivial things, like clothes or social activities, which didn't interest me very much.

MGP: Weren't you interested in having a social life?

AA: No, because I'd always been the ugly duckling, and I kept on being the ugly duckling for my mother and for everyone else, too. I was more interested in sports. I was a very good student but only earned one degree, a diploma from a business-oriented high school. My father didn't think it was important for me to go to the university. He wanted me just to take a few business courses so I could manage his business. That was his plan, and when I was sixteen he did have me run his business. I was in charge of twenty employees and kept the books. That lasted three years.

MGP: A clear sign your father thought you were capable.

AA: He thought of me as a son. Pereira bored me to tears, though, and one day I accepted an invitation from one of my uncles to go to Barranquilla for Carnival. There I discovered Colombia's Caribbean world, and that's how I made it part of my adolescence. I lived next to the sea. It was truly an experience of independence. Once my parents realized what was happening, it was already too late. When I was only nineteen, I surprised them by going to Bogotá on my own. There I enrolled in the School of Philosophy and Letters of the University of the Andes, which caused an incredible uproar. My father hinted that he'd get the police to take me back to Pereira, because I was underage and parents have the privilege of *patria potestas.* At first, one of my women friends, who was very important politically, defended my decision and took me under her wing, and my family let me stay for a year, but then one of my aunts, along with some other small-minded people, accused me of living a Bohemian life. They thought they were losing me, because I'd started singing at parties given by people my family didn't know. This time, my father got serious, threatened me with the famous *patria potestas,* and forced me to go back to Pereira. So I interrupted my college education, which I never finished. Before I quit, however, I had the opportunity to study art history with Marta Traba. Then I became self-supporting. I worked in various businesses in Pereira until I was "of age" and could return to the university and continue studying literature and art history, which I did at an intense pace.

MGP: Why the hurry?

AA: Because I was mad for knowledge. I'd never had the chance to learn anything anywhere, except from my own books. I read a lot about music, which was the only thing I studied that my father accepted and learned to like. Music even became a form of companionship for him when my mother died. I was the one who introduced him to music, and it rescued his soul from a lot of pain. Through music, I could explain the other things I needed, which weren't very unusual. When I told him I was going to Europe, he didn't comment one way or the other. That's how I ended up going to Europe with a cheap Japanese guitar, pretending I was a singer, a guitarist. He thought I'd come back as soon as I ran out of money, but twenty-one years have gone by since I left.

MGP: What did your mother say about such a daring decision?

AA: She was like a mummy. She didn't say a word. Her disapproval of my life and what I was doing was expressed through her total silence. She accused me with an overwhelming silence, because she knew she couldn't fight me with words. That was useless because I'd overcome her easily. Many years later, I tried to change our relationship, but she never went along. I don't think she ever read anything I'd written. One day she confessed that she'd tried to read the first few pages of one of my novels but that she would never do it again. She thought she saw herself in one of the characters, and it frightened her (she wasn't too far off the mark, either). She thought I was going to blame her for something; she was afraid of discovering some sort of message from me that she didn't want to hear. So it seems she opted for silence once again. And she was right about the messages. I've sent my family many messages, but because they hardly ever read my books, they hardly ever receive them.

MGP: Where did you publish your first books?

AA: I took the first one to Colombia myself in 1970, when I decided to accept my father's invitation to visit, seven years after I left Pereira. I showed up with a manuscript entitled *Los girasoles en invierno* [Sunflowers in winter], which I published in Bogotá with some financial help from my mother.

MGP: There was a lot of ambivalence in her attitude, wasn't there?

AA: Yes, as a matter of fact, there was, because she never made any comments to me or asked me what the money was for. I simply returned her loan a little later. Every two years or so I'd send a book to my family. I always dedicated them to my brothers, my mother, my father, as though I were begging their forgiveness.

MGP: Why did you have to beg their forgiveness?

AA: I don't know. It was as if I were begging them to understand me, to listen to me, to let go of the hostility they felt toward me because of their tremendous disapproval of my life and what I'd accomplished, which was the source of a monumental disagreement between us. For example, today my brother calls me a pornographic and obscene woman. He thinks that's all I can write about. He accuses me of having sunk the family into slimy depths. Now I can no longer attempt to beg their forgiveness, but in those early years I tried to prove to them that my work was indeed valid, that it had a future, a richness that would never earn a great deal of money but that was going to give them something far more valuable in return. I made a gesture of rapprochement: The love I felt for my brother led me to offer him that beautiful, raw, violent dissection of my life, of our lives, that is *Estaba la pájara pinta sentada en el verde limón* [The petite colored bird perched in a green lemon tree]. It was incredible torture to write because it opened up a lot of hidden areas of my life, and I wanted to dedicate it to my brother because I loved him so much. And that was how he responded. It was a real shock. The gossip in Colombia that has sprung up about my work has produced a double rejection on my family's part. Only my sister has read what I've written. She tells me that I killed my mother with all of the problems the books caused, with what the newspapers said about me and my work, and by ruining my reputation.

MGP: What do you think of that Colombian world today? What kind of feeling does your country inspire in you?

AA: I think I'm beginning to cross the many sound barriers that one has to cross in life. I'm beginning to see moments of Colombian life in clearly outlined stages. I see my childhood as something magical, a magic I used to write *La pájara pinta* and from which I continue to draw. It has generated an inner source of nourishment within me that will never take leave of me. That earthy nourishment, my Colombian adolescence, has produced three books—the hues, the heat, the tropics, everything I was in those days—it's all part of that ancestral "something" I revere as a ritual. To be born in Latin America at a particular historical moment, to be extremely Colombian—this gives me a kind of vitality that constantly jolts my system with emotional and psychological shocks. It's very stimulating. It has formed a dynamic, and a personality structure in me that seems complete, definitive. Then I tried to search for another part of myself, the part that wasn't disclosed by the immense kaleidoscope of my mirror. The culture had enchanted me before I really knew what it was. *Dos veces Alicia* [Alice twice over], my second novel, was the mirror I had to shatter, to penetrate, to break through to seek Alice in her own element. I only knew that Alice came from England.

✣ ✣ ✣

The Story of the Lady in the Rose-colored Bonnet

She saw the young woman in the white gown and rose-colored bonnet. She was walking around absent-mindedly, barely looking at her when she said, "I like your outfit." "Do you know where everyone is? I'm lost," was her answer. "Who?" Alice said, who didn't know who everyone was. "Never mind: I'm going to look for them," the girl in the rose-colored bonnet said. It was very peculiar clothing to be wearing, especially in those days. She liked the gown that seemed to be of silver, with fringes floating down.

She followed her across the park. She looked at the trees one by one, and then she repeated, after examining them: "It's very strange, they should be here. . . . It's very strange." Alice felt considerable curiosity, because it didn't seem at all strange to her that everyone wasn't in a tree. They couldn't even be in a baobab. "Maybe they could be over there, in that big one," she suggested, more to cheer her up than anything else. "That's right, it could be . . ." she said, smiling, and began to run impulsively toward the tree Alice was pointing out to her [*From* Dos veces Alicia].

✣ ✣ ✣

MGP: Leaving for Barranquilla also helped you go out into the world and begin a new life.

AA: People may say that I plagiarized García Márquez, but I also "arrived at the sea," so to speak. The problem is that suddenly we all spoke as he did because that's what Colombia is. The people I met in Barranquilla were different because the women my age spoke English, they'd traveled or studied in the United States, and they were quite liberated. In my case, I had been educated in a convent in the Andes, and I was deeply religious, a complete mystic to the point that I wanted to be a discalced Carmelite like Teresa of Avila and Francis of Assisi. They are the pillars of my life to this day. The people from the coast desacralize all rituals. They would go to Mass, but it was more like participating in a *cumbia*. Through them, I also lost my faith: by learning, by living and absorbing that culture.

MGP: Is your obsession with the mystic saints and your admiration for their lives related to your religious education, or does it come from somewhere else, perhaps from your grandmother?

AA: Of course, my grandmother's Bible unleashed everything. There was Saint Ines and Saint Cecilia or Saint Ursula, or the strong woman in the Gospel, and also the story of the Maccabees—all hair-raising and unique tales in my literary memory. After my grandmother's stories came those of the Franciscan nuns' academy, which had a bookstore filled with that sort of reading: Saint Tarcisio or Maria Goretti. We had to read them. We were forced to imitate their lives because if we didn't, we'd never go to heaven. So nightmares and dreams of being a martyr filled my head, stamping my brain with a ferocious burning brand that can never be erased. When I was six years old, Saint Lucia kept me from having only one eye, thanks to the fact that she'd always been an intimate friend of my father's aunt. Francis of Assisi was our patron saint and the impossible love of my life. The song of Brother Sun and Sister Water and Sister Tiny Ant is a voice that always calls me back to his shining footsteps. Teresa of Avila was the most seductive. How can one not fall into the traps set by her audacity, her lucidity, her sense of humor and the transfixing pulse of her words. You'd have to add the stories of Joan of Arc, Krishna, Che Guevara, and Mafalda.

MGP: When did your musical vocation begin?

AA: When I was four. But when I was a teenager, I got the idea that I had to go to Russia because that was where all musicians came from, according to what little I knew. When I wanted to go to a conservatory after one of the nuns suggested it, my father said no, because a young girl simply could not go to a school that had male students. That put a stop to my musical career.

MGP: Was it your father's politics or philosophy that young women should be completely segregated from men?

AA: Indeed, both.

MGP: Then when was it suitable to interact with the opposite sex?

AA: Only after one got married. That's what my sister did. She fell in love when she was sixteen years old and got married right away.

MGP: It's clear that a number of things distance you now from your home and your people.

AA: Yes, I'm growing away from the paternal homestead and from Christian norms, Catholic norms.

MGP: Were your parents devout Catholics?

AA: I convinced my father, who was quite indifferent, to convert because of a promise I'd made when I took my first Communion. Afterwards, he took it very seriously. Colombia has an authentic Christian culture. My mother was more than just a Catholic, she was profoundly Christian. And that helped me clarify my life; that passage between to be and not to be, between belief—. My religious education went through a number of stages until I found a middle ground, a personal one, where once again I became integrated into a spiritual world in which I believe profoundly. I believe in an organized cosmos. It fascinates me to think about it, to know it, to feel it, because then I no longer feel like flesh and blood. I've dedicated a large part of my life to that search—something that has alarmed some of my friends. These concerns are visible in the last piece I wrote. It's a search for cosmic organization, the one so many others have undertaken before.

MGP: I think you're in very good company since it has been a universal preoccupation for a long time. Surely your friends' alarm is because you're a woman, so you shouldn't be worrying about the cosmos because it's not your concern.

AA: It also made my parents doubt my mental stability, even though I didn't go to the extreme of setting up permanent residence in Tibet. I believe in one essential truth.

MGP: But you're very personal and very persistent. There is conceptual clarity in your vision of the world.

AA: I'm tenacious.

MGP: It's clear that you aren't off in the clouds somewhere, that there's no lack of adjustment on your part, so the accusation that you are mad is obviously invalid.

AA: What I'm telling you about isn't something I've pulled out of the air. For example, when I won first prize in a competition that takes place in Colombia every other year with *La pájara pinta sentada en el verde limón, El Espectador* in Bogotá ran a four-column headline that read: "*Desvirolada* from Pereira wins Vivencias contest." *Desvirolada* is a Colombian word that means "crazy woman." That's the kind of association my name carries in "respectable" newspapers like the one mentioned before. What's happened is that the way I've broken clichés has really frightened some intellectuals in my country.

MGP: Do you consider your Bogotá phase important for your literary development?

AA: It's not central, but it reveals a channel of direct knowledge that resulted from my entering the university, which seemed like a dream come true to me.

MGP: Meaning that at long last, you had entered the world of culture.

AA: Exactly. I spent many hours at the library. I took courses with Marta Traba and began to go out with Gonzalo Arango (which excommunicated me from the entire world), and I dressed in black like Juliette Greco, the French actress, who was so popular in the sixties.

MGP: Who is Gonzalo Arango?

AA: He was the beautiful human being whom we called "The Prophet" and who initiated *Nadaísmo,* an important poetic movement in Colombia. He died in an accident seven years ago. He was one of the most enlightened intellectuals Colombia ever produced, a poet who was among the most daring of iconoclasts. When he died, *El*

Espectador and *El Tiempo* ran headlines such as: "From Madman to Mystic." That's how they bade farewell to Gonzalo. That's Colombia. Gonzalo had been translated into several languages, but in Colombia they did nothing but subject him to harsh criticism. What's more, Gonzalo's own peers, those poets who had begun *Nadaísmo* with him, claimed he was a madman [before he died], and they burned him in effigy in Cali. After that happened, he went to live on an island and stayed there for the rest of his life.

MGP: But *Nadaísmo* is the vanguard of the poetic movement in Colombia.

AA: Certainly. It's been one of the most important [literary] vanguards in Latin America. He was my close friend and one of the most important men in my life.

MGP: Do you think that your relationship with Gonzalo served as a stepping-stone to writing literature?

AA: I spent my entire life watching people who wrote poetry or painted. I began playing the guitar and singing, and I studied all I could. I wrote things for Gonzalo, and he called me "la Maga" [the female protagonist in *Rayuela* (*Hopscotch*) by Julio Cortázar] before Cortázar did!

MGP: And you also studied art history, as you said.

AA: I was a complete slave to art history, to that fascination Marta Traba exerted over everyone who knew her, to that catalyst, that magnet Marta held over me. I was to be a kind of projection of hers—the next major art critic in Colombia.

MGP: What did Marta teach you to see and to search for?

AA: It's difficult to say. I was attracted to her daring, because I saw a great deal of myself in Marta's small-town rebellion that she manipulated into national importance, not only within art history but also by expanding upon an idea much more exciting than mere opposition to one's parents. Marta spoke out against Rojas Pinilla on Colombian television without his finding out; she discussed the great dictators of the Middle Ages, and no one ever said a word about her critical attitude.

I met her when I was very young, and I loved her devastating sense of humor. Marta taught me how to use that other sharp-edged sword called irony, to use a refined style of humor to head off severe blows, which Marta always headed off very well. Then she taught me how to develop my intellectual capacity, how to administer and manage it for my own benefit. Our temperaments were very different, though. She taught me to analyze. She taught me the necessity of developing, as quickly as possible, the knowledge and intelligence necessary for attaining a moderately important position within Colombian culture, something she had already achieved. I wanted to get there, to be there, to participate in and always be a part of that.

Marta was tenacious, and I became part of her tenacity. I didn't weaken. It caused me a lot of problems, not the least of which was involvement in the stormy politics of a man who wanted to have her thrown out of the country for reasons I will not go into now. Marta exposed herself to the kinds of emotional storms I knew quite intimately and which depressed her a great deal. And when she went into the street, I could see how she confronted her adversaries.

MGP: I think that was part of Marta's special kind of intensity. Returning to your training in art history, how do you think it affected you?

AA: Marta's influence made me study that material for eight years.

MGP: What have you done with it?

AA: Nothing. I simply have it for myself. Marta wanted so much for me to become an art historian and critic that when I went to Europe and started growing away from it and instead became a gypsy, traveling all over the world with my guitar, she was very disappointed. And she objected to my absence. One day in Paris she discovered some pages of a novel I was writing, and she didn't like the idea that I was becoming a writer. I had been doing art criticism for some time. Then a friend of mine, the Chilean poet Alberto Baeza Flores who also lived in Paris, encouraged me to continue writing fiction. That's how I seized the aphrodisiac that is literature.

MGP: So the task of art criticism took up quite a bit of your time.

AA: I wrote art criticism for four or five years. It was published mostly in Colombia. I also wrote a book of essays about art that was the only thing that helped sustain me during a very crucial period of my life.

MGP: Critical writing served as preparation for your later work, didn't it?

AA: Yes. Deep down, at the very core, people of my sign, Virgo, produce that criticism. It was written in my horoscope. We are analytical beings. In those days, analyzing still did something for me. Alberto Zalamea—he was Marta Traba's first husband—praised my work and published a few of my things in his *La Nueva Prensa*.

MGP: And what exactly is *Nueva Prensa*?

AA: It was like the *New York Times*, a splendid political review during the fifties and the beginning of the sixties. It had sections of art, literature, cinema, and politics. I contributed interviews with Colombian painters in Europe and commentaries on all the art shows in Venice, Paris, Germany, or wherever. But the academic dialectic began to stifle me. The only one I was interested in was Argan, the

Italian art critic, who enlightened me a great deal. But Baeza Flores frustrated me, because he kept insisting I should write literature.

MGP: Who was Baeza Flores?

AA: A Chilean friend of Néstor Almendros, a Cuban photographer I knew in those days, and of Julio Hernández, a Cuban painter—people who soon appeared in Latin American history as Cuban exiles. Elsa Baeza, his daughter, is a very important singer in Spain. It was a very tense time for me and a time of conflict for the Cubans, who went to Europe and then felt they had to return. I also met Myriam Acevedo, the actress. I lived the horror of the dichotomy experienced by Cuban artists who left their country. Then Baeza came along. He had lived in Cuba but didn't agree with the thick wall Castro had built around it (which made him rather ahead of his time) and left the country. That was the man who stimulated me to write. Two years later I began my first novel.

MGP: Had you written anything before?

AA: I had written a few stories when I was eighteen, but I didn't really begin to write until I started my first novel, *Los girasoles en invierno,* in 1964. I was twenty-five when I finished it. For me, writing is a part of everyday life; it's not something unusual. I consider it another piece of my life experience, and that is *Los girasoles en invierno.*

MGP: Where did the title come from?

AA: From the fact that it was horribly cold in Paris. What made me think of it was that someone once compared me to a sunflower, always searching for light and sun in a miserably cold Paris. It's a story of bitter cold, of a terrible winter when I sang in the streets or in La Candelaria, in the Latin Quarter, or sang for the Spanish exiles, the workers on Sundays in Banlieue. I sang ceaselessly in order to survive, because that's what it took. The most tenacious, most difficult, drawn out, tense test of survival for me was the time I spent in Paris.

MGP: Why was Paris so awful, as compared with London or Rome?

AA: Because, as Fernando González, a great Colombian writer, says, in Paris it seems so dark you can't see God. Paris was terrible for me, and I think it always will be. Without God, without a soul, utterly bare. Oppressive. It has a most fiendish beauty, perverse and attractive. It's an aphrodisiac with a purgative. It's more punitive than any other city. Like New York, soulless. But Paris has much more fantasy, more beauty than New York. It's more bewitching. New York is like the Eiffel Tower: a twenty-first-century machine. Human beings are irrelevant, and there is no way to measure its enormity. Paris is designed for poets, for dreamers, for people of great sensitivity. It has a plastic beauty that represents the entire city, but that's the great pitfall of Paris: one dies consuming the poison of the arrogant French, who are impossibly chauvinistic and aggressive, though they've become a bit less arrogant since the war. Things went very badly for me. But I had to learn to live on my own, and when you're twenty-five you can put up with anything. I couldn't even see what was happening to me. Now I look at it from a distance, and it doesn't frighten me. But when I was living there, I remember being paralyzed for days by its intensity.

MGP: You didn't speak French, did you?

AA: No. And that was awful, too.

MGP: During the nomadic life you led in Paris, when did you have time to write?

AA: I wrote like a person obsessed. I wrote the novel seven times over. I'd get home at four or five in the morning, when the street cleaners did, after eating onion soup in Les Halles, where the musicians eat. Instead of going to sleep, I'd write down a few impressions and important notes, in a frenzy, very quickly. Then at four in the afternoon, when I opened my eyes again, I'd rewrite everything until seven in the evening, when it was time for me to go sing again. I didn't perform as the main attraction, but rather to fill in time between acts. My adventure had to be complete, and I felt I couldn't withdraw from it just because it was difficult. I'd arrived in Paris in the wintertime with clothes suitable for a tropical climate. That's why I remember cold weather with such intensity. I survived until the following summer. Then I would travel because I knew I could always sleep in a park if I couldn't find anyplace else. Every year I went to explore a different country, to learn the language and see the countryside. Also the French police wouldn't let me stay in France as a tourist for too long, so I'd have to leave anyway. After my stay in France, I went to England, where I began to write my second book *Dos veces Alicia* and the seventh version of *Los girasoles en invierno.* My time there coincided with the Beatles, the Rolling Stones, and the centennial of *Alice in Wonderland* and *Through the Looking Glass,* all of which taught me a great deal. Alice was getting inside me, and she ended up writing the book, but I didn't compose all of it in England. I wrote sixty pages and lived through all of them, and then I reworked it in Rome and included everything else I had lived through. I'd told so much of it to my friends that they wanted to paint or illustrate it, so, of course, then I had to write the final version.

MGP: So you talked about it first, and then you wrote it.

AA: Yes—with numerous notes and good bits along the way until I was able to find a form close to what could be called a novel. Carlos Barral, an important publisher from Barcelona, published it, but he said he couldn't decide to which genre it belonged, which is what people would say later about my most recent narrative works, *Las andariegas* [The wayfarers] and *Misiá señora*. It seems no one knows what to do with my work. Perhaps the short stories are not so difficult to classify; however, there are some texts among them that are quite anarchic in form.

MGP: When were those texts published, then?

AA: When I went to Colombia in 1970. I was a finalist in a literary contest that was later declared to be without winners, in spite of the fact that Zapata Olivella, Mejia Vallejo, and a woman from Pereira—myself—were finalists, together with an army colonel, Valencia Tovar, who wrote a book about guerrillas. They did make a big deal out of the last one, and his work was published. In spite of the results, however, I got a lot of publicity out of that unsuccessful competition. When *Los girasoles en invierno* came out, I'd almost finished *Dos veces Alicia*. I mailed it to Carlos Barral, and eight months later I turned up in Spain because I'd made up my mind to go there. He also published my other books. But back in Colombia, I had considerable difficulty publishing my work.

MGP: Wasn't publication of the novel part of the prize you won?

AA: Of course, but they told me they couldn't find a suitable publisher. That was an excuse, for it had become an extremely controversial contest. Alvaro Mutis [a prominent Colombian poet] was on the judging panel, and he supported my book. Gloria Zea, the head of Colcultura [Center for Colombian Culture], finally published it in her popular collection of 1975. Two or three years later, I offered her my short story collection *¡Oh gloria inmarcesible!* [Oh boundless glory!]. Gloria published it, but it was then used as the Trojan horse to fire her from Colcultura on the grounds that my stories were pornographic and that, by association, she was supporting it.

MGP: What kind of distribution did *Dos veces Alicia* get and what finally happened to it?

AA: Carlos Barral gave it a thousand-copy run. Years later, I still keep buying copies to give people as presents. These kinds of things happen often to both Carlos and me. Alberto Custe, from Argentina, sold some contraband copies of *Dos veces Alicia* to a book-of-the-month club in Argentina, and the club sold twenty-six thousand copies. It was never reprinted.

MGP: Why do you think you have so much trouble with your books?

AA: I think it happens to a lot of people and that I'm only one of many.

MGP: Do you take charge of promoting your books?

AA: Yes. For example, I gave two hundred copies of *Los girasoles en invierno* to Gonzalo Arango. I think he distributed them well. I'm sure of it. I gave other copies to *Tercer Mundo* [Third world], which was partly owned by Belisario Betancur. *Dos veces Alicia* was distributed by Carlos Barral, but it didn't sell very well. As for *La pájara pinta,* it has had a very long and complicated history. There are four editions: the first was by Colcultura and was very good, selling ten thousand copies. It sold out and went out of print in Colombia within fifteen days. Then there was the Seix Barral edition, which was pulled despite the fact that the galleys were ready and proofed; the third was the Plaza y Janes edition, which they took out of circulation in Colombia after two months, alleging that the public "wasn't interested," and finally that of Carlos Barral from Argos Vergara Editores in Barcelona.

MGP: How do you envision your writing career? Why do you think you write?

AA: First, I've discovered that I love to get things across through song, so I was writing for the work itself, for all those spears I had to throw. I go through life well armed because I'm defending myself against many things. And that's my orientation toward life: elbowing my way in. García Márquez says he writes so that his friends will love him. With me, the opposite has happened. I've alienated some of them. One of my friends insulted me publicly in Bogotá because he thought I was pulling his leg by dedicating one of my stories to him. So the love of my friends can't be very important to me. I want to have within me all the beauty of writing, the beauty of life, the experience of joy and sorrow, even though it may be heartbreaking at times. You go through periods when your soul, your blood, your life takes leave of you, for a page, for a chapter, for five chapters, for a thought you're going to write down and then don't. It's a lifetime job. It's a tremendous joy for a paragraph, and it's sorrow for what you've just said. My conception of my literary work is that if I was able to survive the tension of writing it, I'd like other people to read it. I don't know who these people may be since I don't know who my public is. My first book had a face or two or three. The second had a few more, and I saw certain people while I was writing chapters. Then afterward, I didn't. *La pájara pinta* turned into an enormous projection of Colombia itself. I wanted to tell that story to any Colombian of any age at any time.

MGP: There's a tremendous difference between your first two books and *La pájara pinta.*

AA: There's a difference in maturity, because I was growing up. At the beginning, writing was a kind of game. It was a rehearsal, an attempt, a glance at what was happening on the other side of the mirror. Once I crossed through the mirror, Alice had already projected a true image for me: my childhood. Then I began to actually look at who I was, and I saw the first image: a six-year-old girl. Now it wasn't a game anymore. I knew the story I had to tell.

MGP: Could we talk about some of the background work you did for *La pájara pinta* now? Because of when you were born, you must have lived through that difficult period in Colombia's history known as "La Violencia." What recollections do you have of those years?

AA: It's my first memory, the most vivid, and the most constant. When I was in Paris, I didn't stop having strange dreams and nightmares about Colombia until I was finally able to write *La pájara pinta*. I lived through La Violencia as I describe it in the novel, from a seven-year-old's perspective. I saw a man killed in front of my house. And I saw the blood, the clubs, the fires. I witnessed Jorge Eliécer Gaitán's execution in a tiny village by listening to the radio and seeing in my imagination the heads of the Goths—as the radio used to call them—hanging from the street lamps; I could see the processions of men with torches, the papers that fell from the Town Hall turning into pyres, a huge fire in the Plaza de Bolívar, one man shooting another. And that was in a small town. It kept reoccurring through the radio and the newspapers and through what the peasants said, with what happened to any man, what happened to his sister, each suffering in his or her own skin. And they weren't just stories. They were people—from my household, from my village, from my own corner. It was the poor, the wretched, those with nothing who were attacked during the first plague of La Violencia. They were the ones who paid most dearly for the blood thirstiness of that political vengeance. Later the aggression turned in the other direction, and then, years after, wealthy people began to suffer for the first time the same displacement, the same murders. But it took a long time. At first it was only the little people, the kind who rode buses with their chickens and their children. They died and so did their chickens. The *asesino bandolero* [bandits], as they were called, didn't even leave the chickens alive. I get scared telling you about it now because I'm still thinking about the chickens cut to pieces. That was how the papers described it. Those guys went that far with the tips of their machetes. The papers told how they'd rape the women before they did anything else. There were no real rules, except the one that women had to be raped, whether they were seven or seventy. That was the law. It didn't matter whether the women were liberals or conservatives, all faced the blade, and if a woman was pregnant they opened her up, took out the fetus, and quartered it. To me, as a child, as an adolescent, and as a woman, La Violencia made my soul, my guts, and my heart tremble thirty times over because of what I heard and read that they were doing to women. If they caught a man, they would cut off his genitals. They did such awful things to young girls that I can't describe them, horrible acts of sexual violence that Colombian men—soldiers, bandits, or whoever—did to women. The worst crime during La Violencia was the sexual violence that Colombian women had to suffer, whatever their political ideology or age.

MGP: I think that precisely because of what you have just described, your novel has a direct connection to the novels that have tried to deal with the horror of human violence that has occurred in Chile, in Argentina, and in Uruguay, the violence that props up a reality that hasn't really been confronted by the rest of Latin America, especially that twice horrible violence toward women.

AA: Another instance of my troubles with publishers occurred when a friend in Barcelona contacted a potential publisher in the United States, who turned out to be Argentine. She read the novel as an official reader would, and her comment was, "Who'll be interested in a book like this, if everyone in Latin America is tired of hearing these stories?" That was the end of a possible U.S. publication of the book.

La pájara pinta came out a little before Cortázar's *El libro de Manuel* [A manual for Manuel]. Afterward, people said I plagiarized Cortázar and García Márquez. *El libro de Manuel* includes some newspaper clippings as part of the text; without having read Cortázar, I used newspaper clippings in my book because they were vital to the writing. Unfortunately, this typographical distinction was ignored in the fourth edition. When I did mine, all these testimony books hadn't come out yet. *País portátil* [Portable country] was the first book that inspired my project. I acknowledge this debt in *La pájara pinta,* despite the fact that the homage to González León, its author, is somewhat anachronistic.

MGP: Why is it anachronistic?

AA: Because my novel ends in 1968, and *País portátil* was published in 1969 or 1970. I'd already started writing in the seventies. My book ends with the deaths of Che Guevara and Camilo Torres because for me, the historical chronicle of Colombia in *La pájara pinta* comes full circle with the deaths of Che Guevara and Camilo Torres.

MGP: When did you finish writing it?

AA: In 1975.

MGP: What was your original goal when you started writing this novel?

AA: When I started, it wasn't a very ambitious project: I wanted to tell the story of my childhood. I remember that Faulkner said you had to tell things from a distance of twenty years. I began with an amusing story about a little girl in a Franciscan convent and her amusing adolescence: then I'm interrupted—like an early memory—with the death of my friend Juliet who was killed by a streetcar. I had to carry her to the cemetery on my shoulders, an image I can't erase to this day. I go beyond Juliet's death, and it's April 9 (Gaitán's death). And the dead start to increase in number. And I go on telling about the nuns, and the dead are more and more numerous. I stop writing the novel and tell myself that I can't tell people a story of my life filled with violence and death. Instead, I was a little girl in a tiny crystal box, well protected, and that's the story I must tell. And I had written a hundred pages, I went back to Colombia to gather the material on the sorrow. But people still didn't want to talk. I asked about April 9, and people looked at me as though I were from the police. It all happened twenty-five years ago and people still didn't want to talk. I got what photographs I could from the newspapers. There wasn't much historical material, but I could resort to the book *La violencia en Colombia* [Violence in Colombia], which I had left in Europe. The whole research project turned into a recollection of that historical period. I returned to Barcelona loaded with additional material. My ambition started there, but it was more like a vision of what I was compelled to write. This story had to combine certain names, the voices of the guerrillas and the voices of the poor who must speak for themselves. In short, I had to give a voice to each group. That is how I began to work directly with the chronicles. The radio that plays throughout the novel was invented because it's fixed in my memory. I remember even the megacycles on the radio. I dawdled for a year planning, putting things together, writing notes. I organized my personal history and arranged the historic moment. I cut out each event, pinned it together with others, and then began to sew. I felt in control of my project, not in danger of being overwhelmed because I was a woman and therefore not able to discuss politics. I talk about Colombian politics, about the history of my country, but as viewed from the outside.

MGP: It seems to me you're also telling the story from the inside when you bring in the young women's voices.

AA: The outside voices are the voices of the guerrillas, as in a historical novel. Furthermore, all the transcripts are in quotations or italics. It makes a considerable demand on the reader. When the witnesses speak, there are no typographical marks that indicate the shift in perspective. I didn't want to make marginal notes, because it's not an essay. But it *is* history.

MGP: Clearly, incorporating different kinds of material has generated a very dense text.

AA: The technical aspect of this narrative was very ambitious. That's where the writer's spirit truly grows within me. I think that's when I realized that everything I'd ever read would have to be put to use; otherwise, the narrative could turn into a pamphlet. Being political testimony, it could have easily fallen into a pamphleteering trap. I didn't belong to any party then or now. I'm saying what I think the truth is, and I'm trying to formulate a very objective analysis of a reality seen by a woman who believes she's mature enough to attest to that moment of history. What I'm saying is I'm a woman, and I have the right to think, to have an opinion, and to write.

MGP: Without a doubt *La pájara pinta* belongs to a body of literature that has been rapidly growing in the last few years because of what's happened politically in our countries. What surprises me is that this novel has remained so marginal for such a long time. I, for example, discovered it by accident. The irony perhaps is that it is the only text you've written that is not marginal.

AA: I can't give you a response to that because I've already resolved it. While my previous books weren't very popular, *La pájara pinta* hit the target by winning a prize in Colombia. Maybe I should have hung a stone around my neck then, because everything happened backward. The book made me very popular with people in Colombia, who don't exactly know who Albalucía Angel is but who do know me as "la pájara pinta." That's one satisfaction I've gotten from that novel.

MGP: Nevertheless, in spite of your great success and numerous awards, Albalucía Angel is not found in the literary histories of Colombia. Now let's discuss your other great novel, *Misiá señora*. How would you characterize it?

AA: *Misiá señora* is modeled on my wonderful grandmother, my Virgo grandmother, the one who read in secret. It is her oldest story, reaching back to the turn of the century, with those nine sons and then the other nine sons who weren't hers. *Misiá señora* is my mother, that secretive woman, that strange difficult woman, the woman of silence. *Misiá señora* is also me, camouflaged, concealed. She's also my great-grandmother who lost her memory when she was fifty-five and lived into her eighties like a Japanese flower, there in Pereira. Together with the landscape and all the tropical flavor the language of that country evokes, it is the life of four women who have the same name. They're all called Mariana. But until now, no one's figured out that there are four of them. I think it's because the novel makes for too dense a reading. *Misiá señora* was highly promoted, and critics gave it a fair amount of attention. Critical essays have been written about it in Spain, but they haven't been very insightful. Before Carlos Barral published it, it was rejected by fourteen other publishers and received very negative comments by the men who wrote the editorial reports. They said it was excessive, a frontal attack on masculinity. When it finally got through the barricades, Ana María Moix and other critics read it with more attention and judged it to be an anti pamphlet. They were very interested in it. The main character is really four. She begins her story in 1970 and finishes it in the nineteenth century. But no one has read it like a deep two-way mirror.

MGP: What have you tried to do in this very dense and complex novel?

AA: I've tried to do what Faulkner says about distancing one's self twenty years from the events to be recounted and apply that method with a woman's knowledge. I was about twenty-five when I learned what being a woman really meant, when I broke the mold because I felt I had to be something more. Then, once I was already on the way, I was better able to deal with many obstacles. Thinking back on the last twenty years, I realized that I could tell the story of how I learned to be a woman. In *La pájara pinta* there are two characters in embryonic stages: the girl who breaks her chains and escapes her gilded cage seeking freedom, even though freedom is only a vague perception, something she's heard people talk about, and the other woman, who is liberated and courageous, who dreams of justice and vindication but is killed by the police. At the age of thirty-five, I knew what those choices meant, so I no longer envisioned my characters as imaginary; instead, I was able to depict myself. This is where the saga of Pereiran women becomes the saga of Colombia and which, I daresay, is also the saga of almost all women in Latin America. It's like an enormous ripe guava just within my grasp. It is myself, my identity, my fulfillment, my integration into the world of womanhood, regardless of differences in place or language. But I know my work is meant for Latin America because that is my race and my womb. It's a way of telling you how the vibration of the saga is born, peacefully. Later, the novel turned out to be a terribly frightening, confusing mess for me, and ultimately nightmares and suffering are what all my writing becomes at the end. When I think I'm pretty calm and can make plans, that neither my identity nor that very beautiful, ripe guava will fall apart, the torture of transcribing it, of achieving it, remains. *Misiá señora* is fascinating as a literary experiment. It's a great challenge.

That's why the language and the form are so complex. I didn't suffer as much as with *La pájara pinta,* though. For four years I lived imprisoned on a kind of island. I isolated myself near Arezzo [Italy] in a convent-hostel for pilgrims, and then in Cadaques, Portugal. I am continually awed by the challenge of language. But it is the story itself, a visceral throbbing, that makes me melt into a river of blood. I tell it without hesitation. Gabriela Mora, a literary critic, was the first one to read the manuscript. She commented that the novel touches on difficult, prohibited, and taboo zones, the daring language of female eroticism that is masculinized when spoken by men. I believe I present women's sexuality in a different light, which links me with many other women who have expressed it the same way, though not like Erica Jong does. She comes across almost like a man. I want to project the experience I've achieved through my own identity.

Nevertheless, *Misiá señora* hasn't been called "pornography," because no one in Colombia has read it yet! That label came out of the reaction to my short story collection *¡Oh gloria inmarcesible!* which was written in male language, macho language. The language men use to talk about women is what I explore and elaborate there. It's obvious that people read that book in a superficial way. No one looked at the way language was manipulated, the way it unfolded itself as a critique.

MGP: Is *Misiá señora* more important for you than *La pájara pinta*?

AA: I've never reread it. I've read bits and pieces of it, and sometimes I get worried when I think about the reader's reaction. A great deal of the readership is going to be female, but the critic-reader, that is, the man who advises the editor, insinuated that my book wouldn't interest male readers.

MGP: It seems peculiar that this kind of unilateral rejection still remains. When your fellow Colombian writer Humberto Moreno Durán published his misogynistic novels, the sales were excellent, and the author's name became well known. Should we conclude that it's more interesting when men offend female readers than the other way around?

AA: I would rather not comment on that author. I'd like a lot of public response to *Misiá señora,* especially from women. I'm insecure—who knows if the novel's as good as I want it to be, as effective, as well written. I put all I had into it, but whether it's as well done as I want it to be will always be a question mark. So the reaction of the reading public is very important. I believe this is a mature novel for me, a novel with a definite identity.

MGP: Where, in the wandering life you lead, do you find the best atmosphere for working?

AA: When I have something to write, I leave for Cadaques, where there is solitude. When Gala and Salvador Dali were still there, I used to go for walks near their house, because every afternoon at five o'clock I could hear the recordings they played of baroque concertos. The music echoed through the mountains. I'll never find anything like that again. Cadaques is magical; it casts a spell; it's full of energy. Many poets have held forth there, great painters, the Bretons, the Eluards, the Duchamps, and many others. There the creative process was violent, especially because I was harassed by my neighbors, who threw rocks at my windows. They seemed to be furious that I was there, that I went places so contentedly on my yellow scooter. They used to call me "that foreign woman." I was completely free. I went to Cadaques because it was so cheap, but then I discovered the village was vital to my writing.

MGP: Did you write *Las andariegas* there?

AA: No, I wrote that in London over a two-year period. I was living next to a forest, and the walks I took there were very different from the walks I took by the sea in Cadaques. For the first time, it took me a year to write only one hundred pages. And I worked constantly to produce those hundred pages.

MGP: There are a number of noticeable changes in *Las andariegas:* the story of Colombia, the family history, is no longer the main theme, and your writing begins to follow another path that takes you away from the format of the novel.

AA: There's a change of genre, of form, of language. Also, when I was in the middle of writing *Misiá señora,* a book of poems called *La gata sin botas* [Puss without boots] emerged. I felt as though images had gotten hold of me. I was possessed, as Alejandra Pizarnik would say. When I finished *Misiá señora,* that poetic text was waiting. In New York I did another book of poems that someday might be called *Cantos y encantamientos de la lluvia* [Songs and enthrallments of rain]. I'm not sure of the title yet. Poetry burst forth after *Misiá señora.* I can't write novels or short stories anymore. *Las andariegas* is a collection of parables. They began to take shape when I was reading Monique Wittig's *Les Guérrillères* and found myself challenged. A splendid illumination suddenly burst into life. I constructed a dialogue between her guerrillas and my wanderers, a dialogue that slowly distanced itself from its original but didn't cut itself completely off. They don't oppose each other; rather, the texts crisscross. They echo each other.

MGP: Instead of being guerrillas, your protagonists are exquisitely beautiful, gowned and bejeweled women who encounter armored men along their path.

AA: They're walking behind themselves and become mimetic with the moment as they walk through time. When you first see them, they're dressed according to the way they live. They arrive wearing crystal armor, as if they came from the moon, from the galaxies, from the sun. They know nothing of history, and they're looking around. They interpret history in a different way, because they're seeing everything for the first time. That's the way I demythicize, reinvent, and renew experience in order to describe it with another voice. It's the version given by those women who witness history in another way. It's a song of many harmonies and voices where, finally, I arrive.

✣ ✣ ✣

They descended holding onto one another. It resembled a chain of shining steel, glittering in the midday summer sun. They seemed like buccaneers ready to strike. Maelstroms, crystals, harsh winds

Of quicksilver, they seemed

Armor and swords of crystal. The chain came down from the ship like a garland of violets and acacias and anemones and roses and lilies of the valley crossing the air, slender like tiny autumn leaves. Like gypsy women, they descended. Like pirates without battles or cries of victory.

The sun beat down as though it wanted to burn them. The earth below awaited, watchful. It heard them go ashore with their songs and laughter; they seemed a band of urchins coming upon a honeycomb. Or discovering butterflies. Or hunting a treasure.

The wise ancient lecherous voracious earth awaited them [*From* Las andariegas].

✣ ✣ ✣

That's where a portion of my writing ends, which also includes two plays—a project that I then expanded into a trilogy—*La manzana de piedra* [The stone apple] and *Siete lunas y un espejo* [Seven moons and a mirror]. I am working now on the third play. I like the theater very much.

MGP: Are these pieces connected with any of your earlier texts?

AA: One of them—*La manzana de piedra*—is *Misiá señora* all over again, transcribed for the theater. The other play consists of several games about many female characters in history. Several of them meet in a very amusing situation—Joan of Arc, Juliet, George Sand, Alice, and Marie Antoinette. It is all handled with irony and humor.

I'm also preparing a book of conversations with Latin American women writers, done in a very intimate tone. I've traveled throughout Latin America discovering women and their work, what they write in secret. When I finish that project, I think I'm going to take my movie camera and go on a long trek around the world.

MGP: A woman writer's literary formation generally begins when she is very young, and certain readings tend to have a strong impact on her imagination. What texts have been important to you besides *Las mil y una noches* and the Bible, which you already mentioned?

AA: I read fairy tales and the stories put out by Callejas [a Spanish popular collection], but they didn't make much of an impression on me. My passion was for Emilio Salgari, Jules Verne, Tarzan, and Agatha Christie. Also, I read the Argentine magazines *Leoplán* and *Cuéntame.* I was introduced to romance through Corín Tellado's incredibly popular books. There was *Wuthering Heights,* which I already told you about, and *El árabe* [The Arab]. When I was fourteen, I started on erotic literature.

MGP: Which author had the biggest impact on you?

AA: Salgari and Verne, but also Dickens and Mark Twain. My favorite character was Tom Sawyer.

MGP: It is remarkable that most women of our generation have read the same books.

AA: Alcott and Rocambole were for adults, but my father gave me the entire collection as a present. I made a deal with the nun who taught our sewing classes. She did my embroidery, and I got to read aloud. We read a lot of Delly. Then I discovered E. A. Poe. I came across Poe and Oscar Wilde by chance in a bookstore. Then came *Madame Bovary.* Also I began to read an Argentinian theater series published by Editorial Losada. I read Ricardo Güiraldes, *Martín Fierro,* Southern literature, and some Japanese writers. At eighteen I discovered the Americans Kerouac and Ginsberg. Then came Françoise Sagan: *Bonjour Tristesse.* That's when I discovered that women wrote. It was very important to know there was a woman writer almost my age. Borges followed and the books published by Editorial Sur together with the American theater. Then I delved into Faulkner, Dos Passos, Tennessee Williams, O'Neill, Carson McCullers, and the literature of the American South. At twenty I was electrified by Lawrence Durrell, Kafka, Henry Miller, Bradbury, Saroyan.

MGP: Who was most important?

AA: Kazantzakis, who redid the story of Christ, because I understood his reinvention. I learned that myths, like those of Christ or Francis of Assisi, were splendid inventions. I read others for ambience, atmosphere, or for autobiographical elements. When I was a student at the university, I read Simone de Beauvoir's *The Second Sex,* which gave me a new vision of what it was to be a woman. She was not the young woman Sagan was. I also read Sartre, who was so important for the *Nadaístas,* but I didn't understand him very well. I wasn't really one of them because I was too young, but I tagged along because of Gonzalo Arango. When I studied literature at the university, I began to read in a more orderly fashion. I read the Greek and Spanish classics. I became an admirer of *Amadís de Gaula* [*Amadis of Gaul,* a popular fourteenth-century novel of chivalry], which I'd read long ago in a children's version. Then I discovered other writers: the Spanish novelist Ana María Matute, the Mexican writer Juan García Ponce, Juan and Luis Goytisolo, Carmen Laforet. The French poets Rimbaud and Eluard. On my trips to Barranquilla before 1960, I met the "students" of the group La Cueva [The Cave] led by the Colombian writer Alvaro Cepeda Samudio. The students of La Cueva read James Joyce, but I preferred the Borges of *Ficciones* and *El aleph* and the writers of the Beat Generation. I discovered the Russians and other classics. When I turned twenty, I finally met Alvaro Cepeda, and I went to La Cueva. I may have been the only woman allowed in the group.

MGP: Why did they accept you?

AA: Because Alvaro Cepeda brought me. Germán Vargas was there as well as many other important men I'd seen from a distance discussing literature. Learning from Alvaro was magnificent, because he laughed his head off (as he always did) at my innocence and ignorance. He showed me his manuscript of *La casa grande.* That was the first time I'd read a writer's manuscript. Of course, I didn't know what to tell him. It was a turning point for many things in my life and, above all, for culture. I paid a great deal of attention to him.

MGP: Didn't you meet García Márquez there?

AA: No. He wasn't in Barranquilla then; he was living in Mexico. I met him in Spain in 1968. I wrote my first stories for Alvaro and for Marta Traba. Alvaro liked them, but Marta didn't. At any rate, they were never published.

MGP: And what happened to your reading when you went to Europe?

AA: I started reading *L'Invitée* [*She Came to Stay*] by Simone de Beauvoir because I'd loved *The Mandarins.* I also read Cesare Pavese, Michel Butor, and the French authors of the Nouveau Roman. I liked Marguerite Duras very much, but I didn't know about Margueritte Yourcenar yet. In Italy, I discovered Elsa Morante and Dacia Maraini. After that, whenever I saw a woman's name, I'd read the book. That's how I encountered Alejandra Pizarnik and Raquel Jodorowski, who published their work in *El Corno Emplumado,* a literary magazine from Colombia. Alejandra was a beautiful and terrible phantom in my life.

MGP: Did you meet her?

AA: No, never, but I read her work.

MGP: Why did you get so interested in women?

AA: Because I was overwhelmed by the fact that they were writing. And when I saw so many women involved in the writing profession, I began to "pursue" them, in a manner of speaking. I remember distinctly when I discovered Olga Orozco and her novel *La oscuridad es otro sol* [Darkness is another sun]. Olga Orozco wasn't very well known then as a poet, but Alejandra was. When I was writing *Los girasoles en invierno,* I read Camus in French and *La ciudad y los perros* [*The Time of the Hero*] by Vargas Llosa.

MGP: What other Latin Americans were you reading then?

AA: When I began writing, they'd recently begun to publish their "great" works, shall we say. Vargas Llosa's novel appeared in 1965, but *Rayuela* hadn't come out yet and neither had *Cien años de soledad* [*One Hundred Years of Solitude*].

MGP: There was Juan Rulfo.

AA: Juan Rulfo and Carlos Fuentes. García Márquez's short stories. The first contemporary Latin American novel I read that shook me to the core was *La ciudad y los perros.* I'd read *La region más transparente* [*Where the Air Is Clear*], but it didn't really speak to me then. After Vargas Llosa, I went through a short political phase, which is when I read *Los de abajo* [*The Underdogs*] and the work by the Mexican writer José Revueltas.

MGP: Were you a political militant in Europe?

AA: No, not yet. My friends, a few painters in Italy, in Rome, were very Marxist. But I had to consider the contradictions posed by the Cubans who had left Cuba. I'd also read Salvador Elizondo, José Agustín, Gustavo Sáinz, Juan García Ponce, and José Ibarbuengoitia. But as for novels, there still wasn't much. I read those of Alejo Carpentier, among them *El siglo de las luces* [*Explosion in the Cathedral*], which dazzled me. But it was Mario Vargas Llosa's work that had the greatest impact on me, because he was part of my generation. Then *Rayuela* appeared, and I felt as if I were buried. There was no way I could think about writing.

MGP: Did you keep track of what was being published?

AA: When I went to Spain, I found that every library and bookstore in the world was there, and I didn't have enough money to buy all the books I wanted. When I eventually met these writers, I'd already read all their books.

MGP: Did they have any kind of influence on your writing?

AA: No, because I was still a singer then. Carlos Fuentes was the only person I told about my writing, and he was very surprised. But no one ever discussed my books. I'd met them all in Barcelona: Carlos Fuentes, Mario Vargas Llosa, Julio Cortázar, García Márquez, José Donoso, and Jorge Edwards. In those days, García Márquez always put me up because I didn't have any money for a hotel, so I'd end up seeing all of them there. Pablo Neruda, too. But the ones I saw every day at García Márquez's house were Fuentes, Vargas Llosa, Donoso, and Cortázar.

MGP: Did Vargas Llosa have a great impact on your development of narrative techniques?

AA: I knew how strongly his presence made itself felt in my work, so I tried to camouflage it since I knew that he was one of my biggest demons then. For the same reason, I had to try to avoid Virginia Woolf at times, because she had always been a great master for me. But nothing I write resembles her work, because I'm very far from her lucidity and transparency. Up to a certain point, Mario was very important for me, but I haven't achieved the level of *La señorita de Tacna* or *La tía Julia y el escribidor* [*Aunt Julia and the Scriptwriter*]. Until *Conversación en la catedral* [*Conversation in the Cathedral*], no one in Latin America was as innovative, with the exception of Cortázar and *Rayuela,* a text that also sheds an enormous light on narrative strategies.

MGP: How is it important for you?

AA: Mario expresses the mechanics, the form, the invention, the eternal rupture. Every time he did a book, to experiment more, he wanted to tell more. That's what made me so passionate about him then. He wasn't content with one form or one system, nor did he put together a literary recipe. He went further; he searched; he broke easily with tradition and found new rhythms, new voices. *La casa verde* [*The Green House*] is an extension of José Eutasio Rivera's last line in *La vorágine:* "they got swallowed up by the jungle."

MGP: Perhaps he goes further than that; they're born swallowed up by the jungle.

AA: *Conversación en la catedral* is an intense novel. It takes everything farther. It starts over, reworks.

MGP: At any rate, in addition to the writers you mentioned, as a Colombian you have a figure that may or may not be a demon for you, but who is inescapable for writers in your country: Gabriel García Márquez. You have referred to him on several occasions here. How do you relate to him?

AA: He's more demonic to me as a friend than as a writer.

MGP: What kind of relationship does your literary practice have with his?

AA: None, I think. My greatest admiration goes to *El otoño del patriarca* [*The Autumn of the Patriarch*] and *El coronel no tiene quien le escriba* [*No One Writes to the Colonel*], in particular, which are two of his masterpieces, though *Cien años de soledad,* without a doubt, is a major work as well.

MGP: Why those?

AA: *El coronel* has already been talked about enough. It's a black pearl, round, perfect, and marvelous. It is flawless. It's a breathtaking story. *El otoño del patriarca* is also breathtaking, an invention that stands out not so much by its imagination as in its words. Until that point, García Márquez had never done much with wordplay. There García Márquez becomes ultrabaroque and deformed. It's quite beautiful. He's approached Colombian language and dialects in a way that he never does in his other books. He lets his hair down in this book. *Cien años de soledad* runs on two tracks—perfectly—but only two tracks mark the rhythm, the pulse. He is very musical and sings *vallenato* very well. But he hasn't yet written anything with that pulse, that syncopation. Perhaps some day he'll do it. There is a visual component as well. García Márquez's imagination doesn't overwhelm me. Parts of it dazzle me, parts of it blind me; but my grandmother and other people talk that way. My small demon remains. Certain of my stories might resemble García Márquez's works because they are set at the turn of the century. He still hasn't told the story of the twentieth century. He's stalled in the thirties. He hasn't gotten to the forties, where the rhythms are. Our stories, what we have to tell, are a common heritage. What's important is not to tell them the same way he does. In *La pájara pinta,* there is a section about a family going to clear trees from a mountainside in order to colonize it and build a village. I've tried to tell the story of the founders, the Araques, not the way Gabo would, but with a different rhythm. That's a part of the novel that could seem like the stories García Márquez tells. The language isn't like his, though. I'm sure the story I told was *paisa* and *pereirana,* not a story from the García Márquez coast.

MGP: I think you handle language in a different way. You work with different levels. You look for ways to reconstruct regional speech. Why do you think it is so important to be aware of the different dialects?

AA: When you try to explain how the atmosphere in each region differs (take, for example, the differences between the *costeño* and the *paisa*), you have to emphasize the way each one's language works. In order to paint different characteristics, I saw that I needed to manipulate the differences between the student from Bogotá or the people who came from the Caribbean or the south through their speech. I fell in love with dialects because of their expressive possibilities. Besides, I discovered all the unknown flora and fauna through the language of Colombia, which is excellent, pure Spanish.

La pájara pinta set me on a conscientious search for expression, for terms, for words that are beautiful in their expressiveness, for idioms. After my quest for form and language, I found the trace and the inspiration to write *Misiá señora.* That novel ended my cycle of searching for words. In *Las andariegas,* I'm more rigid. A few short parables emerge, but they're much more precise. The voyage in search of language is much more refined. It's entirely another process. I wanted to go on that quest myself, because although I've detected hints in certain Latin American writers and seen certain signs (in poetry as much as in prose), as a reader I've found that expressive richness lacking. Perhaps with the Venezuelan writer Salvador Garmendia it is possible to perceive this work. The Cuban José Lezama Lima has been a lesson, as well. At my level, keeping my distance, I resolved to plunge directly into language without letting any obstacle get in my way. *Misiá señora* has many dialects, especially Colombian ones, but dialects from other places—Argentina, Chile, Peru—appear, too, so that all Latin Americans will recognize themselves. I wanted my literary endeavors to be able to incorporate something it seems to me our literature has lost a little—the quest for language.

MGP: How is this kind of working through language different from the literary task of the woman writer that appears in *Las andariegas*? Does it connect?

AA: While I'm constructing those images, I'm very conscious that this is a sequence that's never been done quite this way before. I'm doing them in this strange way because of my identity as a woman. I also very carefully reproduce many masculine voices. They can be identified. But with the women's voices, my inventiveness gets carried away and I permit myself any irreverence—many would call them atrocities—because as a woman I allow myself not to be identified with masculine language and instead fashion the sounds and voices that might contribute other realities to the Latin American environment. So I think women's language in literature does exist, and that it's in the process of taking shape. It is becoming a kind of delta for many different streams. New forms will appear. We shall see the ocean someday. For the time being, we are busy with threads. We are the weavers that weave words. And not only do I participate in this dynamic consciousness, but I'm ready to defend *Misiá señora* as an integral expression of it. That's what my vision is.

MGP: Is *Misiá señora* a feminist novel?

AA: Completely. It's a novel of women, for women, by women, and from women.

MGP: Is it a "*feminaire*" à la Monique Wittig?

AA: Perhaps. I was drawn to Monique Wittig when I read *Les Guérrillères* because of her courage. She, along with Hélène Cixous, invents languages. Now we are substituting what we need for forms that are phallocentric and patriarchal, and we're rejecting false masculine premises. *Misiá señora* is proof that feminine language exists, by its expression of liberation through its irreverence and in the way it shatters beliefs and myths. Adrienne Rich says that throughout their lives female writers have been treated as though their works were solitary heroic exploits; no one has ever looked for any sort of context or whole or anything of that sort. Women's work has been viewed as something unusual, uncommon. People have taken us out of context, and we've had to come back again and again to show them that we do have a context. Finally there will be so many of us that they can no longer drown us with such comments. Now they're unearthing female writers who were never a part of literary history before.

MGP: Why are you a feminist?

AA: Because I'm a woman.

MGP: What is your position within feminism?

AA: The winner's. And I'm a revolutionary because I don't believe in revisionism. I admire radicals enormously. I wanted to be able to get to that point myself, but I realized that while we encounter problems in life that we shouldn't compromise on, we need to possess the necessary rhythms and modulations to prevent ourselves from getting crushed or broken. I understand that the revolution must have its radical component, and I praise radicals for their commitment. As far as I'm concerned, I'm becoming more radical every day. But there's a certain part of patriarchal society that must be listening to our proposals and cries, so painful at times, and we're going to have to adjust our position, but without softening. This is the moment in women's history, in the feminist revolution, that is crucial, and we need a tremendous revolutionary tension in order not to give in.

MGP: Feminism is a way of being in the world.

AA: It's a state of the soul, a state of being. There's another kind of superficial feminism, which consists of speaking and writing about certain topics, but many women haven't made feminism a part of their souls. We need to develop a feminist structure, especially in Latin America, and to become less afraid.

MGP: In fact, much remains to be done in Latin America.

✣ ✣ ✣

Rosario Ferré

✣ ✣ ✣

MGP: Let's start with your memories of growing up in Ponce, Puerto Rico.

RF: I lived in Ponce until I was twenty. Then it had two hundred thousand people, but now there are half a million. It was a commercial town. In the nineteenth century, it was the second most important commercial port on the island. All the sugar and coffee was shipped from southern Puerto Rico to the rest of the Caribbean and the United States. We also did business with Santo Domingo and Caracas. Ponce was very different from the North. San Juan was the center for the bureaucracy, where the government was very Spanish. There were a lot of *cachacos* there.

MGP: What are *cachacos*?

RF: In Puerto Rico, the sons of Spaniards are called *cachacos*. They sold codfish oil, the kind of oil most people used on the island.

Ponce's personality was quite distinct from the capital's. San Juan was the city of the *gachupines*, or Spaniards, who controlled business and government. Ponce was the capital of the southern part of the island. The Creole bourgeoisie was there, the people who did a lot of contraband business, which flourished among the Caribbean islands during the colonial era.

The town always had a personality of its own. It had a beautiful theater, La Perla [The pearl], quite large for a town of that size in those days. It burned down and was later rebuilt. Many great artists, Caruso and other opera singers, gave concerts there. It was like another country. But everything changed when the island began to industrialize, which happened when Muñóz Marín and the *populares* came into power and formed a government of social bureaucracy. They initiated a series of key social reforms and changed the island's economic structure. It was transformed from a feudal agricultural society to an industrial one because of American influence, which became more obvious as the highways expanded in the seventies. When they built the Ponce–San Juan highway, Ponce lost its personality. In the last twenty years, I'd say that all my friends in Ponce's small bourgeois society have moved to San Juan. Today, all that remains of Ponce is its appearance as a cultural center. Because now, although it's bigger and has more people, it's just a satellite city. There used to be wonderful formal parties in the casino and a lot of social goings-on. The gossip situation was awful, as in all provincial cities, because everyone knew everyone else.

I remember the first time Alicia Alonso came to Puerto Rico, when I was seven years old. She performed in La Perla theater, where she danced the Dance of the Black Swan. She returns to Puerto Rico often, but she'd never think of coming to Ponce now. She only performs in San Juan where the big theaters are.

MGP: So when you were a little girl, the cultural center was Ponce. Was there a university there?

RF: There was only a parochial school or convent—where the Instituto de Cultura is now—a Hieronymite convent where the nuns provided a religious education. Those were the days when the American church had the island under its thumb. All the priests spoke English. When they gave sermons, they gave them in very clumsy Spanish, full of anglicisms.

What was positive about American influence on education in Puerto Rico was that the Americans founded the University of Puerto Rico in 1902, four years after they came to the island. My mother graduated in the second class. There wasn't any university before because the island had always been Spain's most forgotten colony.

MGP: What school did you go to?

RF: I was raised by the Sisters of the Sacred Heart of Ponce. It was a peculiar world. These women were nuns who had arrived at the end of the world, at the edge of hell, in a town where they were submerged in the convent and had to be chaperoned in order to go to the dentist. Imagine wearing those wimples and veils in that heat, since Ponce is as humid and hot as a tropical jungle.

There is a portrait of a nun in the school, who is one of the saints of the Sacred Heart, with a folded head cloth around her face. On top of that, they wore black veils that fell almost to the ground and silver crosses hanging around their necks. I don't know how they could stand Ponce's heat in those outfits. I guess it was part of the torture involved in getting closer to God.

MGP: And they also lived in tremendous poverty, because most of the convents had no money.

RF: That's right. One needed a dowry to enter. But because Ponce was such a small town, the church probably didn't spend much money there, so the nuns had to live in an old house with very high ceilings, balconies, and a patio with adobe walls and windows high above, where you couldn't bring a male guest or even mention a man's name because it was a mortal sin.

MGP: Did you start going there when you were very young?

RF: I attended first grade at a boys' school. That's part of the reason I've been fairly rebellious. I started school during the war, and in order to economize on gasoline, my family sent me to the same school as my brother so the chauffeur wouldn't have to make two trips. The Jesuit school was fantastic compared to the nuns'. I went there from first through fifth grade. When I finished fifth grade, my parents transferred me to the nuns' school because boys and girls weren't really supposed to be together. The difference in teaching quality was like night and day, because the nuns didn't have the educational background the Jesuits had. They did teach us French from the start, though, which the boys' school didn't. I wrote a long story about that for the magazine *La mesa llena* published by the Mexican writer Jorge Aguilar Mora's group. It was called "El regalo" [The gift]. It's about two students at the nuns' school who are friends. Today, that world seems beautiful to me because all the little things and that uniquely Latin American poverty are all lost. Now everything is plastic, hamburgers, the Roy Rogers [fast food restaurant] and all those things.

MGP: North American culture is a very strong presence on the island, without a doubt.

RF: What's sad is that we've forgotten Spanish and never learned to speak English. We have no language of our own. There's definitely a problem of expression, which I share. Perhaps that's why I don't like to speak in public. I can write and formulate my thoughts much more clearly on paper; when I have to speak in public I feel constrained. Margo Glantz or Sylvia Molloy, for example, have an amazing mastery of language that reflects an instantaneous unfurling of thought and word that I find quite difficult. I think part of the problem stems from my education in the nuns' school.

MGP: It wasn't unusual that convent schools were dedicated to educating young girls in the social graces, and so the acquisition of knowledge was left behind.

RF: The education the nuns gave us was based on the principle that women should be hidden and never appear in public. Women were limited to anonymity. Anonymity was considered a virtue; the more quiet and insignificant you were, the more virtuous. My aunts still attack me when I publish a book, not only because I inevitably use autobiographical materials and describe today's society—not only that—but also because my name appears in the press and my picture gets printed in the paper. That for them is in the worst possible taste.

MGP: Are you considered the black sheep of the family?

RF: You said it!

MGP: How would you describe your family? How would you characterize them?

RF: My family is a bit contradictory but interesting. My mother was from a very old Puerto Rican family. They owned sugar plantations and were very traditional. They lived on a hacienda in Mayagüez, a town in the western part of the island. In terms of the island's society, they were aristocrats, with autochthonous values that were almost quixotic. They'd go down to ruin before they'd sell their land, even though they might be dying of hunger. Slowly they lost most of their property. They lost their homes little by little. Finally they were left without servants but still held on to their land, worthless now because nobody works it, but they stayed on as the masters of what is now barren land.

MGP: Do you come from a big family?

RF: Yes, my mother was the oldest of eight sisters, and she also had two brothers, which made ten children all together. I have more than sixty cousins on my mother's side. That side of the family would get together religiously for dinner at my grandparents' house in Mayagüez. All my cousins would come. It's a tradition that's still very much alive in Latin America. Families were matriarchies, and the central figure was the grandmother. Everybody on my father's side, on the other hand, was completely crazy.

MGP: How did that happen?

RF: Because, to begin with, my great-grandfather was French. He came to America with Ferdinand de Lesseps to build the Panama Canal. De Lesseps' project failed, and my great-grandfather settled in Cuba, where he lived with a Cuban woman whose last name was Sánchez: Rosario de Sánchez. He never married her, but they did have two children, my grandfather and a girl who later became a nun because she was very independent. And in those days the way for a woman to be independent was to seek refuge in a convent.

MGP: Reminiscent of Sor Juana Inés de la Cruz, the seventeenth-century Mexican nun.

RF: Exactly. It's something that ought to be studied. Many women entered convents because they wanted to be free, a terrible and contradictory phenomenon.

This Frenchman, my great-grandfather, had a wife and family in France that he was sending money to. He had a lawyer who disappeared with all the money, and the shock made my great-grandfather commit suicide.

MGP: How did the Ferrés arrive in Puerto Rico?

RF: My grandfather went to live with his mother's family, who were *mambises,* or rebels, against the Spaniards. They fought along with the nineteenth-century Cuban revolutionary Antonio Maceo. I've made use of some of that history in "La caja de cristal" [The crystal box].

✣ ✣ ✣

My great-grandfather had arrived in Cuba dressed in a frock coat, tuxedo and the like, complaining "It's so hot!" as though it were cooler in Panama than in Havana. Despite the fact that he looked like a magician fallen into disgrace, his having crossed the Atlantic with Ferdinand de Lesseps provided him with a certain aura of prestige. They had been friends united by the same dream: to divide the New World in half by opening an artery of communication that Western man had sought for centuries: to set out in a straight line from France to India, reaching the throngs of silk, the cinnamon and chinaberry forests, the pitchers of musk and aloe. But if Ferdinand dreamed of the geographic feat of the century, of excavating the furrow in the virgin continent, Albert dreamed of building the most beautiful bridge in the world, a bridge that would open and close its jaws just as the fabulous alligators of America do when they are making love. . . .

It was in those days that he met the Creole woman he was to marry. Ileana didn't speak French and Albert could barely manage day-to-day vocabulary in Spanish, but she never forgot the innocence of the interlacing geometric patterns she saw reflected in his eyes the first time she met him, nor the delicacy with which he held up exotic constructs made of thread between his fingers to illustrate his way of creating things. . . . Albert had joined a family of mambises *and never realized it* [*From "La caja de cristal"*].

✣ ✣ ✣

My grandfather, at fifteen, had joined the Cuban revolutionary forces against the Spaniards, but his mother packed him off to Puerto Rico so he wouldn't get killed. That's how he came to the island. His aunt, the nun, also went to Puerto Rico, but she probably got there before he did. She had served as the mother superior of a convent in Cuba for many years. When she got old she went to

Puerto Rico to die, at the age of ninety, and shortly after that my grandfather died.

My grandfather had an uncle who worked in a foundry, and he worked with him until he built his own foundry. He sent his children to school with the money he made, and all of them studied engineering, except one who studied business administration. In 1950, the first time we went to France to meet the other side of the Ferré family, we discovered that all our French relatives were engineers, too. A veritable Caribbean odyssey.

MGP: How were you received by your French relatives?

RF: Very well. We were the rich Americans. They were going through rough times because they'd just come through the war. Now they're doing very well. To get back to my family history, my father's brothers had built an industrial complex. On the other hand, my mother's family looked down on them because they were the *nouveaux riches,* the ones who earned money from industry. That was inconceivable.

MGP: It wasn't a noble way of earning a living, according to the old Christians of the Spanish Empire.

RF: That's right. My father had a sister who became a nun, too. She lived in Brooklyn for about fifteen years, doing social work with drug addicts in one of the worst slums in town. Now she lives in Puerto Rico on the beach in Ponce, which is also a slum. She is still a hard-working social worker. She's a missionary of the Holy Spirit, and they don't wear habits. A reactionary bishop once ordered them to wear habits, and my aunt replied that if he made them do it, she'd leave the order, even though she'd been a nun for forty years. She won.

The oldest in the family built a cement factory with some of the money from the sugar business, since some of his brothers had married into hacienda families that helped each other financially. That was how he got started. The uncle who made the most money went to Florida, where he built a cement factory called Moll Industries.

As I was saying, being crazy runs in my family. My millionaire uncle went mad after he made investments on such a grand scale that he ended up $200 million in debt. Now he doesn't have a cent. His son, Maurice Ferré, became the mayor of Miami.

MGP: Do you go back to Ponce when you are in Puerto Rico?

RF: No. I go to San Juan, because there's no one for me to visit in Ponce. Everybody lives in San Juan, and those who don't have gone to the United States because things are so bad in Puerto Rico.

MGP: How does your writing relate to that world?

RF: It's a question I've asked myself many times. How did I get so interested in literature, in the midst of a world where I was raised to be a wife and mother, to have a house and a position in society. I think genetics had something to do with it, the vein of madness in the Ferré family, or rather the vein of vanity, combined with a great imagination and an adventurous spirit. From my mother's side I got the desire to observe the way everything was changing. Perhaps deep down what I'm trying to do is recover a world that has disappeared, even though it's a world based on such tremendous injustice that I'm glad it's changed. There's a frivolity to it now that didn't exist then. For me, it's a world full of memories and terrible rancor, a mixture that makes for excellent literary material. It's a fight over the bones and the leftovers, since nothing else remains. The island oligarchy no longer exists, because they've all left and taken their money with them. Belonging to the United States has caused a sort of diaspora by creating an extraordinary social mobility. In Puerto Rico, people who have something stand out immediately, because the majority of the population has nothing.

Another reason I started to write was because I was having personal problems. To write was to try to recover a lost world, but it also seemed important to write from the vantage point of a society in transition. From a historical perspective, I think it is important to note how people change as well as how we try to hold onto the past. Writing was my salvation, because if you have everything, the earth falls away from under your feet and you're left with nothing in which to root your spiritual life. Puerto Rico isn't very religious, but it is superstitious. Still, the bourgeoisie maintains a religious façade. Also, there are some very powerful Masonic societies in Puerto Rico. It so happens that if you don't belong to any religious group, you have no social standing or recognized place in society. If you don't have a productive life, life becomes a mere frivolity, which is what's happened with most people.

For me, literature has been a way to sublimate certain things. It endows my life with meaning. If it weren't for literature, I don't think my life would have meaning.

MGP: When did you begin to write?

RF: I began writing when I was a young girl. I wrote poems and other little things. But I didn't start writing seriously until my mother died. That was a terrible year. My father, who was governor of Puerto Rico, lost the elections the year after my mother died. Her inheritance gave me the financial independence I'd never had. I could do whatever I wanted. That was also a determining factor. That's when I began to write. I wasn't terrified of the future anymore. Up to then, if I had dared to publish something or if I fought with my husband, I'd have found myself in the street, or I'd have had to go home to my parents. That would have been just as bad because I'd already been married ten years, and I led a relatively independent life, even though it was somewhat removed from the spheres my husband moved in. When all these things happened, I began to write.

MGP: When did you get married?

RF: In 1960, when I was 19. I had two children ten months apart. After four years, I had my third child. Everything happened after I'd been married ten years. The year my mother died, I separated from my husband and then got divorced. I was already writing and had begun to publish a magazine. Every time an issue came out, a new story of mine would be in it. This was very important for me because it made me realize I could have a literary career.

MGP: Was this when you were living in San Juan?

RF: Yes. I'd started going to the university earlier in order to finish my master's degree. I'd go between frying eggs in the morning and doing my other housework, because the children were small. My husband thought it was a good way for me to amuse myself, but he never anticipated what would come of my education, the poor man.

MGP: So the university was decisive for you?

RF: Indeed. The University of Puerto Rico was very important. I fell in with a group of friends, writers and artists, who are still like family to me. When I got divorced, I lost all contact with the world I'd belonged to before. I divorced the bourgeoisie of San Juan and Ponce as well as my husband. I became part of a world of artists, of people I felt understood me. That was my world.

MGP: When did you enter the university?

RF: In 1968. I'd gone to high school in Puerto Rico and then went to Wellesley College. I finally graduated from a college in New York. I studied English and French literature. When I went back to Puerto Rico, I studied Spanish and Latin American literature. I studied until 1971. In 1972 I took my master's exams and began to publish the magazine *Zona de carga y descarga* [Loading and firing zone]. I published it until 1976. Also, *Papeles de Pandora* [Pandora's papers] came out that year.

✣ ✣ ✣

pandora was the first woman on earth. zeus put her beside the first man, Epimetheus, and gave her a box with all humanity's good and evil inside.

pandora opened the fatal box and its contents scattered all over the world, hope being the only one remaining in it [Epigraph from Papeles de Pandora].

✣ ✣ ✣

In 1976, I took my children and went to live in Mexico City, but that didn't last long. Now they are all studying in the United States, and I've moved to Washington.

I always think of Puerto Rico as my home. I want to keep going there, and I do go all the time—but it lacks a stimulating intellectual atmosphere.

MGP: Was the magazine important for your development as a writer?

RF: *Zona de carga y descarga* was a crucial factor in my life. Its title was very political because there people would fire and get fired upon. We published every critical article people sent us. We got as many from the right as from the left because it was a rather anarchistic magazine.

MGP: Who was on the staff?

RF: We had a very good group. One of my cousins wrote a lot. In fact, she is a fantastic poet.

MGP: What was her name?

RF: Olga Nolla. She and I are the same age. We were like sisters. Life has separated us recently. Now she writes television scripts and leads a very active professional life. Also a poet, Luis César Rivera. Neither of them has left the island, but both are great artists. He was also a bohemian, from an anarchist group, and he helped us a lot. Waldo Lloreda, another one of our collaborators, was a doctoral student when Olga and I met him. He wrote literary criticism. Eduardo Forestieri, who is a professor of philosophy today, collaborated only on the first issue, because he realized that the atmosphere was too bohemian for him. Other people joined in: Manuel Ramos Otero, an excellent short story writer; the poet Iván Silén; and the short story writer Tomas López Ramírez. At that time—from '72 to '75—the atmosphere was one of intellectual effervescence.

MGP: Was *Zona de carga y descarga* strictly a literary magazine?

RF: Yes. We also did the layout and design ourselves. We met Zilia Sánchez, a Cuban graphic artist and a very good painter. Her erotic painting and sculpture is better than what you may see in the Guggenheim Museum in New York, but no one has heard of her because she lives in Puerto Rico. She showed me how to do all the layout for the magazine, so both of us ended up doing all the work. It was tabloid size, twenty-two pages long. We were able to publish ten issues, two thousand copies of each.

Those were very good years because we could introduce talented young people who didn't have any other place to publish and who, since the magazine disappeared, still have no place to publish and get their work recognized. There's only a magazine called *Reintegro,* put out by some young men who worked with us back then. It's very good. There was also *Sin nombre,* Nilita Vientos' literary magazine. That was a forum for well-known writers and critics, for the sacred cows. They weren't about to publish some unknown who emerged from who-knows-what slum or who-knows-what middle-class suburb in *Asomante* or *Sin nombre.*

MGP: Did you know Nilita Vientos well?

RF: I didn't know her very well then. Now I do, because we've become literary colleagues, and I respect her very much. We call her the grande dame of Puerto Rican letters.

MGP: Not only in Puerto Rico, but in all of Latin America.

RF: She's done more for Puerto Rican literature than the Instituto de Cultura in all the years since it was founded. And besides, she's helped a lot of people. She gives scholarships and organizes literary contests and prizes—she's amazing—and she does it without government help.

MGP: Does the magazine generate the income for this?

RF: No, very little. She *had* a little money of her own. She's a lawyer and has her own law firm. She does it all with the help of friends and intellectuals who know her work and donate money for it. There must be only two or three literary magazines in Latin America that have been published over such a long period. *Asomante* has been around for about twenty years and *Sin nombre* for some fifteen.

MGP: Similar to Victoria Ocampo's *Sur* in Argentina.

RF: Yes. The day Nilita Vientos disappears, the magazine will surely fold. It is recognized more outside Puerto Rico than inside.

MGP: Getting back to your magazine, why did it provoke such a reaction? What were the ideas and objectives behind it?

RF: We believed in social reform, but we didn't want to be identified with any political party. We were always on the defensive. We supported an independent liberal position on the right as much as on the left. We quoted Artaud, Rimbaud, and the first books of Octavio Paz. It was an exciting period for us.

We got attacked from all sides. To some, we were reactionaries; to others, we were communists. In Puerto Rico, where everything is clearly defined, anyone who can't be pigeonholed is a suspect. You are an anarchist whichever way you choose to go.

MGP: Were you trying to succeed at some political objective?

RF: The people in the *Partido Popular* were very conservative at heart, even though we supported Muñoz Marín during his first years. Then the same bureaucratic disease infected them as it had all the others. Instead of taking a political position, the magazine had an existential position.

MGP: Who read *Zona de carga y descarga*?

RF: Good heavens! It sold like crazy! It was incredible! Women all gossipped about it. They all hurried to read the magazine because it ran the most outrageous things. And besides, it contained bad words and used street language. We published a story by Manuel Ramos Otero called "El esclavo y el señor" [The slave and the master]. Good grief! That was incredible! It was issue number eight, in pink, with a doll's head on the cover, and it had a quotation from Oliver Wendell Holmes about witches.

✣ ✣ ✣

Look out, look out, clear the tracks!
The witches are here, they've all come back
They hang them high, no use, no use
What cares a witch for a hangman's noose?
They buried them deep
But they wouldn't lie still
For cats and witches are hard to kill
They swore they wouldn't and shouldn't die
Books said they did
But they lied, they lied
[*From Oliver Wendell Holmes, in* Zona de carga y descarga *3:1, 1975*].

✣ ✣ ✣

All Puerto Rican society thought the issue had been inspired by the devil, so they burned it on their patios.

MGP: Like an auto-da-fé.

RF: Yes. On the back cover was a story by Juan Mestas, "Un joven demasiado hermoso." It was a detailed description of the sexual act between two men. Today I think it's a horrible story, but it seemed wonderful then because it expressed the kind of symbiosis between the magazine's existential position and its political position. And that sometimes clouded our vision a little concerning quality.

MGP: Did you publish your short story "Cuando las mujeres quieren a los hombres" ["When Women Love Men"] in *Zona de carga y descarga*?

RF: Yes, and it caused a terrible scandal. That issue was colored black, an issue in mourning. The cover was black with white letters. It was about Isabel the Black. My story was published on the left side of page 1. On the right, in the other column, parallel with mine, appeared Manuel Ramos Otero's story, also about Isabel the Black. The titles were in very small type. Because the two stories were so much alike and so terrible, people thought they were the same story. Manuel's was called "La última canción que cantó Luberza" [Luberza's last song].

MGP: Had you both decided to work on the same subject?

RF: Yes. We came to an agreement because Isabel Luberza, who was a very famous prostitute in Ponce, had just died. When I was a little girl, all the local bourgeoisie went to her brothel. Manuel knew her story too. The woman had made millions with her house. Then came the day she wanted to give the bishop a donation for the church, but he wouldn't take her money because of where it came from. It was a great scandal, and she was killed in a drug ambush not long after. It all seemed wonderful material for a story. I split her real name—Isabel Luberza—in two and made Isabel into the society woman and Luberza into the prostitute. The two began to merge until they became one person.

✣ ✣ ✣

Now I'm getting close to her because I want to see her face-to-face, to see her the way she really is, her hair no longer a cloud of rebellious smoke curling around her head, but thin and delicate, wrapped around her neck like ancient chain, her skin not black but white, spilling over her shoulders like burning lime milk, without the slightest suspicion of a colored strand, I'm strolling with my hips swaying back and forth on my red heels, and through them flows, slow and silent like the tide, the blood that had so long ago begun to rise through me from the bottom of my fingernails, my blood polished with Cherries Jubilee [*From "Cuando las mujeres quieren a los hombres"*].

✣ ✣ ✣

MGP: I think that's a wonderful story.

RF: Luis Ramos Otero's story was later published in a book called *Con-*

cierto de metal para un recuerdo [Concerto in metal for a memory]. He's homosexual, and his story is centered around homosexual relations. It's excellent.

MGP: And the Cuban painter helped you with graphics and color?

RF: We did the mock-ups, and she showed us the colors we needed to use. It would have been impossible to do the magazine any other way. We learned to move the type in the typesetting machines in order to save money. We met the Ramayo brothers (some reactionary Cubans who had money), and they didn't care if our magazine was communist. But when the story with every obscene word in existence came out, they got furious and told us they wouldn't publish the magazine anymore. The last three issues were published in New York.

MGP: Why did you stop publishing?

RF: Because it was so expensive. We distributed the magazine all over but only collected payments from a small number of the subscribers—more or less half. It was too much work because the men were always, constantly taking breaks, and the women had to run the machines. They wrote and published, and we had to do the "cuisine" of writing.

MGP: Where did the magazine sell?

RF: We had subscribers in Mexico and Colombia, but it was very hard to collect the payments. In addition to the text, the magazine had plates of paintings, portraits, and photographs. My brother, who was the editor of the newspaper *El Día,* helped with the prints. The magazine was designed to reverse the standard reading and layout format. Some poets took advantage of this and did drawings to go with their poems.

And you know, everything really began with Angel Rama, who was the father of the magazine and a very important figure in my life. He came to Puerto Rico in 1971, and Olga Nolla and I took his courses. It was a time when the university began to open up, when it began to bring Latin American writers to Puerto Rico.

When Angel and Marta Traba came, they made an important contribution to the cultural world of the island. Angel and Marta came to Puerto Rico on their honeymoon and stayed a little more than two years. Olga and I were their favorite students, and Angel supported Olga through the publication of her first books. When Angel left, he put us in charge of creating a literary magazine. Angel wanted to publish Olga's first book in *Marcha,* but her husband wouldn't have it. Then she got divorced, too, like everyone in Puerto Rico did. Marta's book *Homérica latina* talks about us and about Nilita, but the names have been changed. She also published a very good book about Puerto Rican painting, which was extremely important for the island's culture. It was too bad they couldn't stay. It was certainly a great loss.

MGP: So you began to publish your works when the magazine started up. What did you publish after *Papeles de Pandora*?

RF: *El medio pollito* and *Sitio a Eros* [Eros under siege], which I wrote when I came back to Puerto Rico from Mexico. This last one is a series of literary essays on literature and women. *Fábulas de la garza desangrada* [Fables of the bleeding heron] came next, and it was published by Joaquin Mortiz Publishers. Now I have a collection of new stories called *Isolda en el espejo* [Isolde in the mirror].

MGP: What are some of the works that you think were most influential in your literary education?

RF: I like the fable genre because I used to read fairy tales in Ponce when I was a child. In a fable, you're always looking through a camera lens that distorts everything. Your perception depends on the lens, in spite of the fact that life goes on the same way it always did. It doesn't change. There was a small bookstore that carried *Billiken* [an illustrated children's magazine published in Argentina] and fairy tales. Later, when I learned English, I became fascinated with *Wuthering Heights*. That novel and *Jane Eyre* were challenging texts for women. For me, *Jane Eyre* is a feminist manifesto, as are the novels of George Eliot, another extraordinary writer. Maybe I was so dissatisfied with having been born female because I was young and because I'd been sent to a nuns' school where the education was of poor quality. I enjoyed books that struggled with those problems, though I didn't know why then. I also liked *Little Women* and all the Tarzan stories. I had a lot of time to read because there wasn't much to do. I couldn't work, and there was no intellectual life of any sort.

Now I'm interested in surrealist writers because at the level of language these writers tried to develop, the so-called demons that impose themselves from outside come into play. Cortázar himself has talked about this. It's like a tiny rabbit that has to be pulled out through your mouth. In *Una vuelta al día por ochenta mundos* [*Around the Day in Eighty Worlds*], every story was an erotic impulse he had to vomit out through his mouth. This happens to me at the linguistic level, but at the level of the plot or anecdote—which is what's hardest for me—the process is one of logical development. I'm interested in pieces whose narrative structure is anecdotal, though I have some narratives like "Maquinolanderas" [Washing machine women] or "Cuando las mujeres quieren a los hombres" in which hardly anything happens. It's language that acts. But what I'm doing now and what I've done in *Papeles de Pandora* is a logical linking of cause and effect. I'm interested in literature that is marked by its tension and that keeps the reader tense, which is what Vargas Llosa does, though I'd wish he'd combine language with anecdote more because he may be excessively logical and anecdotal.

MGP: Moving to another subject, do you consider yourself a feminist? How do you feel about feminism?

RF: The victories that have been won can no longer be reversed. I think feminism is the most important revolution in the twentieth century. Many people don't agree with me. But no social progress will be achieved in any part of the world if it's not through the medium of feminism. It's more important today than social struggle.

MGP: It has to be a struggle that stems from feminism, somehow independent from political ideologies, because women haven't been included in social reform projects, so they haven't been able to make much of a difference.

RF: We women are the ones who have to take issue with women's problems. I don't think any system or political party will do it for us.

MGP: Are you familiar with American and/or French feminism?

RF: I'm familiar with the works of Simone de Beauvoir, which seem very important to me. I've also read Erica Jong, and I like her poems much better than her essays. I've read Kate Millet's *Sexual Politics* and some of her other works. I've read Hélène Cixous also. As far as these subjects go, I think the essays I've included in *Sitio a Eros* are contradictory, particularly when I maintain that women are intuitive beings. I've changed considerably since then because I now see how limiting that position is. Awarding women the monopoly on passion is confining. Empires are not ruled by passion.

MGP: Do you think there's such a thing as feminine writing?

RF: To give you an answer, I'll read you a fragment of an essay entitled "La cocina de la escritura" [The cuisine of literature]:

✣ ✣ ✣

Does there exist, in the end, a body of writing? Does there exist a literature of women that is different from that of men? And if it exists, must it be passionate and intuitive, founded on sensation and feeling, as Virginia wanted, or rational and analytic, with its inspiration in historical, social, and political knowledge, as Simone wanted? Must we, today's writers, be defenders of feminine values in the traditional sense of the word and cultivate a harmonious literature, poetic, neat, devoid of obscenities, or must we be defenders of feminine values in the modern sense, cultivating a literature that's combative, accusatory, unconditionally realist, and even obscene? Must we be, in the end, Cordelias or Lady Macbeths? Dorothys or Medeas? Virginia Woolf said that her writing was always feminine, that it couldn't be anything but feminine, but the difficulty lay in defining the term. Although I don't agree with many of her theories, I'm completely in agreement with this one. I think that today's women writers must, above all, write well, and that one succeeds in writing well only by mastering the techniques of writing. A sonnet has but fourteen lines, a specific number of syllables and a determined rhyme scheme and meter. Thus, it is a neutral form, neither feminine nor masculine, which means that a woman is just as capable of writing a perfect sonnet as is a man. A perfect novel, as Rilke said, must be a sublime cathedral, built brick by brick with infinite patience, and therefore it too is genderless and can be written just as well by a woman as by a man. Nevertheless, for a woman to write well signifies a much more arduous fight: Flaubert rewrote Madame Bovary *seven times, but Virginia Woolf wrote* The Waves *fourteen times, surpassing Flaubert no doubt because she was a woman and knew critics would be doubly hard on her.*

What I want to say with all this may smack of heresy, of cooking that is pernicious and mephitic, but this essay is, after all, about the cuisine of literature. Despite my metamorphosis from housewife to writer, writing and cooking often become confused in my mind, and I discover some surprising correspondences between the two. I suspect that no distinct feminine literature exists. To insist that one does exist implies, in a parallel fashion, the existence of a feminine nature, distinct from the masculine, when to me it seems most logical to emphasize the existence of a radically different experience. If a separate feminine or masculine nature did exist, that would imply distinct capabilities in men and women as far as, for example, executing a work of art, when they really have the same capabilities, because men and women are, above all, fundamentally human.

An enduring feminine nature, a feminine mind perpetually defined by its gender, would justify the existence of an unalterable feminine style, characterized by certain features of structure and language that would be easy to recognize in studying past and present works written by women. In spite of the theories that currently abound on this topic, I think these features are debatable. The novels of Jane Austen, for example, are novels of reason whose structure is meticulously closed and lucid, diametrically opposed to the diabolical, mysterious, and passionate novels of her contemporary Emily Brontë. And both women's novels can't be more different than the open, fragmented, and psychologically subtle novels of modern writers like Clarice Lispector or Elena Garro. If style is man, style is also woman, and it differs profoundly not only from human being to human being, but also from work to work.

What I do believe distinguishes feminine literature from masculine literature is its themes. In the past, we women have had very limited access to, for example, the world of politics, science or adventure, although that's changing today. Our literature often seems to be determined by an immediate relation to our bodies: it is we who carry children and give birth to them, who care for them and worry about their survival. The destiny nature imposes on us creates some very serious problems when we try to reconcile our emotional needs with our professional needs, but it also puts us in contact with the mysterious forces that generate life. That's why women's literature—much more than men's literature—has been preoccupied with the past, with interior experiences, that have little to do with the historical, the social or the political. That's also why women's literature is more subversive than men's literature, because it often dares to dive into forbidden areas, closer to the irrational, to madness, to love and to death, areas whose existence, in our rational and utilitarian society, sometimes ends up being dangerous to acknowledge. These subjects, nonetheless, interest women, not because women have a different nature, but because they patiently and minutely harvest their experience. And, to a certain point, this experience, like men's experience, can change; it can be enriched and become broader.

Ultimately, I suspect that the interminable debate over whether feminine writing exists or not is now vain and insubstantial. What is important is not to determine whether we women should write with an open or closed structure, with poetic language or obscene language, or with the head or the heart. What is important is to apply the fundamental lesson we learned from our mothers, who were the first, after all, to teach us to fight fire with fire: The secret of writing, like that of cooking, has absolutely nothing to do with gender, but has everything to do with how skillfully the ingredients are combined.

Only a woman can confront a woman's themes. But you can't say there's a feminine language.

✣ ✣ ✣

MGP: Don't you think women approach and use language in a different way?

RF: The diary form is a feminine genre. I make a distinction between the structure of language and its themes.

MGP: Are there any writers who particularly interest you?

RF: Yes. Felisberto Hernández was very important for me. I did my master's thesis on him: It's called *El acomodador: una lectura fantástica de Felisberto Hernández.* Of women writers, I've most recently become familiar with Silvina Bullrich, Clarice Lispector, Elena Garro, Elena Poniatowska, and also Lillian Hellman. But it's occurred to me that because my themes are outside my own self and because women's literature is more introspective, men's literature has been more of a stimulus for me, except for Brontë and Woolf. I went crazy when I discovered Virginia Woolf.

As far as structure and textual framework are concerned, men have been more important: Mario Vargas Llosa, Juan Carlos Onetti, Julio Cortázar. I learned from them the instruments of narrative technique I didn't learn from women. I don't know why, since Virginia Woolf has mastered these techniques perfectly. But that's not the reason. When I read a woman, I look for other things. When I read men, I read a series of technical questions. With women I look at myself in a profound and intimate way. Sylvia Plath is a good example. After having read all her works, I can't reread them because I get too depressed. They made a deep impression on me, and I fell into the abyss. In poetry, César Vallejo is most important for the way he deconstructs language and for the conflict of forces that his poems create, especially in *Trilce.* It's the same linguistic violence we attempted to create in our literary magazine *Zona de carga y descarga.* The erotic element in Vallejo has also been very significant for me.

When I was working on my book of fables [*Fábulas de la garza desangrada*], I read the *Iliad* and Sophocles. The character of Antigone is of great importance to me.

MGP: *Fábulas* is a very beautiful and major work. I think there is great potential for rewriting mythology by using the multiple possibilities offered by fiction. Another essential aspect of feminine writing is the reinterpretation of cultural history. Why did you choose only female characters for that book?

RF: The idea was to give a new history of women, interpreted as it should have been and given a different ending: Desdemona kills Othello, Ariadne leaves Theseus. It's a book of rebellion, and I identify very much with Albert Camus in that regard. The most authentic existential position is that of the rebel.

Vargas Llosa's book of essays *Entre Sartre y Camus* is very good, and I agree with his defense of Camus against Sartre. The book of fables was really a pleasure to write.

MGP: Why do you incorporate myth as a literary theme?

RF: Because it is a world, as García Márquez says in *Cien años de soledad,* where everything is there to be named. It is the world of the founding people. Inside that world all the feminine conflicts can be found. If you read the *Iliad* from a feminine point of view and take into account the female characters as well as the goddesses, it's a truly dazzling work. In "Contracanto" [Countersong], my best piece, I work through all of that. I think Helen of Troy is one of the victims of humanity—not only Helen, but also what she signifies, which can be extended to the contemporary female figure. An example would be the American woman who must have perfectly done hair, long and blond, like a gilded cloud, et cetera. She must follow Helen of Troy's ideal of beauty. It's a terrible phenomenon that goes beyond objectification and ultimately poses the existential question of what feminine beauty signifies.

✣ ✣ ✣

a face whose beauty may provoke
the final feat of arrows
that weave in the battlefield,
inevitable yet invisible
a face in which to forget even forgetfulness
that drags down with its fatal silver gauze
into a tide of other spent faces,
of wives nearly transparent, leaning
over fires in the hearths
of ruined rooms and barren epochs

. . . .

O Helen,
you who were born between white Leda's wings;
not in vain did Nemesis, on contemplating your fate,
flee, terrified of her offspring!
Let what you see here convince you that
from one side or the other
of your dark contrite heart
fly two faces of the same death!
pallid Paris, to whom, as a pledge, you uttered sweet life,
and Menelaus, the golden Atreidae,
they who together reveal to you the bitter truth
of your already vanished and arcadic existence:
for one man you were the consummate courtesan
who ruled his destiny, wedded to the bed,
between sheets moaning with delirium;
for the other you were the able administrator
of the gold accumulated by the greedy bridal bed

in slow drops.
but I now know that in this hour
when you understand and are prescient of all,
the remorse of having been what you once were
and your sorrow at not being able to go on,
you predict inside this horizon's boundary
a third torment that is certain;
Achaeans and Trojans, the noble flower
and cream of ancient youth, the young men
tall as ash trees, the seed of the kings
and the Fates, delicate as deer and the
brown princes of Asia, perfumed with spices,
the dauphins, heirs to diadems,
the primogenitors and the bastard sons
of happy Argolis,
men consumed in the eager
exercise of war, ironclad outlaws
already grown up and advanced in years,
they whose long manes trail in the dust
their disdain for honest defeat, they who arrived
in their wine-sodden ships to sack Troy
and to make widows in her streets, and they who today
defend Troy, the diamond-like whistling of her arches
exalting the high towers,
they who today cover from sea to sea the Scamander
before coloring with purple murex dye her millenary sand
they who roar, bubble, boil at your feet,
around the flowers of glory,
destroyed by the fields,
the statues distilling blood,
pretending to shine in your name;
that for your love satiate the entrails
of the hard earth with heroes' flesh;
which in your memory the greyhound, the wild boar and the wolf
claw, in the whirling eddy of their necks,
the memories of other men and other times [*From "Contracanto"*].

✤ ✤ ✤

MGP: In your essay "La autenticidad de la mujer en el arte" [The authenticity of women in art] from *Sitio a Eros* you emphasize women's experience as a source for literature, but you also remark that experience is limited, so women's creative capacity may prove limited.

RF: She limits herself. I limit myself.

MGP: Due to external forces or conditions, social or moral ones. You underscore the importance of individual experience as a productive source. In the story "La muñeca menor" [The youngest doll] we see this aspect very clearly in the game of the doll's image and when the infection in the protagonist's leg oozes and smells like an overripe mango. But in *Fábulas de la garza desangrada,* direct experience is less visible.

RF: Yes, it is. Every woman has a mask, and behind that mask the same voice is heard. In that sense, there's a continuity between *Papeles de Pandora* and *Fábulas de la garza desangrada.* The mask changes. Instead of Isabel Luberza we have Antigone.

MGP: Nevertheless, I believe that you treat one differently from the other, in that the second is much more of a literary elaboration.

RF: Yes, it's more literary. Those are characters who have certainly been worked through at length throughout Western literature. They've been written into a context that always contains conflict that eventually gets resolved in a tragic way. They're always being bent to fatal destiny, or to force, or to the will of men and gods.

MGP: The first time I read the book, I thought you were taking on a new responsibility in the task of rewriting history, of discovering—in the sense of lifting the veil—a scarcely known world that turns out to be something new. The project is utopian and fascinating at the same time because of the possibilities it offers to the female imagination. Also, the language that you're creating links you to the rest of Caribbean literature in its baroque boldness and audacity of literary production.

RF: Isn't Borges' language daring or that of any other Latin American the same?

MGP: Although you see it as one gesture of the way Latin American writers express themselves, I think this literature also can be thought of as a revision of the canon, a subversive undertaking, rather than think it's caused by conditions set by underdevelopment. In your immediate writing plans, will you continue working with the short story, or are you thinking of tackling the novel now?

RF: The novel requires a longer time commitment than I am able to make yet.

MGP: It has been remarked that many women tend to write in a fragmented style, and some tend to cultivate the shorter genres as well.

RF: I believe that's a situation or circumstance that life imposes on us.

MGP: Borges is of the opinion that the novel is a minor genre. He says the best form is the short story.

RF: Amazing!

MGP: You once said that one way you write is by "copying" the masters. Could you tell me what you mean by this, and how you put this ingenious formula into practice?

RF: OK, look. You have to read their stories. For example, you take a book by Felisberto Hernández, you read it through, and then you go to sleep. The next day, you make an *arroz con pollo,* mix everything together, and then out comes the story.

MGP: What do you like in Felisberto, for example?

RF: I'm interested in how he enters the process of imagination. He struggles with madness, and his images come very close to it. He's very close to the surrealists, who also interest me very much. If I read much Felisberto, I start hearing echoes. It's like doing the same thing but in a different tone. Nevertheless, what's hardest is not the work with language but spinning the plot, because it's trying to impose order on chaos in a process in which you don't know what the order should be. You must disperse the ambiguities until you find the right order. Then you suddenly discover the order because it existed all along.

MGP: Vargas Llosa has talked quite a bit about this style of composing. These texts seem wonderful to me because it's like being in the middle of the kitchen, cooking up literature right next to him. He says that narrative material eventually finds a form that takes shape very slowly. Then it needs to be reworked, but in some sort of way the material begins to find its own form. Those are Vargas Llosa's famous demons, which have caused more than one discussion in the past.

RF: With me, it's a bit different. I begin with a visual image or metaphor that I have to develop in all directions. I work with one image, a seed, from which I begin to extract a tiny thread that I have to start weaving around it. That makes me confine myself to short texts because it's easier to finish weaving something than to write a novel. You would have to write a novel with many tiny centers, which is what many novelists do. By the way, I've finished a novel called *Maldito amor* [Damned love].

✣ ✣ ✣

From the windows in the car, adorned with gray velvet, well-to-do citizens would greet one another, craning their necks to figure out who was going in or out of such-and-such a place in order to guess whether so-and-so or what's-his-name had or had not been invited to the party, if he had been blackballed or if he would be accepted by Don Fernando Arzuaga. It wasn't that they'd never had similar festivities in town. The lofty society of La Perla del Sur, which until recently was chiefly composed of landowners and sugar magnates, had gained fame for its extravagant parties, where the sugar and rum barons unfurled the full scope of their power without thinking about it. But in the final years, the character of these celebrations had changed. The sugar cane aristocracy was no longer the ruling class, because its lands and estates had already passed, for the most part, into the hands of huge foreign corporations. Political power was now in the hands of the new industrial class, which was allied with foreign interests, and the sugar barons had passed overnight, from the florid speeches recited from their benches in the Senate (from which, dressed in coarse linen twill, they planned the elaborate filigree of their Ciceronian oratory) to heroic deeds of another caliber. They gave themselves body and soul to burning the candle at both ends, to throwing the foundations of their homes through the window without much regret.

It was clear there was no way out for them, and it was said that they occasionally came to the point of inviting the agents of their misfortune—the people who ran the North American corporations—to their parties. Devoid of all intellectual cultivation, as well as true refinement, they decided, as did the citizens of ancient Rome, to commit gradual suicide by devouring their own entrails. They shut themselves up in their stone mansions in the small towns where they had moved when they were forced to abandon the estates that were impossible to maintain and ate and drank what remained of their vast fortunes [*From* Maldito amor].

✣ ✣ ✣

✣ ✣ ✣

Margo Glantz

✣ ✣ ✣

MGP: To begin reconstructing your chronology, I would like to start with the first books to which you were exposed. Do you remember what you read when you were a child?

MG: I've been reading since I was a little girl. The only prize I must have won in my entire life was for learning to read very rapidly in school. They gave me a talking doll. I took her in the tub to see if she could take a bath with me, but because it was a deficient machine, she died there in the tub and never talked again. But, getting back to my first readings, my father had a rather extensive library with a variety of books, many volumes of poetry in Russian and also in Yiddish. Papa was a Jewish poet who wrote in Yiddish. That's why he had a large library of poetry in these languages, and when he arrived in Mexico he became interested in Spanish and Mexican and Latin American poetry. I remember he had an anthology called *Florilegio de varia poesía* [An anthology of poetry] in which I read the Greeks and other foreign poetry in translation. I began to read Calderón de la Barca, Shakespeare, Alexandre Dumas, Jules Verne, Emilio Salgari, Mark Twain, and pulp novels by Pérez and Pérez. At that age you read whatever falls into your hands, what fascinates you and moves you.

MGP: Were you interested in the serialized novels that came out in the papers?

MG: My father used to buy *Novedades,* a newspaper that published novels in serial form and also in hardback. I also used to read Rocambole de Ponson du Terrail and Gaston Leroux. Those kinds of books fascinated me when I was a young girl. I also read all sorts of adventure novels and even some pornographic novels my father had lying around. This was all when I was about thirteen. I must have started reading when I was between nine and ten. I also got interested in some collections of Greek mythology adapted for children. That was very important because the stories of Jason, Perseus, Prometheus, and the rest have become a part of my fiction. I was drawn to the adventures of Columbus, Cortés, Robert Peary, who discovered the North Pole, to the Himalayan expeditions, to stories about inventors, about Watt and many others. In other words, I read whatever fell into my hands. Since I was a very shy child, what I mainly did was read. And when I was an adolescent, I read even more.

MGP: I'm surprised that you say you were a shy child.

MG: The shyest. I don't seem so now, do I?

MGP: So not only reading but reading a great many books is a consequence of your being very shy?

MG: Yes. Reading was a kind of protection: first, because I liked it so much; second, because I was often left alone to take care of my parents' business, their many businesses. But my job was always to be in the shoe store we had on Tacuba Street near Calzada México. We had the store from the time I was thirteen until I was sixteen. We kept a business schedule that no one keeps anymore: from 9:00 to 1:00 and from 3:00 to 6:00. We'd close the store from 1:00 to 3:00, but we had to be inside taking care of things. My mother would go upstairs to make lunch, and I'd stay downstairs.

MGP: Did you live above the shoe store?

MG: Yes. That's why I'd stay and watch the store and read. I got annoyed when it was my turn to wait on customers because they interrupted my reading.

When I was about fourteen, I joined a Zionist organization called Hashomer Hatzair. It had a lending library that seemed pretty good at the time, though I don't know if it really was. It had important books—most of all, books by North American authors. I began to read John Dos Passos, Steinbeck, Upton Sinclair, Sinclair Lewis, Sherwood Anderson, Faulkner, and others. I'd read translations published by Editorial Sudamericana. I also read literature in translation published by Salvador Rueda Publishing House and the trilogy *Manhattan Transfer,* plus Faulkner's *The Wild Palms,* translated by Borges, though people then still didn't know who Borges was. I read a lot of the Séptimo Círculo collection, whose editors were Borges and Bioy Casares. I didn't discover Borges' own writings until much later—when I was thirty—though I'd read his translation of Kafka's *The Metamorphosis* and also of some of the works by Hermann Hesse. *Manhattan Transfer* was very important.

MGP: Could you explain to me why it was so important? What was it that made an impression on you or attracted you?

MG: It was a very interesting novel—epic, with changing places and characters. It was about contemporary problems, a novel of social consciousness, engagé, according to Sartre's philosophy. I remember that Faulkner used to intrigue me in a morbid way. I also remember getting wrapped up about twenty times in a couple of Jules Verne novels—*A Two Years' Vacation* and *A Captain at Fifteen*. I read *The Children of Captain Grant* even more than those two. I can also add Fenimore Cooper to this list, with *The Last of the Mohicans,* and Walter Scott with *Ivanhoe.* Everyone in Hashomer Hatzair read a lot. My friends there were mostly older than I—almost all of them were fifteen. We got to take the books home, and I devoured them, because I've always been a fast reader. I read all those books passionately several times over. When I was sixteen, I'd already read Huxley's *Point Counterpoint.* And the next year I began to read Proust, but I didn't like it because it seemed boring. I remember the German writer Jakob Wasserman, a Jew who lived in Germany until he had to emigrate because of the rise of Nazism.

There were other novels that people don't read much anymore, like *El caso Maurizius* [*The Maurizius Affair*] and *El hombrecillo de los gansos* [*The Little Goose Boy*] and *Etzel Andergast* by Wasserman and *Jean Christophe* by Romain Roland. Feuchtwanger was another German Jew I used to read when I was a little girl. He wrote an important novel called *El Judío Süss* [*Jud Süss*]. I also remember Max Eastman, the North American whom I saw reemerge in the movie *Reds* because he was a friend of Jack Reed's. I tried to read *As I Lay Dying* then, but it took a lot of effort. And reading *Sanctuary* left me with an impression somewhere between morbid and violent. I read and read and read and didn't understand a thing. Faulkner was about things that were very hard to understand—abortions, rapes, and a eunuch that orders a woman's rape—so I had trouble grasping these subjects. Nevertheless, I later read Faulkner passionately and very carefully. *Crime and Punishment* made such an impression on me that I've never been able to get through it a second time. It always seemed so violent that I couldn't read it through to the end. Then I began on the French authors, including Flaubert and a little Balzac.

MGP: Did your father help you pick out books to read?

MG: No, he wasn't interested in giving me books. I got what I wanted from his library.

MGP: You didn't talk about what you read with him either?

MG: No, no. I might have talked with children my age about what I was reading, especially the romantic novels. But it's really a time I don't remember much about, except that I read and read like crazy.

By the time I got to Public School No. 1, I began to calm down and get along better with people. I had a circle of friends then, which was very important, because it's so basic for an adolescent to have friends. I got along better with my non-Jewish friends than with the people from the Hebrew institute to which I went. I didn't get along very well with them because I hadn't gone to a Hebrew academy before. By the time I started high school at the academy, the other students had been going there since kindergarten and were lifelong friends. When I came, they treated me like a foreigner and made it hard for me to fit in because I didn't know Yiddish. My parents never had much money, because my father had never managed to become much of a businessman. We were always going from one end of town to the other, because his deals would flop and then we'd have to move. It was a disaster. And if most of my classmates weren't rich, they were at least pretty well off. They had money and came from well-to-do middle-class backgrounds.

MGP: Did that make a difference in your relationships with your friends?

MG: A big difference. We lived in a working-class neighborhood, and my classmates lived, if not in very well-to-do neighborhoods, at least in very comfortable ones. Sometimes I lived in some of the nice neighborhoods, too—the Colonia Hipódromo or the Colonia Condesa. Later on, it became fashionable to move south of town. Then we moved to the Polanco district. Many Jewish families were migrating down there in those days, but we never made it. I had very little money, few clothes, and few occasions to do much traveling. My classmates would always take vacations in Cuernavaca or in Acapulco, but that was impossible for me. I got acquainted with the ocean when I was fourteen because my father took us to Veracruz, but I had never been to Acapulco. Yes, there was a difference, especially in education. Even though my father was a very important Jewish poet and Yiddish was his main language, he didn't teach it to me or to my older sister.

MGP: And why didn't he teach you Yiddish, as seems to be the case with most Jewish families?

MG: My parents spoke Spanish with us and Yiddish and Russian with each other. I went to a month or two of fourth grade at the Jewish school, and then we had to move because of family problems. The Hebrew institute was very expensive. Besides, we lived in neighborhoods where there were scarcely any Jews, so the institute's schoolbuses didn't stop there. Hardly anyone had a car, and I'd have to take two or three buses to get to where the institute bus stopped—so going to school there was really out of the question. Then later a group of neighborhood children began to go to the Hebrew institute, and they managed to get a special bus to come get us. By then I'd already started Jewish high school.

I was propelled into the Hebrew high school after something really decisive happened. We were living in a neighborhood where families lived crowded together and everyone knew everyone else.

My father's shoe store was at 517 Tacuba Street near Calzada México. Next door to the shoe store was another store, and above my father's store we had a tiny apartment with two bedrooms—one for my parents and one for us four daughters—a living room, and a dining room. Our apartment was next to another one that had been built earlier. Very poor people lived there in very difficult conditions, as many people in Mexico do, in tiny little flats where various family members are all crowded together and where we were the rich people in the house. Our apartment was much more organized, much more modern, much newer. It was on top of the annex, which means that besides the building, besides the bedrooms, there was a place where we could have a business. In front there was a *mixtamal* mill where some people from Spain worked, making dough for tortillas. One of the men fell madly in love with my sister Lilly, who was very pretty. He started flirting with her, and my father gave her some terrible beatings because he didn't approve of that kind of carrying on. I'm probably just exaggerating.

Next door lived a man, a doctor, in a place he kept for his mistress, with whom he had four daughters and one son, a rangy, skinny boy named Rubén. Our houses had flat roofs with terraces on top and low ledges from which you could jump from one side to the other. This boy lived up on the terrace because there were nothing but daughters below, and he'd flirt with all our maids. He'd go to bed with them, as I later found out, and once he even made a try for me. I fell in love with this fellow in a platonic way. Back then I had very strange ideas—very conflicting, very morbid and very dark, very murky—of what sex might be like. I didn't know much about anything, and my mother never even explained to us what menstruation was. Your older sister would tell you, your cousins, your classmates—anyone but your mother. I was in high school. One day I went up to the roof, and we were talking about something when he grabbed some pieces of rope and tied me to a post that divided our two houses. And then he kissed me. He clung to me, and I felt him grow hard against me. I shut my mouth tightly, and he moved his tongue around the outside. I remember the sensation very well.

Well, after this happened, I went to talk it over with one of the maids. My mother, who was in the next room, heard our conversation and got scared, because she thought he had raped me. They took me to the doctor, who examined me to see if I was a virgin or not. The doctor asked me if I had had relations with that boy, and of course I said yes, because I thought "relations" meant friendly relations. They shut me up in the house, and I got a terrible thrashing. That's when my mother decided that I had to go to Jewish high school, because I was in danger of marrying someone who wasn't Jewish. A school like that seemed like a punishment to me. I didn't have friends. I didn't have a very clear identity. My family was very Jewish but quite unusual. My father was a poet and had lived through the Russian revolutionary era with poets from all over the world. He was born in a small and very Jewish ghetto, a small town the czar had granted to the Jews.

My father's first language was Yiddish, and then he learned to pray in Hebrew. He came from a very religious family, and his parents kept all the traditions. He was really a very Jewish man, but when the revolution broke out, many refugees from the big cities came to his village because they were being persecuted. The years of that era, from 1905 to 1918, were both terrible and interesting. Anyone who was having problems and belonged to the underground movements left the cities for the villages. On the other hand, many of the revolutionaries were Jews.

MGP: Did your father join any of those revolutionary movements?

MG: My father was very young then, but he was indoctrinated by people coming to the agricultural settlements. They told him about their lives as militants—what they had done up to that time—and they told him about their theories.

MGP: When was your father born?

MG: He was born in 1902. When his father died, he went to a large city called Jerzon. He lived with one of his uncles, the only one that had more or less prospered and made a career. He was a mining engineer, but he didn't have a degree, because in those days the universities didn't accept Jews.

MGP: Was there very strong anti-Semitism during the czarist era?

MG: Yes, very strong. In certain parts of Russia, Jews were only allowed to practice certain professions.

MGP: Part of your family history is included in your book *Las genealogías* [The genealogies]. Did your entire family come from Russia?

MG: My parents remember their grandparents but no one before them. My father's grandfather came from Vitebsk, the same village as Chagall. They had divided the population in half because there wasn't enough room for everyone, and they sent the second half to another little village they named Novo Vitebsk. It was a Jewish agricultural colony. My grandfather was a farmer and glassmaker.

MGP: Why did your father come to Mexico?

MG: Because all his family had emigrated to the United States.

MGP: What year did they leave Russia?

MG: In 1925. The situation was already bad for them. My father had been put in jail because of a problem he'd had in a workers' meeting. He'd become a strikebreaker because the Stalinists didn't allow any critics, and so people started getting sent to jail when they protested on behalf of the workers. In one meeting, one of the workers threw himself from the fifth floor of a building.

My father was a friend of a newspaper reporter who was beginning to be a spokesman for dissident ideas, and my father had already started to write there, in spite of the fact that the paper wasn't recognized by the Bolsheviks. After the accident in which the worker committed suicide, the police came and put a lot of people in jail, including my father. That was when he met my mother, who came from a more well-to-do family.

MGP: Did your father come to Mexico alone?

MG: No, they both came. They got married and then left for Mexico, to her family's great sorrow. And as I told you before, I didn't have much of a Jewish education, because my father was very bohemian. We never had much financial stability, because he kept going into different businesses all the time. Later in his life, he studied dentistry. He'd sell bread in the mornings and work as a dentist in the afternoons, but it bored him and he got sick of it. What he really liked to do was write poetry, go out to eat with friends, and meet poets. He made good friends among Mexican and North American poets and painters and other artists who lived in Mexico then. He didn't lead a very orthodox life. His link to the Jewish community was through cultural activities, and he had very intense relationships with the exiled Jews who had recently arrived in Mexico, with whom he met frequently to talk things over in Russian and in Yiddish. He never taught those languages to us. He also continued to be very much of a leftist, a socialist. He supported leftist causes and supported the Spanish Republic. This was the era of Lázaro Cárdenas—the years between 1930 and 1936 were the years of socialism in Mexico. He was very Jewish and very liberal. He was very disillusioned by the Nazi-Soviet pact.

In regard to my own development, I didn't have a very clear identity. I was very shy, and getting to know people took a lot out of me. So reading, besides being something I liked, was very important. Besides, I identified a lot with my father.

MGP: That can be seen quite clearly in *Las genealogías.* Is there a connection between the fact that you were very close to your father and your later dedication to writing?

MG: I wanted to devote myself to literature ever since I was very young, but I wasn't sure I could do it. I began to write very late, when I was about thirty-two or thirty-three. I always knew I wanted to study literature, and I'd kept a journal since I was young. I was shy and didn't have much personality, but I felt a very clear vocation. My relationship with the world, nevertheless, was rather cloudy. I wasn't very much in tune with things, and I didn't get along well with my mother. In time, I did get along better with her. My parents lived in their own little world. They often left us alone. They also invited people over a lot. We had a great family life, but my mother and father were like a completely separate entity. My dad was always pretty selfish, fascinating but selfish. My mother, as far as she was concerned, was completely dedicated to him. Sometimes it bothered her to have to take care of us and not be with Dad, so they'd leave us at home with the servants. My mother, playing the wife's traditional role, was the more stable and dependable one. She was the head of the family more than my father was. She was the one who broke her back raising us, getting money for us, pushing us to work hard. She helped us to live and supported us financially for a long time. Dad was always working, but he was more fragile. My mother had to be stronger to survive.

MGP: Do you think that was to counteract your father's bohemianism a little?

MG: For my mother there was no difference between my father's work and hers, and she was right. My father did what he did because of her. If she hadn't been by his side, he wouldn't have been able to do anything. She wouldn't have been able to be who she was without him, either.

I think my father missed out on a lot, because he'd get bored with things. He did very important work with poetry, but there were few people in the Mexican Jewish scene who were interested in culture. This was terrible for him.

MGP: What cultural possibilities were there for the Jewish community in Mexico then?

MG: There were some newspapers, *Der Weg* [The way] and *Die Stimme* [The voice], which he worked on for fifty-five years. He founded the first Jewish newspaper in Mexico with two other poets, Saul Glikowski and Isaac Berliner, who were very good but not as well known as he was. After so many Jews died during the Nazi holocaust and the state of Israel was created, the Yiddish language moved into the background.

MGP: Where did he publish his poems?

MG: He published many of them in the United States. When the Yiddish newspapers began to die out because young Jews were writing in English, he published in Israel, where there were still people who spoke Yiddish—the survivors of the Nazi hecatomb. He was very well known there and won a number of prizes, but unfortunately the Yiddish-speaking Jews had died. Jewish culture had been kept alive by the persecutions. Now that's all changed.

MGP: What books and authors were important for the development of your writing?

MG: I've talked to you about the books that were important for me when I was an adolescent. Later, when I went to live in France, after I was married, I learned French quite well and read Proust and Stendhal. I read French literature very systematically, along with essays and criticism. Dostoyevski, Proust, Stendhal, and Flaubert made the biggest impact on me, most of all, *Sentimental Education*. Lately I've been working very hard to write more like Borges. There was a time when I couldn't write if I didn't have one of his books by my side. Borges has helped me tremendously with language, as he has so many people, because he taught me to synthesize, to handle certain phrases and certain expressions, to avoid using series of useless introductory phrases, to avoid the *that*'s—all those things. Besides, I'm fascinated with how he handles adjectives, his capacity to concentrate an enormous quantity of thoughts in very little space. On the other hand, that very important Borgesian relationship with erudition and the encyclopedic are basic for me. It doesn't mean that I have this master's erudition, because what he's read and assimilated, in addition to his capacity to handle linguistic and mathematical elements, is truly impressive. I'm saying it's the relationship that's fundamental for me.

Another author I find essential is Georges Bataille, specifically in relation to the question of the body. I read him many years ago, and I've kept that textual relationship ever since. I've also translated two of his books, *La historia del ojo* [*Story of the Eye*] and *Lo imposible* [*The Impossible*].

MGP: You also wrote prologues to these texts, didn't you?

MG: Yes. Those prologues are included in one of my books, *La lengua en la mano* [The tongue at hand].

✣ ✣ ✣

The obscene tearing apart, the most dishonest *parts of one's person (according to the religious vocabulary), in Bataille return to a world that does* not *signify but simply* is, *to a world where the mystical interior experience is indivisible from the body, tied at the sinews, bound to its excrescences: urine, sweat, and, in the same nature, the eyes, which through their softish composition, liquid and sticky, unify the two sexualities, the exterior sexuality that produces semen and that of the eye-*

balls, mutilatable, castratable, Oedipal: "Laura's face bore a horrible resemblance to the face of that horribly tragic man: an empty and half-crazed Oedipal face. This similarity grew during her long agony, while the fever seemed to penetrate her, especially during those terrible attacks of wrath and hate against me." The Eleusinian mysteries that Bataille distills in his obscure texts—miry, often badly written—tears of consciousness that never abandons its corporeal territory, that are secret *because of that, because of a kind of linguistic juggling: what the body keeps* secret *by its being impossible and what that body keeps, it* secretes [*From* La lengua en la mano].

✣ ✣ ✣

I'm also interested in the Sartre of *L'Imaginaire,* his text on Baudelaire, and his critical essays, though not the philosophical ones. The one that had the biggest impact on me, that was most useful to me, and the one I've almost torn apart by the number of times I spent reading it is "Saint Gênet," in which the problem of holiness and the body are basic. Roland Barthes has become a very important author lately. I've read all his books and applied his work to my own ideas. He's a truly fascinating writer. His concept of the fragment, along with his relationship with erudition and creation, nourishes me a great deal and delights me. I really enjoy reading Barthes: *El placer del texto* [*Pleasure of the Text*], *Fragmentos de un discurso amoroso* [*A Lover's Discourse*], *La cámara clara* [*Camara Lucida*], *Mitologías* [*Mythologies*]. One of the columns I wrote for *Unomásuno* was called "Mitologías" [Mythologies] in honor of him. Walter Benjamin is another important author, as is Albert Beguin, who wrote a book called *El alma romántica y el sueño* [*The Dream and the Romantic Spirit*], an essay about German Romanticism that was published in Mexico a few years ago by the Fondo de Cultura Económica. I read Barthes' *Michelet.* In other words, these essayists have been basic for my own writing.

MGP: Would you add any other authors to the ones you've already mentioned?

MG: In general, reading many books is what is important to me. I've worked with Kafka—like a psychological process—since I was very young, as I mentioned to you. I'm also particularly interested in fragmentation.

MGP: I know you're very interested in theater and that you've done several different things in that genre. Could you talk about some of them?

MG: As a matter of fact, I've read a lot of theater and translated various works into Spanish. I've also worked on adaptations of novels for television and radio. All this has been very useful as writing practice.

MGP: You still haven't mentioned anyone from Spain. Is there a group of authors that has especially interested you in connection with your writing?

MG: I've read a lot of Spanish theater. Quevedo, although he didn't write plays, has been a big help to me through his poetry. I've worked through Calderón de la Barca intensely in one of my books, *De la erótica inclinación de enredarse en cabellos* [Of the erotic inclination of becoming entangled with hair], which has some one hundred pages dedicated to Calderón.

MGP: Have you been working through any Calderón pieces in particular?

MG: I've done *La vida es sueño* [*Life Is a Dream*]; *La gran Cenobia* [*Xenobia the Great*], which isn't very well known; *En este mundo todo es verdad y todo es mentira* [In this world everything is truth and falsehood]; *La hija del aire* [The daughter of the air]; *El monstruo de los jardines* [The monster in the gardens]; and *Las manos blancas* [The white hands], which is a lovely comedy. I have some fifteen pages on it. Tirso de Molina is also important. *La celosa de sí misma* [The woman jealous of herself], which isn't read very often, is a very beautiful work (evidently I'm interested in Don Juan). Finally, I've been through Garcilaso and Lope, the chronicles of the conquest of America, and *Las mil y una noches* [*The Thousand and One Nights*], which seems to me to be a fundamental text.

MGP: Why is this a fundamental text?

MG: The character of Scheherazade fascinates me, and I'll tell you why. I've always read the Parisian *Le Nouvel Observateur,* which I think is a very important newspaper. In a 1962 issue, they published an excellent and comprehensive article about Michel Foucault's first book, *Histoire de la folie de l'âge classique* [*Madness and Civilization*]. I realized how important this book was, and it proved very useful to me in conceptualizing madness, a theme I was writing about at the time. Foucault said something about a book I'd read a few years before, *Les Bijoux indiscrets* [*The Indiscreet Jewels*] by Diderot, which appeared in the mid-eighteenth century. Diderot wrote it, in a style that had become popular in that century, about 1705 or 1706. The first French translation of *Las mil y una noches,* by Galant, had already been published, but with a lot of omissions and parts censored out. Then came a series of libertine books—very sinful, very violent, very critical—and among them was this text by Diderot. Foucault studied this work and pointed out that the discourse of sex wasn't a silenced discourse but rather a discourse that spoke constantly. But the discourse that Diderot addresses is only feminine discourse. I studied Diderot a second time. I think it's an important book and needs to be taken up again. It was very important in the eighteenth century and also in the nineteenth century because there was an entire literature full of translations, parodies, and paraphrases of *Las mil y una noches.* It is the discourse of the body and of erotic art that was so important in Europe in that French-dominated century, a very libertine era. I did a short paper ["Al borde del milenio" (On the brink of the millennium)] on Diderot for the Third Congress of Canadian Writers in Ottawa, and it was very successful. It's a brief but violent paper, quite incisive, in which I deal with the problem of sexuality and the character of Scheherazade.

✣ ✣ ✣

In exchange, Scheherazade proposes another kind of tale, which serves to redeem her from death. And, in fact, Scheherazade is the most absolute image of life: a being who squanders herself and speaks through all her mouths, because through the first she gives birth to all her tales, and through the second to all the beings that the Sultan engenders within her [*From "Al borde del milenio"*].

✣ ✣ ✣

MGP: This work is linked to others you've done about hair, nudity, and blood. They seem to make a trilogy.

MG: I think you're right. I want to continue reflecting on *Las mil y una noches,* because with that book I have a complete theory of sex and the feminine text.

MGP: Are you interested in surrealism? Your texts have some elements that link you with certain surrealist writers or with that approach to literature and writing.

MG: I think my texts *are* surrealistic, in fact. I use a logic of association typical of automatic writing. Bataille and Artaud, who are the dissidents among the surrealistic writers, interest me. I'm also very much interested in that great surrealistic painter Marcel Duchamp. There is a book by Octavio Paz entitled *Apariencia desnuda: La obra de Marcel Duchamp* that really fascinated me.

MGP: I detect a project of self-representation in your books that works on many levels and suggests several interpretations. I'm thinking of *Doscientas ballenas azules . . . y . . . cuatro caballos* [Two hundred blue whales . . . and . . . four horses], *No pronunciarás* [Thou shalt not pronounce], and *Las genealogías* to begin with. Each text incorporates a part of you that becomes a link in the biographical—or, better, autobiographical—conception of your writing, to an obsession with your innermost being.

MG: I feel that the world I've chosen is a marvelous world, so I feel a great joy that I need to communicate. But it's been difficult to look inside myself and to work, because of all my inner struggles. Writing has redeemed me as a being, as a body. In that sense, writing is very important to me because it's a way of putting myself back together, of remaking myself tissue by tissue, cell by cell. I'm also very interested in doing interviews like this one because it makes me realize so many things about myself.

MGP: It's somehow like a dialogue with your mirror.

MG: Yes, a kind of poetics, perhaps, of putting together a poetics. This kind of dialogue provokes a chain of ideas, and you begin realizing things that had never occurred to you before.

MGP: How does a text like *Doscientas ballenas azules*—such an intriguing title, by the way—arise?

MG: For a long time, whales—whales with an identity of their own—had been swimming among the shipwrecks of my imagination. Whales fascinate me because they're fat, they're mammals, they have milk and breasts and a long gestation period. They suckle their young, make love very gently, and when they can no longer endure the world, they commit suicide. Man persecutes them and writes poems about them, too. *Moby Dick* is the great epic of destruction and of the sadness caused by that destruction. At the same time, it's my way of relating to the world of adventure that I've been able to live only from the shore of a book. Then I decided that whales have their own facial features and, at the same time, I was obsessed with the two hundred blue whales remaining in the world.

MGP: How did this idea of wrecks come about?

MG: I decided that shipwrecks and wrecks were a class by themselves, so I began with floods, cosmic hurricanes, that is, meteorological, majestic, or cosmic convulsions of nature taken from the Bible and the flood of Gilgamesh. Then I took the conquest of America, which for me is a truly fascinating phenomenon. It seems at once horrible and attractive to me, because I saw how men killed other men, how they subjugated them without giving them the right to be different because they believed that only one culture should rule. Man's self-destruction by lusting for power, by the need for not allowing anyone to be different, is an old obsession of mine.

MGP: I know you've just completed a trilogy you've been working on for quite awhile. Why a trilogy?

MG: It's a trilogy because my books, like the text and its shadow, start leaving behind seminal traces, and those traces begin forming a kind of organic waste, textual fragments that are being fed internally. I'd begun with a syndrome of shipwrecks and a treatise on nomenclatures. The latter followed its own course, and *No pronunciarás* came out, which includes certain biblical questions, such as the name's relationship with the person, the person's signature, and the person's writing.

MGP: Why do these things interest you?

MG: Because handwriting is a form of biography that defines you, since there are no two identical beings, not even twins. Neither fingerprints nor voices are identical, and your writing has your particular style. Writing your name forms you, it identifies you with yourself. In addition, I'm interested in individuality, in not being part of the crowd. The world would be better off if modern societies wouldn't tend to make everyone the same. I'm interested in democracy, but not the kind that makes everything anonymous and plastic. I'm interested in the democracy that allows pluralism, that allows for thousands of distinct forms, that gives you individuality. I think that looking for your individuality is what makes you completely different from other beings. *No pronunciarás* like all my other texts has a cosmic preoccupation that includes the religious and the sacred. I have the heritage of Jewry I denied for such a long time, but it is my heritage. I'm forever linked with the Bible, with the prophets, which is where the title of *No pronunciarás* comes from: "Thou shalt not take the name of the Lord thy God in vain" [Exodus 20:7].

MGP: Let's go back to the shipwrecks and destruction for a moment, to the hurricanes and floods. How did you bring all these universal preoccupations together in your current work?

MG: I realized at last that little by little the external hurricane, the external flood, the external destruction go back in part to my own destruction, which was the love relationship. I also realized that one can drown in a glass of water, and that storms can be small at times. My book is my own life, my own cosmos, and my own heart, which become a small history—a small death and a small orgasm—that in some way takes part in the universe.

✣ ✣ ✣

Madame de Chatelet knew it, knew that you have to fear those great upheavals of the soul, the sources of ennui and sorrow. Order banishes the tempests and prevents suffering, also life, but you don't have to fear it, maybe it's better not to give it a name, just to call it a gale if it becomes a whirlwind, or to call it a fright if it's a hurricane. Sorrow arrives (in spite of life) and ennui is used to being banished with the north winds. Passion leads us only to unhappiness. If actions were preceded by reflection, we would live with decorum [*From* Síndrome de naufragios].

✣ ✣ ✣

MGP: What led you to write a text like *Las genealogías*?

MG: I wanted to know where I came from, who my parents were. I was curious to know what my childhood had been like. I wanted to understand how it could be that, though I loved my parents so much and they were so close to me, I didn't really know who they were. I wanted to know what world they came from, what their reality was like—so different from mine. At the same time this kind of writing is like a voyage inside oneself. I wanted to live that sort of interior voyage, like the interior voyages of medieval women, which were so important in that era. Once I translated a book by an Elizabethan contemporary of Shakespeare's, *La tragedia española* [*The Spanish Tragedy*] by Thomas Kyd. The story is about revenge but is also a descent into the inner self. I think that *Las genealogías* was a way of recovering my parents, of forgiving them for a childhood that was painful, as all childhoods are. It was also a way not to feel aggression and anger for the way they'd stamped my life and, simultaneously, to bring them back as human beings with great tenderness and affection with all their faults and at the same time to put myself together—that is, a kind of biography of exiles. The book has been very well received, but for me it forms a completely logical part of my entire development as a writer.

MGP: *El día de tu boda* [The day of your wedding] represents another change in your writing, because it more clearly incorporates the Mexican cultural context.

MG: It's a text that has something of Barthes and Benjamin. It's almost a homage to them, a silent homage but one that these readings touch, especially that of Barthes' *Camara Lucida*. It's an essay about love letters and postcards—a particular sociological characteristic of the era.

MGP: What text was hardest for you to write?

MG: I think the one that's taken the most out of me is *De la erótica perversión de enredarse en cabellos* [Of the erotic perversion of becoming entangled with hair], which I later changed to *De la erótica inclinación de enredarse en cabellos* [Of the erotic inclination of becoming entangled with hair], because *perversion* seemed redundant. It's a text I've been putting together for many years. I started it in 1977 and began publishing fragments by submitting pieces of it to *Unomásuno.* I didn't have a clear idea of what I was going to do with them, but I knew I had a continuing obsession with the problem of hair. When it seemed to the editors that I'd done enough with hair, I continued working on my own.

I remember that I once read a prologue to a work about Calderón by the critic Blanca de los Ríos. It said that Calderón had various Segismundos, something obvious to a reader of Calderón, but not fully developed in terms of treating hair as a theme, which is what I decided to do. I examined thirteen or fourteen works and found that, in fact, there was a repetitive and constant obsession with the idea of hair. I observed that one of Segismundo's characteristics was that his conduct was as disorderly as his body: his body developed in an unruly way and so did his behavior.

MGP: Why, then, does the question of hair in literature interest you?

MG: Probably because I was never content with my own hair or with myself. I never liked my hairstyle. If I combed my hair back, the boys didn't like it. I felt an unending sadness when I'd go to a dance and just sit there the whole time. I decided it was partly because of my personality and partly because of my hair. I let my hair grow out wild but not long, like a blackamoor, like that fighter who wore his hair in dreadlocks the way some of those screeching pop singers do. Your hair was a sort of frame of your self. Every time I went to a beauty salon, I'd think that was the day I'd look great, and I'd make plans to try to preserve this treasure. I felt like Cinderella when I went to the beauty salon, like someone who would be rescued one day, because she had something other people didn't see. It's a type of character all we women have inside ourselves.

MGP: In the midst of this hair struggle, you've still used literature to untangle other people's hair—

MG: Because now, retrospectively and a posteriori, my biography is personal and literary: it's a kind of judgment on what I'm writing, that is, a kind of inquiry into the type of writing I do, writing that apparently is completely fragmentary and amorphous. When I realized that I was interested in hair—by the way, it was King Kong, the hairy monster, who got me started on hair—I did research in anthropology and mythology to learn about the themes and motifs of hair in various cultures. Later I went looking for hair in literary texts, as well as in interpretations, to put together a theory of hair, not an anthropological theory but a Calderonian poetics. I wanted to incorporate all the texts about King Kong, because for me both literary and critical interpretations are one and the same, so I decided to put them together. When I started to do it, I realized that it was impossible and that there was no way to write the book. Then I found a crucial phrase from Barthes that said that every text has its shadow. I then realized I had two texts, *De la erótica inclinación a enredarse en cabellos* and the shadow text. Since the text on Calderón was already written, it remained for me to write its shadow, so it would be a textual composition in which the academic work could be handled like the shadow of the text, like excrescences, like a woman who keeps removing her mustache, though it is always there underneath.

Suddenly I realized that the other text was there, that what I had to do was put it in the context of the beauty salon that obsessed me. There's a very long chapter called "Beauty Salons and Laboratories" that puts together in two columns—with white space and different typefaces—two ways of looking at the world: that of vanity and frivolity and that of death, because hair is frivolity and death. The third part of the text is called "La cabellera andante," a parody of *Don Quixote*, the "*caballero andante*." Wandering around in search of windmills and hair seems amusing, ridiculous, and marvelous as well. I've made a braid.

I realized also that this text was a reliquary. Because there is so much hair in the world, it's futile to put the ones I'm writing about together with the rest, because you'd end up with a shapeless mass. What I had to do was gather my own favorite hairs, the ones that had to do with love.

I think my book is structured somewhat like the books Macedonio Fernández talked about, books in which the relationship among quotations gave another kind of textuality. My book would turn into the book of roving knowledge, of wandering knowledge.

MGP: You've mentioned masculine hair, but you've left out women's hair. Feminine hair is related to literature.

MG: In a crucial way. There are a number of important traditions. In the Middle Ages and up to the beginning of this century, women didn't show their hair. I remember that in the Spanish ballads known as *Romanceros* women who were looking for a lover wore their hair loose. Or in the beautiful German fairy tale, Rapunzel lets her hair down, and it was so long that it fell all the way to the ground. Even though she was high up in a tower, the handsome prince was able to climb the wall to reach her. Hair is one of the things that most identifies a woman with her body and her sexuality, so hiding it was the worst kind of repression and caring for it the best way to show love—a very special form of eroticism and a very feminine way of organizing the world, because it's like putting threads together, beginning to embroider your world because you're shut up in a room, like women of the past, like nuns in the convent. It was a way to begin using your fingers to spin life into other universes utterly disdained by men but equally rich. One way that a woman can relate to the world is and always has been to embroider, to knit, to cook, because in the kitchen she could invent a series of exquisite combinations to present to the men—father, bishop, or whoever it might be.

My book is a way of stringing together those scattered beads that I couldn't interweave at first.

✣ ✣ ✣

Sylvia Molloy

✣ ✣ ✣

MGP: When you think back to your childhood, what's the first thing you remember?

SM: Being afraid. That's what I was when I was a child—afraid. And I have a feeling that I felt very lonely before my sister was born. I don't really have any memories from that time. I have an image of myself walking alone in an enormous garden and picking up scarab beetles—the ones we call *vigilantes* in Argentina—which I found fascinating. That image of great solitude and fear is carved into my memory.

MGP: And what were you afraid of?

SM: Of doing things badly. We had very high standards set at home that I had to learn, and I had trouble understanding them. So I was constantly asking one of my aunts—I adored her! She's the one who appears in *En breve cárcel*—things like how I should pray, for example. I had very conflicting feelings about that because I thought I could either think about God or say my prayers but not do both. It seemed impossible to do both at once because the way I saw it, one or the other had to be right. That's the feeling I have of my childhood, except for the times I threw myself into games. And I played a lot. I had a very active fantasy life based on concrete objects; for example, I played with dolls until I was thirteen. I was also fascinated with the marbles that rolled from the garden next door. I could spend hours making up stories for the dolls, doing a thousand things.

✣ ✣ ✣

Her childhood—she does not see it as a prologue to her future as an adult, nor is she trapped in the longing for a lost paradise. She remembers it full of disguises (the funny, grotesque ones she made with her father's clothing) and long periods of self-scrutiny, with or without disguise, in two facing mirrors. A habit of doubling and of order, in endless series. Marbles got away from the boys she spied on at the school next door and rolled into her yard; she hoarded them and spent hours setting them out in rows. She always marked the beginning of a row in the same way, with a yellow cat's-eye, much prettier than the others. She cannot forget that ritual, not the facing mirrors [*From* En breve cárcel].

✣ ✣ ✣

MGP: Did you play alone?

SM: I played a lot with my sister, who went along with my games, almost like another doll. I'd make up the games. We'd pretend to be the mother and the aunt, but she was really more like another doll because she did what I told her.

MGP: Did you dominate your sister because she was younger?

SM: I was very bossy and daring in all of the games I made up but not in real life. I loved our vacations at the seashore. They were a source of freedom. I went to the beach, rode horses. For me, that was freedom.

MGP: You mean being outside, getting out in the country.

SM: Yes. I can still remember something terrible that happened to me in Miramar, by the way. It was Mardi Gras time and so the *Billiken* magazine, which we all read every week, had all kinds of masks in the centerfold that children could cut out. I'd invented a funny disguise for myself that year. I remember I wore gaucho pants, and I went to the parade, where I was a big success. But suddenly some children started making a circle around me, and one of them tore off my mask. That was the end of spur-of-the-moment fun for me. When people say they want to live childhood all over again, I always think about mine. Although I can't tell you it was bad, I don't have the feeling it was very happy.

✣ ✣ ✣

If you would help me get through this week, this day, this hour in which I write to you. You feel far away and you've doubtless always been far away, although I was sure you belonged to me. Last night someone told me I pontificate in a vacuum, that I play in solitude, and I know that it didn't used to be like that. In the garden you and I were together: I startled you, riding on a broomstick and taking away your dolls, but when you cried, I was the one who was startled. Sara (whom I know you haven't seen for a long time) sat in the sun and laughed. I don't think we remembered Mama at those times: she'd be having tea inside; she'd be thinking about the weeping willow propped up with concrete that was always about ready to fall but never did [*From "Tan distinta de mamá"*].

✣ ✣ ✣

MGP: What was your relationship with your parents like?

SM: Mother was a very distant figure, very authoritarian. Her authority didn't come from shouting, though, but from a distance she created that always seemed vast to me. My aunt was like a mother to me as far as anything you'd call affection. I loved to look at my mother because she seemed so lovely, but I didn't feel very close to her. I had a very complicated relationship with my father. He loved me very much, he'd do whatever I asked, and he wanted to play with me, but I'd put him off most of the time. Much later, by the time I was twenty, I started being able to communicate with him.

There was also something else that began to get clearer and clearer—a division of nationalities between my parents—to which I felt very sensitive. My mother was from a French family, and my father was from a British family. They spoke Spanish to each other and to us, but we used to speak English with Father, even though Mother didn't speak it. She really rubbed in the way the British had colonized the world and dominated everything, and besides, she always saw herself as a victim of my father's family.

MGP: That family spoke only English, then?

SM: Yes, they were very insular. They'd speak English with each other, and Mother would feel like a foreigner. That kind of attitude is pretty typical of the English. For me, it was a problem, because I went to an English school, and I didn't know what I was—English, Argentine, or French. It was very unpleasant, and because of all this I threw myself into everything French, very innocently, as a way of vindicating my mother's side of the family or making her more important. Argentina loses out a lot in all this, or perhaps this conflict itself is precisely very Argentine. At any rate, I began to go crazy over everything French, which somehow felt like something marginal, and I began to disdain anything English. Later, as a teenager, I had a teacher at the Alliance Française who instilled in me forever a passion for literature.

MGP: Do you remember what type of things you wrote when you began?

SM: I wrote stories with a moralistic tone. The characters were children. I wrote a few, I remember, until my aunt, who was the one who read them, started liking them too much and began asking me to write more. And that's how the first stage of my writing career ended.

MGP: Did she try to correct you?

SM: No, she thought they were terrific.

MGP: It's strange that such a good reception didn't stimulate you but instead acted as a negative influence.

SM: But only to a certain point, because I always said I was going to be a writer, from the time I was very young. I was also attracted to journalism. I was extremely curious about everything that happened around me, especially unusual things, like the lifeguards in Miramar swimming out to save people from drowning. Of course, all this happened when I was a very small child. I wrote those stories in Spanish. I think that going to an English school had something to do with it, because I stopped writing and never wrote anything in English. I think something got cut off there, though I continued to read a lot.

MGP: What did you read then?

SM: Naturally, until I was twelve or thirteen, I read all kinds of things, many of which weren't very good. I'd take books I saw around the house and then sneak off to read them. One book that made a very strong impression on me was *Cuán verde era mi valle* [*How Green Was My Valley*]. I remember a rape scene and a sentence that left me completely absorbed: "That day they closed all the stores because a woman had been raped." I immediately had to find out what "rape" meant, so I went to ask my mother. She happened to be with a group of her friends, so it was a bad time to ask. She tried to avoid answering me, and because I was insistent, she sent me away to my room without an answer.

MGP: So the topic was taboo and discussing it was forbidden. And you couldn't ask your aunt, either?

SM: No. I saw my aunt as an asexual being, as an equal. She was like a playmate.

MGP: And the French teacher you mentioned?

SM: She was a young woman of twenty-nine; I was fourteen. She fascinated me, and I identified with her and with her life, too. I needed to know all the details—her husband, her children. I realized, quite clearly, that I was obsessed with this woman. Because of her, I began to read and to get interested in another type of literature: Gide, Malraux, and others. Proust interested me for different reasons. Gide satisfied my moralistic side, the side that asked questions, that looked for the meaning of life. Proust, on the other hand, represented the pure pleasure of literature, of storytelling and gossip—a literature not moralistic but pleasurable.

MGP: Did you talk about these texts?

SM: Yes, she was a very good teacher. Literature went together perfectly with the passionate intensity I brought in, so it was an ideal relationship. It combined the pedagogical with the erotic.

MGP: What did you do when you finished your studies at the Alliance Française?

SM: I left for France when I was twenty. I was absolutely terrified but had wonderful fantasies, like a turn-of-the-century poet, about what I'd find in France. I hadn't lived very much. I had led a very intense literary life inside myself but was quite detached from reality. Anything sexual was completely repressed. Finally, I got to Paris, and it seemed much different from what I had expected. It seemed smaller. I'd thought everything was going to be together: the Arc de Triomphe, the Eiffel Tower, the Louvre—all in one block. I lived in the Argentine college in the Cité Universitaire, but I didn't want to take courses for foreign students. I wanted to study with French students. I felt like a fish out of water. I wanted to study at the Sorbonne, even if I felt I didn't quite belong.

MGP: How did the French students take to you?

SM: I had very little contact with them. I found them aloof and more distant than university students in Buenos Aires. I didn't want to be with Argentines but couldn't make friends with the French. But one day I came upon a solution. Up until then I'd been a Protestant. That was another strange thing about my house. My father was Protestant and my mother was Catholic, but they had been married in the Catholic church. And then they baptized their daughters Protestants. Finally, in Paris, I got involved in a very active Catholic congregation at the Catholic student center, which had a very open, leftist priest. It was during the war in Algeria. I made French friends there, and I also converted. It was a very serious, important thing for me to do, even though it didn't last very long. I stayed in Paris for four years, but I was always thinking I wanted to go back to Argentina. When I did, it was very hard for me to adapt, and things went pretty badly for me at first. I felt as if I didn't know where I was. Besides, my French degrees were not recognized officially, so I decided to join the Alliance Française as a teacher. I taught from 1962 to 1967. I left home and went to live alone, to the despair of my mother but with the complete approval of my father, who helped me and supported me during that time. That was when I became very close to him.

MGP: Is that when you decided to start writing again?

SM: In France, I'd met Alejandra Pizarnik, who became a very good friend. Around that time I began to write in Spanish. I wrote poetry, prose fragments, nothing too structured. When I returned to Buenos Aires, I saw a lot of Olga Orozco, whom I'd met in France through Alejandra. At that time, I also met Victoria Ocampo, María Luisa Bastos, Enrique Pezzoni, and Héctor Murena. I began to write pieces for *Sur* about Güiraldes and Valéry Larbaud, about Edith Sitwell, about many different subjects. I met a lot of new people then. It was a very confusing time of life for me. I was trying to catch up on many fronts. I was looking for a way to make up for the feeling of loss from my unhappy and chaotic adolescence. Coming back to Buenos Aires meant reassessing that adolescence and rescuing the lost time by living everything very intensely: the literary, the personal, the sexual.

MGP: It was a time of definitions, of finding yourself.

SM: Yes, I felt very vulnerable and unprepared. I didn't go on writing very much, though at first I wrote a number of poems.

MGP: Did you publish any of them?

SM: No, but I worked a few passages into the novel. They're fragments filled with despair, written during a time when I was trying to find myself, but they aren't publishable by themselves. It was better to think of them as preparatory exercises.

MGP: I have the impression that you're very critical of your own work and that maybe that attitude keeps you from publishing.

SM: I think I owe that partly to my childhood, because my mother was of the school that believed if you didn't have anything important to say, you were better off keeping quiet. I didn't have the pleasure of the word.

MGP: You said you were in Buenos Aires some five years. What happened after all the upheaval?

SM: I got a scholarship to go back to Paris in 1967 to finish my dissertation and decided I would come through the United States on my way back to Argentina. And here I stayed. At that time I started working on the articles about Borges and Silvina Ocampo that mark the true beginning of my critical work. Fiction writing was postponed until 1970, a few months after my father's death. Then I had a dream in which a friend of mine and I were looking at the same scene: a tree and a bench. He could see my father there, but I couldn't. It was as if there were fragments I couldn't put together. I thought that when the remaining things became fragmented—that is, the bench and the tree, which were what propped up reality—I was going to go crazy.

✣ ✣ ✣

She would like to last. That is why she struggles to forge pieces that should form a single face, or, at the very least, a single mask. She must bring those pieces together, merge them even for a moment; the alternative is madness—the collapsing façade, the helpless eyes. She had dreamed of being with someone before the same landscape: a park, a bench, a tree, and one character, her father, who is dead. The two visions, hers and the other person's, coincide in all respects except one: her father. The other person sees him as a whole, projecting his shape. She, however, searches for her father and sees fragments that she cannot bring together. She tells herself that a mediated vision, capable of being composed, is sanity. When not only the image of her father but also the images of the bench, the tree, and the park are fragmented, then she will know she has gone mad. All at once, with an effort, she turns her mind to good dreams as a way of warding off evil. She would like to sleep [*From* En breve cárcel].

✣ ✣ ✣

I remember I wrote that down while staying at a friend's house, one day when she wasn't there. It was suddenly as if I'd discovered myself in that place. I was all alone and I could write again. I still had no idea it was going to be a novel.

MGP: Did you compose a fragment?

SM: I composed a fragment similar to the ones I'd been writing down in Buenos Aires. From 1970 on, I began to write fragments and to write down my dreams. I was in analysis and I began to have dreams that were symbolic, very structured, and very architectural. I was starting to write down very clearly framed landscapes or scenes. I wrote a few prose poems, but they were all small fragments oriented toward something I didn't understand very clearly then, a few dreams about my father. The strange dream that appears at the end of the first part of the novel, about Diana, is a dream from that period.

✣ ✣ ✣

She has had to stop writing. She lay down exhausted past midnight, drunk and disgusted, and fell into a stupor. Near dawn she was awakened by a strange dream. She is in her parents' house, where her mother now lives alone, a house that has to be emptied. The dining table is piled with plates, cups, everything that has to be moved or auctioned off. While she looks over the table, reminiscing—I once ate a favorite cake off that plate, once broke a glass just like that one—the phone rings. It is her dead father calling. The connection is bad; she can hardly hear his voice. She slowly begins making out individual words: first the urgent word Aegeus, then the word Ephesus, which is repeated several times. It is necessary to leave everything—her father's faint voice is telling her—and travel to see Artemis. As she listens to him, ever more distant, she looks at the plates on the table (one of them seems to be full of blood), at the flowers out in the yard, especially the star jasmine. She does not want to go on that trip, does not want to tear herself away. When she asks her father why she should go, the connection is cut off. Then she hears her mother's voice, from her bedroom upstairs, asking who that was. She does not answer [From En breve cárcel].

✣ ✣ ✣

Although I was starting to write all this down, I didn't really have a good idea how it was going to come out because I still didn't see any form or unity.

MGP: Were you writing every day?

SM: From that time on I didn't stop writing, and I even began working on what would become the book on Borges [*Las letras de Borges* (Signs of Borges)] in 1972. By then, I'd already come to Princeton. The Borges book came out of my preoccupation with Borges' characters. It was an attempt to track down those characters and to see how Borges made them work. One discovery I made was that Borges didn't compose characters but fragmented them, decomposed them. And through that idea of decomposition, I began to get interested in the idea of writing fiction.

MGP: Based on this process of decomposition and fragmentation?

SM: Yes, totally. It's very much like Felisberto Hernández, though he has not marked my work directly—a way of seeing the world in pieces, of lingering with each of them and then trying to put the fragments together, or looking at everything in disintegration. I see a lot of myself in this way of looking at the world.

MGP: As criticism has pointed out, a great deal of feminine fiction is based on fragments that serve as an organizing principle for the inner world of feminine characters. Would you agree with this interpretation?

SM: In my particular case, the idea of fragments had been with me a long time, ever since I was an adolescent. I thought that if I ever wrote anything, it would be very fragmented. Since the time I was very young, I couldn't imagine a whole, a block of something, something unified. I was starting to accumulate these things in an unorganized way, without daring to think about a connecting thread. Everything happened totally by chance. Suddenly one day, something external allowed me to begin elaborating a more extensive text. Eventually that lengthening resulted in the text of the novel.

MGP: When did you decide to give shape to your fiction?

SM: When I went to Paris in 1973. What I tell at the beginning of the novel is completely true. Finding through an ad an apartment where I'd lived before seemed so uncanny that I took it as a challenge, and I sat down to write what was going on to get it off my mind, because that house was heavy with memories.

✣ ✣ ✣

The story began some time ago, in the same place where she now writes. In this small, dark room, someone who did not know her, someone she herself did not know, waited for her one afternoon just as she now waits, with the same uncertainty, for someone who is about to come. (There is no difference between a person one thinks one knows and a new acquaintance, of that she is sure; in a moment, if the person she is expecting arrives, that person will be for her once more a stranger.) While she waits she writes, or perhaps it would be more accurate to say that she writes because she waits. Her words prepare for, call for a meeting that might not happen. It is getting late [*From* En breve cárcel].

✣ ✣ ✣

Besides, I wasn't doing very well. I had just broken up with someone, and really the only thing left to do was to get rid of all the ghosts in that apartment and *do* something: write to keep myself alive.

MGP: You said at the Amherst meeting on Latin American women writers [1982] that all fiction is autobiographical—

SM: Yes. There are many things in my novel that are autobiographical and many things that aren't. What I meant to say was that all fiction is autobiographical, though all the content may not necessarily be autobiographical. I believe I find my voice in this novel, the intonation of my voice. Autobiography isn't necessarily facts, it can be—and in my case is, I want it to be—that voice. I've found my language and my word in my novel, but it is the same word as in my text on Borges.

MGP: Do you need to fictionalize reality and experience through memory? If it's a process of dismembering or breaking up in order to put back together—rethinking, you once said—then would some kind of exorcism be called for?

SM: Yes. My first impulse was to see if I could rid myself of these ghosts. The only way was to keep them at a distance by writing, but not as I'd done before. I now had a clear idea that what I wanted to do wasn't an analytical or psychological or merely cathartic exercise. What stimulated me wasn't just the intuition that I was trying to get something out of myself but that I wanted to distance all this in order to do *something more.* My goal had changed.

Now I was composing, actively inserting this material into a fictional context. That is why I decided never to use first person. From the beginning, it was written in third person.

MGP: To objectify all that experience, to look at it from a distance.

SM: Yes. Also because there was an element that always fascinated me and that I still haven't talked about. There's a writer who really attracts me because of his voyeurism—Onetti. I've always been attracted to spying, which is what I did when I was a child; it's the idea of seeing the forbidden, the hidden, of coming upon what is strange. And the novel was a way of spying on myself, of spying on the material I'd tried to take out of myself by using third person. Without doubt it's very narcissistic, looking at yourself in third person.

MGP: Could it be the recapture of the female Narcissus? There's a great temptation and curiosity to find out what we're like. I remember that when I started your novel, the barrier caused by the third person bothered me, but after a few pages that distance stops getting in the way. I think it's one of the successes and innovations of *En breve cárcel.*

SM: There are occasional cracks in the use of the third person, places where, as if by an affected carelessness, the first person appears, a strange "I." For example, when the protagonist imagines seeing a rope to hang herself with. The invasions of this "I" are deliberate, another way to break a comforting surface. But the places where this happens in the novel aren't deliberate. I picked them by chance, though now I think they turned out to be almost perversely pertinent.

✣ ✣ ✣

She has pointed out clues, and now feels at peace. She is aware, however, that she has fallen into these tardy revelations so as not to go on facing those feminine presences, to protect herself from them. Suddenly they descend on her, like fearsome divinities, and all she can say is: "I summoned you here." And, more modestly: "I wanted all of you—mother, sister, lovers—to be here, I live only in you" [*From* En breve cárcel].

✣ ✣ ✣

MGP: Can both the violence of the word and the physical violence involved in the act of writing be explained by that necessity to objectify certain experiences, certain memories?

SM: No, I don't think so.

MGP: Why is there violence in the act of writing?

SM: Because the act of writing is an act against nature, so I don't agree with some women writers who speak of the almost physical naturalness of the act of writing. For me, writing entails pulling out demons or ghosts that are extremely violent. I perceive myself as a very violent person, always critical of myself, always keeping myself under control, always like a pot that's about to boil over. That is, it's a question of taking off the lid and at the same time imposing the violence of the word on what emerges, channeling it through writing. It seems like a very unnatural thing to me, because instead of starting to break things or hitting somebody or starting to scream, I sit down to write. An extremely contained and extremely distanced fiction that is doubly violent. I feel my novel to be very passionate and very violent. What comes out has those characteristics. At the same time, I'm forcing the story to be cold or to seem cold. I gag it with words. For me, writing is not at all "what comes out of me," which would dilute the effect and the function of literature, but exactly the opposite.

MGP: It's in the forces of opposition, of bringing out but dominating, controlling to the point—

SM: Of ending up without air.

MGP: To put together a text that has to come out naked. You also said you're working on a second project. What are you doing now?

SM: I want to finish some stories I'm writing about sibling rivalry. Sibling rivalry doubtless attracts me for personal reasons. Almost all the stories are variations on antagonism between brothers and sisters or people who could be brothers and sisters.

I've got another project, which is another novel that would be more rooted in a tangible, real-life reality, which would be Buenos Aires. *En breve cárcel* was like being nowhere. It was an aseptic story. Now I want to seek a Buenos Aires that I always felt has somehow eluded me. I see Buenos Aires as a very mysterious city, full of myths, and there's something—a key, a path—I have yet to discover. It's like a rite of initiation. I have to find what has gotten away from me, what I haven't lived. This is due to exile, no doubt, and distance, but I want to work in that search, that mystery of Buenos Aires in this novel where there would also be a lot on memory, a lot on mythification, more and fuller characters, but I don't know yet. Mansilla's texts or Borges' early poetry, both of which mythify Buenos Aires, interest me a lot. They mourn a belated, vanished Buenos Aires, and I'd like to use them a little, work them into the novel in some way. I think it would be a novel with much more space than *En breve cárcel,* much less pressured. I intend to continue to write both fiction and criticism. I ended up feeling quite empty after I finished the novel, but luckily I still have the short stories. At first, some of them were part of the novel, but I took them out and held onto them as leftovers. I worked up stories out of the remnants of the novel, and I still have some unworked fragments. There's a whole aspect, a field, that remains unexplored, the realm of the father, of friendships or relationships with men. There's a whole masculine field I'm interested in exploring.

MGP: You mention a relationship with a man, but only in passing.

SM: That's the relationship that will appear in this other novel.

MGP: You mean there are threads left hanging that you might rethink and then develop in future texts.

SM: Yes. I feel more settled now, more secure in my storytelling. Maybe even less violent.

MGP: To move on to something else important about you, what, in your opinion, is the relationship between literary criticism and fiction writing?

SM: I think there is a relationship. In fact, I need to do both things at once. I was writing *En breve cárcel* at the same time I was writing *Las letras de Borges.* Right now I've started on a dual project: fiction on the one hand, criticism on the other. I like to write about authors I enjoy and in whose work I recognize something of myself. For example, when I write about Onetti, I'm interested in gossip, in voyeurism, because I use both in my fiction. The practice of criticism strengthens my fiction, and my fiction is made of the threads of all the writers' voices that come together in my own.

MGP: When you're writing, working through your text, does the critic appear to take a look at it?

SM: No. Writing the novel, for example, was very impulsive. I didn't give it a conscious, detailed critical eye. It was a very passionate activity. I even found it difficult to reread myself, to organize. There were two stages to my writing the novel. In the first, I started and then stopped when my stay in that room ended. The year was up. My lease ran out and I left. And later it was very hard to go back to it, so much so that I started writing it again from the beginning, trying to find a new burst of energy. It worked. I went back and followed it through without thinking. At one point I realized that I was shutting myself in and closing off all the exits. It was turning into a kind of solipsistic silent exercise. I realized that I had to get out, that I somehow had to get the protagonist out for some air. But how? How would I get her out, if the woman was being gradually stripped of everything? That was when I forced my way out of my tendency to keep on mulling things over, in a kind of endless self-contemplation. I deliberately put in the drive to the country, then the encounter, and in the second part I began to include a few elements of action. This was a novel in which I wanted to avenge myself, and part of the plan was to attack the character named Vera, to torture her. The question was how to do it. Then I hit on the trick of having her return to the room so she would be humiliated. There I resorted to a literary loan: in *L'Educación sentimental* [*Sentimental Education*], the last time Madame Arnoux sees Frédéric, she goes to his room. They're sitting in semidarkness and suddenly there's a light from outside, from a carriage. He then sees that her hair has gone white. That white hair was a perfect revenge and a literary revenge. And besides, they were taken from Flaubert, a writer who marked me greatly.

MGP: How did he mark you?

SM: I had a passion for Flaubert when I was a student. Here's the distinction I'd make in what I read then: Gide and Malraux were the formative readings of an adolescent who needs values. These values were subversive, but nonetheless they were values. Then there was literary reading, which is how I would classify Flaubert and Proust. Disillusionment in Flaubert fascinated me. I had a notebook in which I wrote down fragments of his novels and criticism about him. The Goncourt brothers said, in discussing the sadness in Flaubert, that there was a squalid kitchen smell about his novels. The gray, the hopeless, the faded attracted me very much. It continues to attract me today. For example, what draws me to Jean Rhys is reading about the disillusionment of passion that has ended or is about to end. Hers is a sickly passion, with a way of holding back that I find fascinating. The quality of delay in Blanchot interests me, too. I'm interested in the apparent neutrality of those texts stifled with power, as though they were gagged.

MGP: You started reading Blanchot later, didn't you? What did you read before that?

SM: I thought Nathalie Sarraute was very interesting, and I also liked *Moderato cantabile* by Marguerite Duras. There's a brilliant scene in *Moderato*—the meal scene where they bring in the duck. There's a distant memory of that meal in my novel. But in general, Duras doesn't interest me that much. Sarraute, on the other hand, does. I was interested in her until she started falling into a rut, until that underlying conversation became so overly detailed, so mannered, that it proved unbearable. But her first works are important. And I also like her autobiography very much.

MGP: Were you interested in Simone de Beauvoir at that time?

SM: No, I wasn't that interested in her, except for *Une mort très douce*

[A death most sweet], about her mother's death. But the self-complacency of her memoirs bothers me, the way she lets everything go without any rigor. I helped translate them, and then Alejandra Pizarnik and I would write parodies of her because she so exasperated me. I read Colette a lot when I was seventeen or eighteen. I liked her irony, her humor, her flirtation with the forbidden—as in the Claudine series—but not so much the ecstasy before nature. I read many English authors, Evelyn Waugh, for example, for his irony—another form of verbal violence that is also important in Borges. Katherine Mansfield, whom I read very early on when I was in school, seemed—and seems—extraordinary to me: I discovered her by chance, because we didn't read her in class, of course. I don't like Virginia Woolf that much.

MGP: Why not? She's the precursor of most women writers.

SM: I'm interested in Virginia Woolf, the critic. All the texts in *The Common Reader* are wonders of precision, of humor, of intelligence, but I'm a little afraid at times of certain lyrical aspects of her fiction. It seems as if she gets a little carried away. I wish there were a little more of Jane Austen in Virginia Woolf. But the essays, all of them, interest me. I've also read a lot of Forster. *A Passage to India, A Room with a View,* are texts in which something is always about to happen, something latent that never occurs. There's something similar in Onetti, something that's left there, that is never said outright. It's a little like what Borges says: the imminence of a revelation that never occurs is, perhaps, the aesthetic act. I'm fascinated by all texts that have that characteristic.

MGP: What North American writers interest you?

SM: I've read a lot of Carson McCullers and Truman Capote. Flannery O'Connor, too.

MGP: Who are the main Latin American writers?

SM: I'm interested in literature of ambiguity. I'm interested in literature that doesn't clarify but rather blurs, digresses, when it's done well and you can't see the seams or the detours. Borges, of course. Also the José Bianco of *Las ratas* [*The Rats*] and *Sombras suele vestir* [*Shadow Play*]. The Bioy Casares of *El sueño de los héroes* [The dream of the heroes] and some stories, where I find that Buenos Aires that is so uncanny. I find Silvina Ocampo immensely interesting from sheer spirit of contradiction. Silvina Ocampo does what I don't do. Hers is a literature of excess, not of language but of situations, of plot. She does what she feels like doing.

MGP: Like Delmira Agustini?

SM: She has the same dimension of excess. That same way of putting everything in, of exaggerating, repeating, that one so often dismisses erroneously as bad writing. It's not a flow of feeling, it's something else; but I'm more interested in Silvina Ocampo than Agustini. I like Juan Rulfo very much for his economy, for how little is explained, for the understatement he uses to get across the most tremendous things.

MGP: And Cortázar?

SM: I see him falling into a parody of himself, very mannered.

MGP: The Cortázar of the short stories also presents a mysterious Buenos Aires.

SM: Yes, I like the Cortázar of the stories very much, the Cortázar of *Bestiario* [*Bestiary*] or *Final del juego* [*The End of the Game*]. I think he's magnificent. Once again you ask yourself what's happening because you know something's going to happen, and nothing is ever explained. That's the Cortázar that interests me, not so much the Cortázar of *Rayuela* [*Hopscotch*]. I like certain Donoso texts, such as *El lugar sin límites* [*Hell Has No Limit*], which is amazing, and *El obsceno pájaro de la noche* [*The Obscene Bird of the Night*], perhaps because I read it at a very particular time in my life and feel I have it very deep inside me. The madness in the novel, the way it comes unhinged, really got to me. I wasn't well and had begun to read this novel almost by chance. That kind of coincidence has happened to me several times; it happened with *Tristana* by Galdós, which I read when I was very sick. I've read a lot of Onetti, of course, and Felisberto.

MGP: What poetry interests you?

SM: I like Darío very much, perhaps because I'm looking at his poetry very closely right now.

MGP: Are you working on a bigger project on Darío?

SM: Yes, I began a book on Darío, and now I've gone over it and I'm going to redo everything I've already done. I'm interested in Darío as a machine that devours everything, that incorporates and assimilates everything, like some kind of monster—

MGP: Like a mill that grinds everything up—

SM: And goes on to write, and incorporates and writes in a frenzy for writing-as-incorporation. Darío's voracity interests me more than Lugones' because in Lugones you already begin to sense the mechanism. In Darío, you don't see the underpinnings as much. I'm also interested in how Darío himself fashions his poetic persona. From a critical point of view, I'm interested in seeing how literary myths are created and what kind of hand the author has in it. In Darío's case, politically, he made friends with every Tom,

Dick, and Harry. He got close to important people, and that's how the public figure began to grow. I'd like to do the same with Gabriela Mistral someday.

MGP: And among Latin American women, whom do you remember in particular?

SM: Besides Silvina Ocampo's stories, I can think of a number of works that have turned out to be important to me through the years. *Los recuerdos del porvenir* [*Recollections of Things to Come*] by Elena Garro. *La última niebla* [*House of the Mist*] by María Luisa Bombal. This novel, which I liked more than *La amortajada* [*The Shrouded Woman*], sounds like a voice in the void, as if these fragments, which seem to be bits of letters, of personal diaries, remained suspended in the text, defiant and somewhat hopeless, without a voice. I like *Las muertes* [*The Deaths*] by Olga Orozco, perhaps because I see there a sustained belief in the word, which I don't have, and certain poems by Gabriela Mistral—"Locas mujeres" [Crazy women] from *Lagar* and the poems about her mother's death. She wrote a splendid, little-known poem called "Electra en la niebla" [Electra in the mist], a poem of matricide or, more accurately, failed matricide. In addition to these people, I'm very interested in the poetry of Alejandra Pizarnik. It's left a deep impression on me.

MGP: As a writer and as a critic, how do you understand the much-debated question about whether there are separate feminine and masculine literatures? On the one hand, as the French feminist critics have done, we talk about a feminine literature that is articulated specifically as a literature of the body. On the other hand, there is the perception held by the male Latin American critics. Not all, but many, consider the distinction false, because they argue that literature has no gender. This last argument could be interpreted as one more attempt on the part of the masculine hierarchy to ignore or reject the possibility of a distinction. Anyway, it's a question one has to confront, to analyze, to think about. Here you are in the middle of the debate: today's women writers have adopted diverse positions about this. Elena Poniatowska, Margo Glantz, and the late Marta Traba believe that feminine literature does in fact exist, and they acknowledge some important characteristics of this type of writing. Luisa Valenzuela, Elvira Orphée, Isabel Allende, and Rosario Ferré do not believe there is such a distinction. What do you think?

SM: There are some things Marta Traba has pointed out that I agree with. There's a kind of detail that appears in texts by women that women make use of in a very characteristic way. Women have a more suspicious way of looking at things. They haven't earned the reputation of being gossips for nothing. I think there's a capacity for observation in gossip and a capacity for interpretation and for different ways of looking at things that women have more than men. Sarraute and Compton-Burnett have been able to get a lot out of those apparently neutral conversations with this capacity for observation and interpretation I'm talking about. Katherine Mansfield, for example, with very few elements, can create a dramatic situation or a narrative knot better than many men can. With very little, some women writers can put something together that is very complex. In "Bliss" by Katherine Mansfield there's a description of a dinner party in the house of a young, recently married couple seen from the wife's point of view. There's another woman there, too—a guest. The wife realizes that something's wrong with her husband, and, in fact, something is wrong at the end. She realizes that the husband helps the other woman on with her coat in a special way, picks up a veiled remark. Then she realizes what's happening. Everything is suggested, not said directly. Or the Virginia Woolf story about the yellow dress. They do a lot with a little, though I also see this in some men. There's another aspect that seems to me to be very important in women—the capacity for a special irony. It goes hand-in-hand with being suspicious and shrewd, but sometimes we forget about it. In my particular case, when I finished the novel, I realized that I'd missed a whole dimension for which I wasn't going to have room. I don't know whether to call it humor or irony. And, in fact, it stayed out, but it's part of my voice. I like to think of my voice as having that ingredient, and I think it can add a lot. It's like using all the little things to turn the world upside down. It's not the big subversions but the small ones, like those you see in Alejandra Pizarnik's prose or Virginia Woolf's.

MGP: The ideological position within feminism also seems important to me. On the one hand, you don't have to be a feminist writer, the same way you shouldn't confuse feminist writing with feminine writing, although "feminine" is the past, present, and future rubric under which all literature written by women is integrated. I think there is an underlying resistance within the Latin American group regarding this very fundamental question that surfaces in the type of argument it evokes. One of them says that male or female writers usually, and on principle, should not get involved with any ideological cause because they'll lose authenticity.

SM: That may be, but not necessarily.

MGP: One example would be engagé literature, or literature of social consciousness that has a Marxist tone. But at the same time, you can be a Marxist and write novels that don't incorporate this ideology. At any rate, I think it's important for women everywhere, in all aspects of life, even when men systematically deny the problem exists. I certainly have a radical position on feminism. I'm a feminist because I'm convinced that if you're not a feminist, you're opposed to the cause of women.

SM: Of course, and for that reason, it would be good to see wider participation in feminist activities to correct injustices done to women on all levels. It seems to me that these problems are difficult to get at through fiction. What one can do through literature is limited.

MGP: In any case, it's difficult to accept the position that there aren't different ways of writing in regard to the parameter of gender. I interpret this position as an insidious way of denying reality and a major way of denying our sex.

SM: I agree. Again, we fall into the simplification that the writer is sexless or bisexual. How telling that the people who say that are usually men! I can't say that I'm bisexual or sexless when I write. I have a sex and that somehow must come out in what I write, in the way I approach language. And when I say "I have a sex," I'm not simply referring to my biological condition. I want to say I have a *way* of being a woman that without doubt affects the way I approach language and writing. That way is conditioned by my gender, by how I perceive myself as a woman and how the society in which I live perceives women. To have gender is a biological and social fact at the same time.

MGP: For example, Josefina Ludmer, who starts out from a psychoanalytic position, proposes that the "I" of writing is bisexual.

SM: I think we all work with one language. But what we do when we write is label or channel that language according to the circumstances. When I use it, I put a mark on it, my personal mark. I'm conditioning anonymous language, which is asexual or androgynous. I'm somehow sexualizing it when I write.

MGP: Hélène Cixous talks about the woman as the *voleuse du langage*.

SM: Why women and not men?

MGP: She's playing with the double meaning of the verb *voler* in French ("to fly" and "to rob") when she says that "for us the point is not to take possession in order to internalize or manipulate, but rather to dash through and to 'fly.' Flying is woman's feature—flying in language and making it fly. . . . It is no accident that *voler* has a double meaning, that it plays on each of them and thus throws off the agents of sense. It's no accident that women take after birds and robbers just as robbers take after women and birds." It's the forging, step by step, piece by piece, of a new language, because phallocentric language excludes women and their word.

SM: It doesn't exactly seem to me to be about an exclusion. More than excluding women, that language assigns women to a subordinate place and, from that position of authority, deauthorizes woman's word. That is, it includes that word but in a position of weakness. This happens on more than one level, from the practice of language—the Bishop of Puebla belittling Sor Juana, Darío belittling Delmira Agustini—to editorial policies. A case in point is the very different fates of two splendid books that are surprisingly alike: *Los recuerdos del porvenir* and *Cien años de soledad* [*One Hundred Years of Solitude*]. Just look at how Elena Garro's novel, which came out four years before García Márquez's did, was set aside, ignored, while the patriarchal novel was triumphantly promoted. *Recuerdos* didn't even win inclusion in the dubious "boom," which is exclusively masculine, of course.

I really don't understand this business of creating a new language, because the way I see it, there's only one language, and every speaker or group of speakers puts it to use in its own way. What women can do and, in fact, have done is establish a new praxis, subverting the authoritarian language that puts them "in their place," dislocating it in different ways depending on the time period. There are those who say you can't make a cross-section like "women through the centuries," and they're partly right, because one must look at women in their own time and in the context of the literature of their time. But one can also make a careful cross-section through the centuries without neglecting the context. After all, the themes and attitudes of masculine novels are usually the same. In the same way, one can imagine a continuity in feminine literature, without falling into excessive, atemporal, and ahistoric generalization.

MGP: Taking another look at the idea of minor genres like the journal or the letter, you can see a continuity within feminine writing.

SM: Yes, but people also exaggerate sometimes. With Sor Juana, for example, people often give her work a kind of interpretation that makes it say more than she's saying, which happens when they take her out of context, and they impoverish her by doing that. That is, I can do a twentieth-century reading of Sor Juana and see certain elements, certain constants—like protest—that you see in contemporary women's literature, but I haven't nor should I forget that Sor Juana was writing in the seventeenth century, and that there is a series of literary conventions that inform her writing, just as there are literary conventions that inform my own.

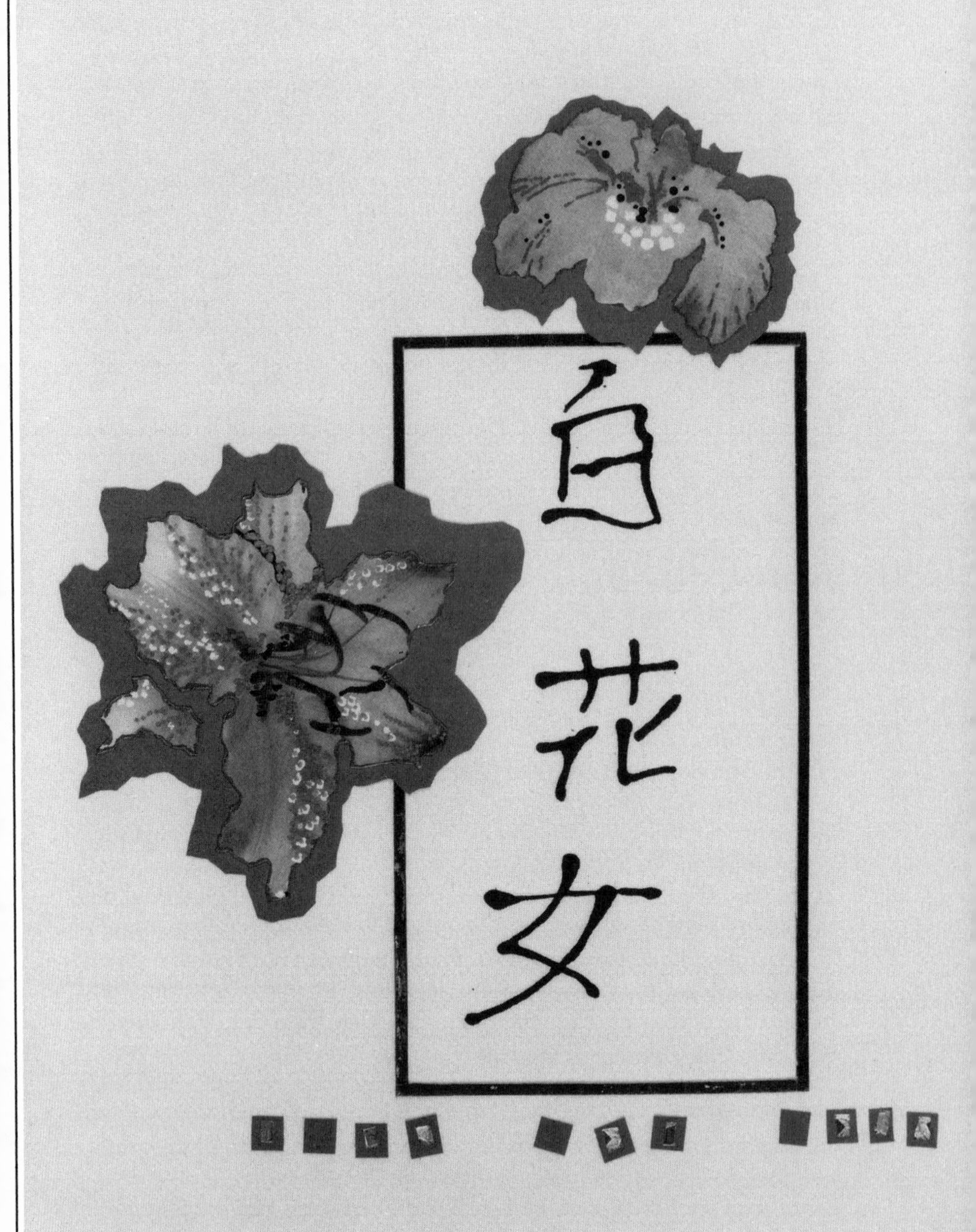
白花女

✣ ✣ ✣

Elvira Orphée

✣ ✣ ✣

MGP: Where do you come from?

EO: I come from Tucumán, a subtropical province in northern Argentina, rich with sugar cane, citron blossoms, and, to some degree, lepers. My last name is a Greek import that took a side trip through France. I've been writing ever since I could hold a pencil.

MGP: How do you remember your childhood?

EO: Illness confined me in my childhood, so I had to create in my room everything I was missing out on. That was how I could fly above the mosquito netting. In my fever-induced delirium, I could see myself fly.

MGP: What was wrong with you?

EO: I had a number of digestive ailments (probably parasites) and gall-bladder problems. At first I rebelled against this importunity, but finally I accepted it as one of the elements that led me to write. If I'd had the same chance for an outside life that other children did, maybe I'd never have written a word. In any case, sickness has the mysterious power of precipitating distant reverberations so that you're converted into a kind of prism that can receive and refract all kinds of light.

MGP: Did you spend much time in bed?

EO: I was almost always in bed. My parents and relatives made a habit of giving me storybooks, so I learned to read when I was very young. I had a huge collection, including, I remember, the stories from *Tesoro de la juventud,* books by Emilio Salgari, but not Jules Verne, because he was too scientific and his novels lacked Salgari's sense of adventure and the exotic.

When I was four, someone in my family gave me a little book of stories to add some color to my long stays in bed. I already had magazines, so I could look at the mysterious pictures. But this little book was something I had to decode. It contained secrets that would open a door toward—flight? I deciphered it with some help and then finished it alone. After that I got a number of similar books, each one with a different story, as if there were an infinite number of stories to tell. My whole family began to ease my illness by giving me coloring books. The drawings helped me pass the time, but they couldn't transport me to the kingdom of true life, where only fantasy is real.

MGP: Were there any kinds of literary incentives in your house?

EO: No, none. My mother didn't read literature, and my father was a scientist who wasn't interested in that type of book. I have no literary predecessors in my family, except its provincial atmosphere—something I've always found surprising. People say female writers have a tactile kind of style. I'm olfactory. It seems strange to me that a province like Tucumán, with so many smells and fragrances, doesn't produce more mystics. Olfactory imagery runs constantly through the works of the Castilian mystics, the fragrance of white flowers—orange blossoms, jasmine, magnolias. As I say in *Aire tan dulce* [Air so sweet], they are flowers whose intensity of fragrance makes up for what they lack in color.

MGP: What kind of relationship did you have with your mother? How did she treat you?

EO: She didn't really know what to do with me. She had no idea how to raise me. For example, she had me start studying piano when I was four, and I continued for eight years. I hated the white keys, the black keys, the eighth notes, the thirty-second notes, and the sixty-fourth notes. I hated them the way only a lover can hate something that keeps her from her love. For eight years, music kept me away from books. As luck would have it, only someone as tone deaf as my mother could believe that what she heard coming from the other side of the house were Czerny exercises. What was really happening was that my fingers were randomly moving over the keys while I was engrossed in a book I had propped up on the music stand.

MGP: So, do you see your passion for reading and literature as being directly related to the fact that you were confined to a limited space—that of your sickroom?

EO: I suppose that being shut in forces you to have an inner life, because there's nothing to do and you're unable to have an outer life. I would have liked to have had an outer biography, to have participated in things, as long as it wouldn't have taken away my capacity for writing. I was never part of anything important nor did I ever work, except for assignments that were sporadic and irregular. Because I couldn't. I had no exterior life, only sickness. Wandering multitudes passed through my adolescence. I worked as if I were surrounded by a fog, cared for by two doctors whom I portrayed in my novel *Uno* [One]. How did I achieve an inner life? I had no inclination for either painting or music, but I did for literature. Besides, ever since I was very young I told myself that I had to have a career, something to do that would show people I wasn't stupid, so that later I could be comfortable being stupid. I needed something to show everyone I could think, that I was a thinking being.

MGP: Why did you have to show you were capable of something? Could it have been, perhaps, a way of compensating for your immobility?

EO: I felt it was absolutely necessary for my survival. There were two things I thought I could try—being a lawyer, which would give me a chance to talk a lot, make arguments, and say interesting things; or being a pilot, which would give me the chance to be in contact with the air and get out of the earth's clutches. Later on, I decided that writers were really failed or cowardly actors.

MGP: Why?

EO: Because I couldn't appear in public. Every time I do, I'm terrified. I've always wanted to be an indirect presence. Everyone wants to have a presence, but actors are encouraged to be direct and to play this or that role. I said to myself that I couldn't do that because I write alone in my house where no one can see me, where I'm in charge of my characters, and where I'm performing, but only indirectly.

MGP: Are you very shy?

EO: I'm shy but daring.

MGP: That's almost a contradiction.

EO: I don't like being the focus of attention or playing a role, the role of Elvira Orphée's interpreter.

MGP: How long were you sick?

EO: Forever. One gift that sickness gave me was delirium. I lived with affectionate elephants and vain flowers like fragrant white lilies. Because I was used to the delirium of sickness, I could start dreaming other dreams, like those provoked by the exhilarating fragrance of white flowers. The scents of the flowers soared; they flew on air.

✣ ✣ ✣

He would have wanted to make the two houses into one. They are already white; he wanted it more white. You can no longer see outside very much, because nothing is happening; he wanted it a more blinding white. Encircled by low walls that formed open corridors to heaven, they chanced upon other corridors, always roofless, crossing over one another until they finally opened out onto a central patio, full of white flowers, and in the middle of the patio is the house, a dazzling white, with freezing-cold floors. A house in the heart of labyrinthine corridors. Saturated with magnolias, with jasmine [*From* En el fondo].

✣ ✣ ✣

MGP: Do you remember your school days?

EO: Yes. I was a very good student. Sometimes I'd miss a whole month, but they always let me make it up. I went to public school first. For high school, I went to a school run by nuns, the Colegio del Huerto in Tucumán.

MGP: Did you keep up your literary pursuits?

EO: More than ever. I remember I'd already started reading Dostoyevski.

MGP: Was your reading censored at all?

EO: Yes, but I could get around it pretty easily. I was really too young to appreciate Dostoyevski. Andersen's fairy tales fascinated me because they were more than fairy tales: they were myths. I didn't know what myths were then, but I remember very well a little mermaid who wanted to conquer her immortal soul, a wrenching prospect. I also remember a little boy who was stolen by the Snow Queen. In order to escape the palace, he had to make the word *eternity* out of ice cubes, but it proved impossible. Everything was foretelling a reality that, apart from the mystery that surrounded me all the time, already existed. I don't know what your childhood in the provinces was like, but for me everything was a mystery. I'll give you two examples. I'd walk by the gratings over convent windows in the moonlight, and I'd be afraid. Something strange was happening, something mixed with the scent of the citron blossoms. I also remember that you couldn't go near certain houses because there was sickness inside, which was considered to be divine retribution in those days. It wasn't simply that some poor man or woman was sick. These things seemed very mysterious to me. Once I found out that the father of some friends of mine lived in a hospital, and they would go to visit him there. But he treated them very badly. Years later I found out that it was an elegant way of keeping him prisoner.

MGP: Did you write when you were a little girl?

EO: Not often, but I do remember that I wrote love letters to imaginary people. One day one of the nuns at school found one of the letters and thought someone else had sent it to me, and she made a tremendous fuss with my mother.

MGP: When did you finish high school?

EO: When I was fifteen, because they put me in first grade when I was five. I was quite a little tyrant. After I got sick, I became a terribly mischievous child.

MGP: What memories do you have of Tucumán?

EO: There was nothing to make an impression of sweetness on my childhood, except the scent of the flowers. The city was ugly. It didn't have much of a winter, but during what little there was of it, it seemed uncomfortably cold. Braziers and weak electric stoves couldn't provide enough heat for houses with mosaic-tiled floors whose doors always stood open. Your nose would freeze even if you were all wrapped up at night. In the summer, everything seemed to collaborate with the sun, even the moon. The nights were white-hot and full of mosquitoes. Under that sun "the only thing it was a pleasure to be was carrion" [from "La calle Mate de Luna" (Mate de Luna Street) in *Su demonio preferido* (Her favorite demon)].

Where I grew up, the mosquitoes could give you malaria. They deposited it within me, and I harbored it for years. I would shiver under eight blankets in the summer when it was a hundred degrees in the shade. Delirium let me fly around my room when I was only three. From my bed, I saw myself between the curtains, touching the ceiling, and I felt a happiness comparable only to how I've felt in later years when I've dreamt I was flying. One of the most beautiful flights I've ever had was through a turquoise sky, at sunset, over a very tall palm tree and people looked up at me from below as I flew over singing a Puccini aria, my voice pure as the air. *Aria* means *air.* It was all air, and a tremendous feeling of happiness. Experimenting with flight dulled my other feelings. No dream was equal to the dream of flying.

MGP: What kind of relationship did you have with your parents?

EO: I had a somewhat difficult relationship with my father because I was always judging him, from the time I was very young. I was always waiting for his next step, gesture, or movement; I would anticipate what he was going to say, and so forth. I'd figured him out. I knew everything about him, and this disgusted me considerably. As far as my mother goes, I wasn't capable of forming a judgment about her most outstanding quality, her sense of humor. Back then, I only passed judgment on her trips to church, her *novenas,* her discipline, her demands, her fastidiousness.

MGP: Were you an only child?

EO: Yes.

MGP: Could that be why you were so hard on your parents?

EO: I don't know. Perhaps.

MGP: Do you think they spoiled you because you were an only child and sickly?

EO: Up to a point. My mother spoiled me, but her affection was a frigid love (though I always got whatever I wanted). She loved me very much, but distantly. She wasn't a mother of the cooking and caressing school because she couldn't cook or give caresses. In those days, I longed for a mother who would make jokes I could understand. I never understood her jokes at all. Only much later did I begin to think she had an excellent sense of humor.

MGP: When did you go to Buenos Aires? Right after you finished school?

EO: My mother died and my father was left alone. With great pleasure, he informed me that I could decide who I wanted to live with, as long as I lived with someone in the family in Tucumán. But instead, I told him I'd decided to go to Buenos Aires. He didn't want to support me if I left Tucumán, but I left anyway because I had an aunt and uncle who adored me. My aunt gave me enough to support myself and get by in Buenos Aires. I was sixteen years old.

MGP: What did you do in Buenos Aires?

EO: I tried to study medicine. I enrolled in a boarding school where I could live and study. But the director talked me out of studying medicine because my health wasn't really up to it. So I changed my major to philosophy. I instantly fell in love with everything I studied: history of religions, logic, French literature, et cetera.

MGP: Did your parents speak French?

EO: No, they didn't. But my grandparents did, and I could read it very well.

MGP: What writers especially interested you at this point?

EO: I know I was passionate about Montaigne because he said things that touched me very deeply, as, for example, this phrase I still remember: "With consummate skill, the Fates begin to unravel our life." Montaigne wanted to live a secluded life, but isolation took away the pleasure of massaging and polishing his mind against other minds. Thinking about Montaigne gave me a very graphic image of everything inside my head that needed to be polished so that only the essentials would remain. The Latin poets interested me, Catullus among them. I wrote something about them. That was the first time I tried to write again. I wrote little things, but I couldn't really connect them. I thought the hero was an aberration, an excrescence of what is human. A long time ago I saw a headline in a magazine that said: Why do women love heroes? Many years later, I turned that idea into a story. I thought you should only live until you were twenty-five, because if you got to be twenty-five and hadn't done all you could do in this world, you'd never do it or you'd do it badly. That story appears in the collection called *Su demonio preferido* and it's called "Círculo" [Circle].

MGP: That's a rather terrible and violent idea. Where do you think this notion came from?

EO: I believe that after the age of twenty-five, life begins to follow a continuously declining path, an interminable descent that gets sadder and sadder the longer it lasts.

MGP: Have you changed your mind since you wrote those short stories?

EO: No. That's why it seems to me that Maria Callas' death was chosen by the gods. What do we do with Greta Garbo? What does she do with herself? They're not heroes. Human beings should reach their peak and then die. When I had my first daughter, I felt very sad without knowing why. It happened with all three of my children. When I went to the doctor, I realized it was a physical kind of depression. When the first one was born, I discovered that once you give something, you don't have it anymore: I have given life; I no longer have life. Then I felt I wanted to die, because I had reached my moment of fulfillment, of the greatest expression of love, which that child embodied. And so it was time to die.

MGP: Many writers use autobiographical material to structure their fiction. Do you think that's true in your case, especially with your childhood memories?

EO: It's difficult for authors not to show up in their own books. Illness appears in my books. As Valéry says, "Pain is the best way to get attention." In our little towns—maybe in every little town—until not too long ago, sick people were considered to be suffering from a curse. They were never sick for normal reasons. Guilt, their own or their ancestors', was the source of infection. A sick person was doubly segregated: once for sickness and once for the sin of having provoked it, as I just told you. Sickness was evil, almost in the demonic sense. For a child, to be segregated was a tragedy. But not in my case. My illness kept me from noticing my surroundings. Later, when I began to realize that I was being excluded from the normal world, it didn't matter so much. I had an "abnormal" world that was much more interesting. As an adult, I cursed illness and anyone who suggested psychoanalysis. Finally, there came a time when I understood how much illness had done for me, how it had preserved my life in lowercase letters. At last, the day came when my sickness was beaten, and I no longer viewed as soothing the image of an oven with the gas on full blast, with no fire and my head inside. But even when vanquished, illness demands the strictest equilibrium, a kind of four-sided time, in which such-and-such must be done at such-and-such a time and under such-and-such circumstances. Much of that appears in my fiction.

MGP: What kind of things did you write first?

EO: I wrote tales and reflections that turned into stories years later.

MGP: Did you keep that material through the years?

EO: Most of it, though I burned many of the things I wrote. They were a reflection of what happened to me on the exterior and on the interior, what I read, what I thought, what I conjectured. There's one story that has to do with Don Quixote. I didn't understand why people loved the character of Don Quixote so much, why they praised him while they disparaged Sancho. In the end, Quixote's madness could be forgiven, but he did nothing except bother people and constantly put them in jeopardy. He's like a horse with blinders on, because he doesn't see past his nose and he ignores what his mind tells him he must be seeing. Sancho, on the other hand, acted out of love—Sancho, who is so ridiculed, who already realizes that everything is an illusion. When Don Quixote retreats, it is Sancho who wants to continue their adventures for the love of his friend. On one occasion he says: "I love you, my lord, from my very innermost being." Out of love, Sancho becomes a knight errant. Those are the kinds of reflections I wrote.

MGP: What did you do when you finished at the university?

EO: I went to Spain on a scholarship. It must have been a lost year, because I didn't feel comfortable in Madrid. I don't remember reading anything there. I loved Barcelona, but in Madrid, even the cobblestones seemed annoying.

MGP: What did you think you could do in Madrid?

EO: They gave me a partial scholarship to study literature, but I didn't go to any classes. I explored museums and took long walks because I didn't feel well when I stayed inside. Finally, I went to Paris, to the Casa Argentina, which offered room and board to students. I took a course at the Sorbonne, and it turned out that I was the most knowledgeable student in the class because I'd read Kafka, Thomas Mann, and other writers from different worlds. I stayed there two years and began to write, and I wrote a lot but didn't publish anything.

MGP: When did you start to publish?

EO: When my first daughter was born. I got married in Paris to a painter from Argentina, Miguel Ocampo, and we went back to Argentina. I spent my entire pregnancy in bed, so I took advantage of the time to write a book. That's when I really began to feel like writing.

MGP: When did you start publishing your first pieces?

EO: My first story was published in *Sur,* and the editor changed some parts of it without asking me. Later on, that story became my novel *En el fondo* [Down deep inside].

MGP: Were you part of the *Sur* group?

EO: No, and I still haven't figured out who was!

MGP: Did you meet Victoria Ocampo?

EO: Well, she was my husband's aunt. I used to see her in Mar del Plata during the summer. But I never perceived her as a writer people admired or as someone who could open doors for me. And she didn't, because when I published my book, I was the one who sought out a publisher. I don't think Victoria would have recommended it, either.

MGP: Why not?

EO: Because Victoria only liked people who were already established. I don't know if she had the critical judgment to recognize people who were just starting out.

MGP: Did you have a circle of friends who were involved in literature?

EO: No, I was never part of any literary circle, and I don't enjoy literary get-togethers.

MGP: Were you in contact with Silvina Ocampo? Did you know Borges?

EO: No, I met Silvina much later, when she had already written two books. I met Borges much later, too. I did a lot of little favors for him after he went blind, like taking him places and giving him rides to the National Library. My husband and I gave him a tour of Paris when he visited there. I also knew a number of people who never left Argentina, like Fernando de Elizalde or Inés Malinov, who aren't very famous.

MGP: Did you settle in Buenos Aires after you came back from Paris?

EO: We spent four years in Buenos Aires and then went to Italy, because my husband is a diplomat in addition to being a painter. We saw a lot of Alberto Moravia and of Elsa Morante there, Morante being Moravia's companion in those days. Morante is an Italian writer who isn't very well known, but I think she's very good. We also met Pratolini and other Italian writers. After that, I traveled in Venezuela quite a bit.

MGP: Some of your books have been published there. Is there any particular reason you don't publish them in Argentina?

EO: They couldn't be published in Argentina. They wouldn't have lasted even one day on display. They would have been taken out of the window. Besides, no book store would have dared sell them.

MGP: Were you ever involved in publishing a literary magazine?

EO: No, because I had a lot of work to do, which took up a lot of time. I don't have much time to write because I also need what I call "subjective" time. A magazine would take that time away from me. As it is, I don't have much time to write. I get interrupted by things in the house. There are taxes to pay, because if you don't pay them right away, you get threatened, killed, or thrown out of the country. Traveling takes up a lot of my time, too.

MGP: Do you travel a lot?

EO: Yes, but now I think I'm going to stay someplace quiet, because I have a book of essays under contract.

MGP: Could we talk about this new project?

EO: I'd prefer not to discuss it much, but I can tell you it's about ancient religions. I'm interested in religion, and I'm fascinated by useless knowledge. I was once reading a biography of Gandhi, in which they mentioned his interest in intestines. There's a rational explanation for that. There are labyrinths everywhere. For example, the swastika is a mutilated labyrinth. Among the Hindus, there is a kind of initiation rite based on the idea that certain parts of the body contain great power and that one of those parts goes through the anus; thus, anal coitus is a form of illumination. For that and for other reasons, the labyrinth of the intestines is very important. The ritual surrounding the goddess Kali also interests me. Kali has four hands: in one she holds a severed hand, blood gushes from another, in another she holds a sword, and in the fourth there is a serpent. The explanation for this iconography is that Kali is the goddess of time.

MGP: What writers have influenced you or have had some sort of impact on your writing?

EO: None, so far as my work goes, because I don't write like anyone else. I wanted to write like the Japanese, but they carry a series of odd experiences within themselves that I can't participate in. I don't think anyone's influenced me.

MGP: You don't recognize precursors, or mentors, either?

EO: No. Every writer has his or her own admirers. The word is something that man has appropriated. There is an old Australian myth that says women used to have all the tools of power and that among them was the word. One day, when the women were asleep, the men took all the tools away. When the women woke up, they said to themselves it didn't really matter, because they would remember everything. But I think it did matter. From that time on, women had lost the word. The unfolded word doesn't have many sympathizers. I'm interested in the concise word.

MGP: Are you interested in and have you read literature written by women?

EO: Yes, I've read Elsa Morante and Colette, whom I like best.

MGP: Are there any Latin American writers who interest you?

EO: There are, but fewer. I would have to be very selective.

MGP: Where would you place your own work, then? Does it belong to a specific group within Argentine literature or within Latin American literature?

EO: I don't know. That would put a frame around myself, and I'm a person, not a portrait. At best, my provincial surroundings could be my frame. Can a portrait know the frame that best suits it? I can only name the writers I like now or have liked in the recent past. But I don't think these preferences mean I resemble them because all human beings process readings through an internal alchemy, which includes both their preferences and rejections. The result is neither resemblance to the writer's favorites nor absolute difference from those whom she rejects. The narrators I like are Japanese: Yukio Mishima, Junichiro Tanizaki, Ryonosuke Akutagawa, Osamu Dazai. Among westerners, I like the Italian writer I've already mentioned, Elsa Morante.

MGP: How has your writing developed?

EO: In the first two books, *Uno* and *Dos veranos* [Two summers], I write about life in the provinces, and I avoid the third-person narrator to avoid falling into the trap of the omniscient narrator. In my third book, I managed to completely avoid that. Instead, the character communicates directly with the reader. When I was in Italy, I remember that quite a few writers strongly disliked the omniscient narrator style, which reinforced my own rejection of it. In *Aire tan dulce* the action is outlined, planned out, and even lived in the moment, not described from the outside but from the inside. Of course, the narrator who writes in the first person is just as conventional as the omniscient narrator, since I don't really know how such-and-such a person thinks. Nevertheless, the first-person narrator gives me more direct access to what I am trying to express than the third-person narrator does.

✣ ✣ ✣

The gentle mid-season rain slips down the grape leaves in large drops. On one side of the grapevine, she is huddled under a blanket. She thinks about her childhood as if it were the past: she remembers the adobe oven, Eudoro's window, the smell of the lime trees around my house, the guava trees where we tied their hammocks. She thinks: This ugliness is unbearable. Help me. But she doesn't know who she can ask for help.

If you came, if you got out from under that dirty blanket, you could see the rain with me and your childhood would come back to you. We'd huddle together and look at the clean water falling; the fragrance of the grape-vines and the lime trees would float by like a slim thread in the wind; to cover you, I'd have a white blanket with colored flowers woven by women who lost their words a long time ago. What have you lost, Sara? What have you lost, little soul made of peach down? A fuzzy chilling skin that leaves me chilled when I want to caress it [*From* Aire tan dulce].

✣ ✣ ✣

MGP: So you feel that you can communicate more directly with the reader when you write in first person?

EO: Yes. I like books that communicate directly with the reader.

MGP: In one of your most recent books, *La última conquista de El Angel* [*El Angel's Last Conquest*], your main character speaks in the first person. Why did you write this book? Why did you choose to elaborate on torture as a literary theme?

EO: Because of hate. But who knows whether it's the writer who picks the theme or vice versa—whether the theme begins to insinuate itself in the recesses of the spirit, choosing the writer, brushing lightly against sensitive zones? That must have been what happened. The theme infiltrated my spirit, touching points of hatred within me, points of repugnance for all forms of insults to defenseless life, like those exerted upon children, animals that are martyred, and other cornered living beings. These are abominations that seem to be transgressions against a divine order or, in any case, are too important to be violated. In *Aire tan dulce*, there's a line that says that blood does not disturb us because of its color or odor, but because of its mystery. Whoever wants to make this mystery-conducting riverbed spout probably feels all-powerful, like an evil sorcerer's apprentice.

One of the characters in the book talks about this phenomenon and says: "Torture belongs to a supernatural order." At some point, one wonders if it is God himself who initiates torture. We see examples of that in the Bible, when God commands Abraham to kill Isaac or when He is so cruel to poor Job.

MGP: How did you develop the theme of torture in literature? How did you begin to conceptualize it?

EO: It was born in me perhaps like a nauseous feeling, an impotence, a frenetic abhorrence of arrogant macho dominance, until one day a little book fell into my hands—it was like that almost literally; I didn't go looking for it—a little book in which a man, Santiago Nudelman, a member of the Chamber of Deputies, wrote memoirs about torture in his time, some twenty-four years ago. He enumerated facts, prisoners' depositions, testimony given by people who saw a stained piece of clothing or who heard cries. After that the first story—perhaps it would be better to call it a chapter—of my book began, in 1970, and the stories continued in heartbreaking succession until 1975. I say "heartbreaking" because each story, each chapter—once finished—seemed to be literature compared with the stripped-down style of Nudelman's little book (entitled *La era del terror y la tortura* [The era of terror and torture]) whose pure, adjectiveless enumeration was far more bruising than any literary re-creation.

✣ ✣ ✣

They should have come already blindfolded. Their eyes shouldn't be visible inside here. Nor exactly where they are nor who we are. The work must be perfect. To fatten fear, yes, but not in the midst of filth.

. . . .

The night-light hanging from the middle of the ceiling sent oblique rays off the green eyeshade. We made a circle, each one of us at the end of a luminous ray. Behind the circle, the darkness barely touched our backs. None of the torture chiefs in charge had appeared yet. But on the table, just beneath the small light-bulb, the man is positioned artistically. His eyes are blindfolded, his clothing partly removed. What other clothes remained, we pulled them up from where we had to pull them up, revealing small parts of his body that prompted Roque Abud to say: "He's just an innocent angel." The other men laughed softly. They couldn't have stuck Tupac Amaru any harder. He began to come out of his swoon or state of shock [*From* La última conquista de El Angel].

✣ ✣ ✣

By the end, I stopped feeling discouraged: my novel wasn't about exposing a reality in itself more sincere, more vulgar, and more scatological than any of its representations could be, but rather about why a man becomes a torturer. What mechanisms, besides the pathological ones, make him into a celebrant of those Black Masses?

We all know that torture exists: the newspapers have repeatedly told us about Nazi horrors as well as those committed by the Ugandans, the guerrillas, the police (either KGB or gestapo). The results are always the same. But the *why* remains unanswered.

MGP: Were you thinking of doing a kind of repulsive inventory of torture?

EO: Besides utilitarian types of torture used to extract information as well as the kind of torture that forces people to collaborate and torture that originates through the whim of a vengeful Señor Presidente who doesn't consider his offended dignity soothed by simply condemning a maimed or elderly person to twenty years in prison. Aside from these examples—none of which are justified but which can at least be explained—there's another: torture applied without justification. There's an aspect of this lack of justification in the previous examples, which takes them out of the realm of the merely human. It is at this point that the *why* emerges. Why the delight in inflicting suffering? Why does the union of contempt with torture seem to elicit such a high pitch of spiritual delight? That's the level of comprehension I wanted to reach. There's something metaphysical about torture. It has nothing to do with analyzing or demonstrating a mechanism. I simply had to write stories with real, known facts. And in order to make them more than merely realistic, it was better not to explore the position of the one being tortured, the one for whom pain was the "supreme attention," but to explore the position of the torturer, for whom this same pain is—what? Trying to approximate that *what* was what I attempted in my book.

MGP: Do you think there is a difference between the way you treat torture and the way other writers have dealt with it?

EO: The norm in Latin American literature is to study the upper echelons of power. Only in certain novels, like *Amalia* by José Marmol, is the victim's point of view pursued. *La última conquista de El Angel* is one of the few novels in which the problem of power is seen from the perspective of the low-level hired guns.

MGP: What made you decide to work with this particular angle?

EO: The upper echelons embody indirect power, while the lower ones provide the manual labor. These people deal directly with the actual materiality of power: human beings. For the upper echelons, power is something abstract, no manhandling. They could even ignore the atrocities carried out through orders emanating from themselves that did not anticipate every move of the executioners. There are many intermediaries between the orders from above and those of the executioners. This is the one in charge of handling the victim's pain, life, and death. Abstract power pertains to the mind. Direct, abominable contact with something that surpasses abstractions pertains to the spirit. That's why literary elaboration seemed like a better strategy—to develop the torturers' mentality, to deduce their psyches. Even the language of torture had to be invented. It's a language that seems real, but, for example, when one of them says, upon leaving the body they were torturing, "The market showed moderate trade in pork," such a phrase can also be read in a newspaper article about the hog market. I don't know if a torturer would have said that, but that's my literary re-creation of the context.

MGP: The character of Winckel is quite humane. Why did you decide to treat him that way, more humanely?

EO: I didn't want to fashion a portrait of a deformed, grotesque torturer, as others have done. It's a literary treatment that leaves no trace of humanity. For example, one of my characters in this story loves music. Another, the one named Cajoncito, doesn't want to see a movie about Nazi torture in Germany because there are too many dead bodies and he won't be able to sleep afterward.

MGP: Where would you place this book in relation to the rest of your work?

EO: There is one critic who distinguishes the objective from the subjective in my work. Apparently, if the author is a poet or a woman, this critic prefers the writing to be saturated with lyricism. If the author is a man, or purely a factual narrator, the critic prefers narration with movement and exterior creations because, as everyone already knows, men—except poets or potential poets—perceive the world in terms of its surface and the variation of facts it offers rather than in terms of individual depth. But "in no part is there a world, O beloved, save inside," as Rilke said, who was often repudiated for not concerning himself with "reality," as if he were a politician. What is the outside world without the internal world but some kind of list? Even psychoanalysts know that.

As far as my books go, *La última conquista de El Angel* could be categorized as objective—that is, the writer is not present—but if it is thought of as my only objective book, it could be thought of as transcending the facts in a nonlyrical form. *Aire tan dulce,* on the other hand, is unabashedly interior yet nevertheless full of facts that are lived as projects, memories, and even as the present.

MGP: Where do you place yourself with respect to feminism and feminine writing? Do you think the movement is important? Do you think women have developed a different literary practice in creative writing?

EO: Up to now, you could make a distinction between feminine writing and masculine writing. Now that the world has opened up to women, we'll see what the future brings. When you talk about violence in women's literature, it is a violence very distinct from masculine violence, which is the violence of slaps and stabs.

MGP: Do you think women use or manipulate language in a different way?

EO: Within the Western literary canon, yes, they have. At least looking back, I think they did, but from now on, I don't know whether they'll continue to follow this model.

MGP: What are the characteristics of this kind of writing?

EO: To begin with, the idea of God. For men, it is something that makes no sense: the burning bush, the spider's web, that which impedes passage, the quest. I'm thinking of Kafka or Dostoyevski. In contrast, I find examples in Virginia Woolf, for instance, that represent the idea of God in another way: as a man who thinks about entering a cathedral to deposit a briefcase containing papers that have to do with the quest. Women have a feeling of divinity that is different from having a God that can be produced at any moment. It is a light, like a reflection in water. Man lives torn by that idea of God; that is, he lives torn by himself since God is the image of man. The proof is in the fact that some men are locked in asylums because they think they are God. Since God wasn't created in the likeness of woman, or vice versa, what woman has ever found herself confined in an asylum believing herself to be the Virgin Mary?

MGP: What other characteristic do you think is important?

EO: I don't say *sensibility* because the term is overused, but women definitely treat the senses differently because, since they're shut out, they have nothing to do. They don't have safaris or wars or trips back and forth. They have to take whatever small things are offered them. I remember once visiting a high school in France and opening a book that the students had made. It was dedicated to "Notre dame de petites choses" [Our lady of little things]. That's what it seems like to me. Women can redeem littleness by intensely focusing on it. One must imagine more when one has less. Sensations unfold the way Proust's work does. In Colette we see what happens with many "little" things.

MGP: Would you agree with Marta Traba's thesis that women's literature has a general tendency to explain a reality that is relatively immediate, as opposed to the way men interpret the world, which is always in terms of mental constructs?

EO: That's exactly right. Men always elaborate mental constructs, which is what I meant when I said that the world of the word belongs to men. People are biased toward what is talked about most. What is discussed with an air of importance matters most. Women certainly touch on these important topics, but in a diffident way—life, death, love, that is, all subjects but religion. But I don't see that as a fault. Anyway, it is not religion but the idea of God that women barely touch. Female narrators have been reproached for being amoral, and I believe that's exactly right. As one Dostoyevski heroine says to a man: "You are just. You are not good. Therefore, you are unjust." That, translated into reality, is immoral. If I were a female judge and decided to set free a woman who killed her husband because he came home drunk every night, because he beat their children, because he set a bad example, because she lived amid insults, filth, and vomit, if she did it to protect herself and to protect the children, if I decided to absolve her, surely I would be considered to be amoral. In that case, fine, I have no morality.

MGP: Feminine moral principles are different. Remember that moral codes were established by men, who, furthermore, both invented the religions that dominate the world and set up the ethical and moral order.

EO: That's right. The state religions are Judaism, Islam, and Christianity. The moral codes for women in the era of goddesses, in the Neolithic age, were based on nature. Nevertheless, that image of divinity reunites the union of opposites, which makes an exact diologema, maternal and abstract at the same time.

MGP: What are you working on now?

EO: I'm working on the book of essays that I told you about and also on a novel, but it's going very slowly. In the novel, which I might call "Basura y luna" [Garbage and moon], I'll use a lyrical narrative style. I'll also treat eroticism as lyrically as possible, because it exists for at least half of humanity. And even if it only exists for a fourth, there's no reason to favor the majority.

HASTA NO VERTE JESUS MIO

✣ ✣ ✣

Elena Poniatowska

✣ ✣ ✣

MGP: Where were you born?

EP: I was born in Paris in 1933. My mother was Mexican and my father was French, of Polish origin. His family was expelled from Poland after the first partition. All the Poniatowskis were French-Polish. One, for example, José Poniatowski, was one of Napoleon's marshals. They had been expelled from Poland precisely because the last one was Stanislaus Augustus, the last king of Poland. My father fell in love with a Mexican woman named Paula Amor. Her name was really Dolores de Amor, but since that sounded awful in Spanish because it means "sorrows of love," they called her Paula after her father, Pablo. She belonged to the Mexican gentry, hacienda owners who lost their lands after the Mexican Revolution. During the Lázaro Cárdenas administration, when the government instituted agrarian reform, they spent most of their time traveling. They lived in hotels and moved from house to house. I don't think my mother ever lived in a house or apartment that she could call home until she married my father, and even then, her in-laws lived there, too.

MGP: Did your mother spend much time in Europe?

EP: Yes, of course. She was born there. My mother speaks French much better than Spanish. When she talks to me, she speaks French.

MGP: So your mother didn't live in Mexico.

EP: Yes, she did. She spent her vacations on the hacienda, where she would ride horseback, galloping through the countryside and over the cornfields. But then she would go back to France. I think she spent one or two years at the Academy of the Sacred Heart in Mexico. She always claimed she liked living in Mexico. She likes to talk about the time she went to where the hacienda had been—in Querétaro near San Juan del Río—an hacienda called La Llave [The key], which is now completely destroyed. I think the social upheaval must have been terribly difficult for her, because of the way she reacted when I went with her to see La Llave. I think she found it overwhelming, but she'd eventually point out everything and tell you incredible stories about what it was like to have been a member of the landed gentry. For example, the train was routed through there just so her family could get off. They were the only passengers who went to La Llave. Behind the hacienda you can still see the train tracks that came by to leave off the family of Don Felipe Iturbe (my grandmother's last name).

MGP: So the hacienda is completely abandoned now.

EP: First it was expropriated, and now it's abandoned. It was turned into a school, but that never worked out. Only tree stumps are left, nothing else. The hacienda chapel is completely destroyed: the once-splendid choir is in pieces; the crosses have been thrown on the ground.

MGP: So you were born when your parents were living in France?

EP: Yes, I was born in Paris, and so was my sister. And then, many years after the Second World War, my brother, Jan, was born. He died in 1968.

MGP: Your books are dedicated to him.

EP: Yes, all of them. He died in a car accident on the eighth of December 1968.

MGP: I'd thought his death was connected to the riots of 1968.

EP: No. He took part, as did all the young students, but 1968 wasn't what caused his death. Of course, one can say that it's somehow connected because social unrest was always simmering under the surface. Still, it means something to see so many young people dying, though, of course, my brother didn't die in the Plaza de las Tres Culturas, nor did he die in a police roundup or in jail. But it means something because a young person has died, doesn't it?

MGP: Of course. How long did you live in Paris?

EP: Not very long. During the war, my mother drove an ambulance and my father was in combat, so they took us to the south of France, to the country. We went to school there, to an *école communale,* or parochial school. I remember that I learned about addition and subtraction, about the pistil and all the different parts of the flower, which I used to draw very carefully. I remember that I was terribly afraid of our teacher. I was always scared I'd spill the ink on myself—violet ink—which they used to put in white porcelain inkwells set into our desks. Each of us had a quill pen. We had to do our letters with very delicate upstrokes and downstrokes—*les pleines* and *les déliées,* we called them. Although I liked to go to school, I was always extremely afraid of it. We got special treatment because we were considered princesses, because of my father's family name.

MGP: Did you mingle much with the other children?

EP: There were a lot of children in my class, but I don't remember making any friends. Perhaps that was why we rode bicycles all the time. My sister had a red bicycle, and I had an orange one. I used to go riding alone quite a bit because I loved to ride through the lavender fields. Lavender fields are a jewel that doesn't exist here, a jewel embedded deep within my memory. I remember those were huge lavender fields. Something else I liked very much was to pet the yearlings on the back, because they were so smooth. I never thought they could be so slippery. They were always so slick with grease that it was like putting my hand in a pot full of butter. Those were very good years. Then we left for Mexico.

MGP: Were you a young child then?

EP: Yes, I was very young. We came on a refugee boat, and later I found out that many refugees came on one called El Marqués de Comillas. We arrived in 1942 or at the very beginning of 1943. Without my father. That's when the separation from my father began. We came with my mother. And that was when I got to know her, because my grandparents and governesses had been taking care of us before, and after that we had *señoritas.* I remember a Polish *señorita* who wore a salmon-pink corset made in the days when they buttoned all the way up, and it was completely lined with money. I never did figure out if she was a criminal. There was also the war atmosphere. When we were in France, I remember that at night they'd paint all the windows blue and listen for the airplanes, and once when my father came to see us, he was dressed in a soldier's uniform.

MGP: Was your father at the front?

EP: Father was in the war, and Mother drove ambulances. Once she saved a donkey, and put it in the ambulance. She got reprimanded for that. They were very young, very good-looking, very irresponsible, and not very conscious of danger.

MGP: How old were they then?

EP: Well, my mother must have been twenty-four when I was born. So during the war she would have been between twenty-eight and thirty. In any case, they were very young. I remember that here in Mexico they went to a lot of dances. My mother was very beautiful and got invited everywhere.

MGP: Did your father stay in Europe?

EP: Yes. We finally got to see him seven years later, which seemed like forever. After the war he came to Mexico, and he liked it. People said he had a lot of possibilities. But he failed at everything because he wasn't much of a businessman. He had fought in the war; he had been in Germany, Russia . . .

MGP: When your parents returned to Mexico, was your mother's family there?

EP: Only my grandmother and Felipe Iturbe, one of the former owners of the hacienda, which was now expropriated.

MGP: And they had no money?

EP: My grandmother did. Even though wealthy people say they don't have any money, they always do. This Felipe Iturbe used to say he had nothing, that he lived off the kindness of his friends, but when he died he left an inheritance. Everyone cared for him very much, because he was such a wonderful person. They constantly invited him over for lunch and dinner, but he kept a notebook where he recorded what he thought of his friends' cooking. I read this little book once. Instead of being grateful for having such generous friends, he'd said terrible things about them. As you can see, all social stigmas can be found in my family.

MGP: How old were you when you came to Mexico?

EP: I was eight.

MGP: And you spoke only French?

EP: Yes. But I learned Spanish from the servants very quickly. From that time on I have always had very sympathetic feelings for housemaids, or whatever you want to call them. That explains why I like Jesusa Palancares, the main character in my book *Hasta no verte, Jesús mío* [*Until We Meet Again*] so much. I learned Spanish because I didn't need to. To some degree, it was thought to be the language of the colonized. It wasn't a language you really needed to know, my household assumed. My parents put me in a ridiculous English school, where we'd sing "God Save the Queen" and where they taught us to count in pounds, shillings, and pennies. I've only been to England once in my life, and that was only four years ago, so you can imagine how useful the British system was for me in Mexico. But when you're a child, you learn just about anything. So I already spoke three languages before I was ten, and that's something I'll always be grateful for.

MGP: What did you speak at home?

EP: We spoke French or English at home because my grandmother had a boyfriend—Archie—who courted her very seriously, and so she preferred us to speak English or French. She finally got married for the second time at seventy.

MGP: Tell me, did Jesusa Palancares really exist?

EP: Jesusa Palancares exists.

MGP: Would you say that your book *Hasta no verte, Jesús mío* is a testimonial?

EP: If you ask her, she says it isn't. I gave it to her to read after I finished it, and she got angry. She told me, "You don't understand anything. What good did it do you to have studied so much? You changed everything. You didn't understand." Now, it's true that the book is based on many conversations with her, but it's a novel, right? It's not what she dictated to me nor does it use exactly the same language, but it's based on her story. She doesn't acknowledge that. It's as though I'd wanted to write a novel about you, and then you'd wanted me to write about selected things.

MGP: Only good or nice things?

EP: No, not only nice things. For example, she wanted me to emphasize something that was very important to her, such as her involvement with a religious group called Spiritual Work, and describe all the people who participated in their meetings and ceremonies. She felt disappointed when I didn't and claimed I made up characters or killed people off—comments like that.

MGP: So Jesusa is an excellent reader and critic.

EP: Yes, I wrote a novel based on a completely real account. Of course, many people prefer to see it differently and think of Elena as a very lucky person to have found someone who dictated a novel to her chapter by chapter.

MGP: There's no doubt that it is a novel and a tremendously powerful one.

EP: It is a novel.

MGP: Recreating Jesusa's entire account of her world is your task as a writer. What doubt can there be?

EP: That's true, but a lot of it is a testimony based on a reality she didn't recognize as hers. That's why she didn't take it very well. I should have used her name. The actual person isn't named Jesusa Palancares, even though the book has photos of her. I wanted to make a text that, though I'm not an anthropologist or a sociologist, would reflect a certain reality that she couldn't acknowledge. She ripped up all the photos when she saw them, ripped them into pieces. She said she didn't want those photos. She wanted a sepia photo of herself, very blurry, that would make it hard to figure out if it was her or someone else. She said she had nothing to do with the book. It was a complete rejection.

MGP: Where did you meet Jesusa?

EP: She's 83 years old now. I met her in a laundromat when I heard her talking. I liked the way she talked, and I sought her out.

MGP: How did you approach her?

EP: When I started out, it was extremely difficult to interview her, because she was very suspicious. She'd say I was wasting her time. Then she'd want to talk about herself. She'd want to spend hours telling me that the pipes were stopped up and that the lady of the house didn't fix them. She did have her obsessions. It was very difficult to win her over. Now I think that I must have been influenced by having worked a month and a half with Oscar Lewis. I met him before he became famous for *Los hijos de Sánchez* [*The Children of Sanchez*]. I helped him with another book called *Pedro Martínez.* I saw him work. I saw how he devoted himself to the people, though I was only with him a very short time. He used a tape recorder, because he had North American equipment. When I went to see Jesusa, I used a tape recorder borrowed from some printers who were the only people I knew who had a tape recorder. It was a huge boxlike thing. The first time I brought it with me, Jesusa didn't say anything. The second time, she said, "Take that damn thing away. Who's going to pay for it? Who's going to pay for the electricity you're stealing"—because there weren't any batteries—"you or me?" and I tried to calm her down and tell her I'd take care of the bill. And she went on: "And how will I figure it out? It's nothing but a bother."

Also, when I took her the manuscript of the book, which I'd had bound in an attractive shiny blue material so she'd like it, she told me, after she started reading: "No, you didn't understand anything. And take that away. Take that damn box away from here too. It bothers me. It takes up a lot of room, and I don't have any place to keep it."

MGP: Could Jesusa read?

EP: No, she couldn't. I read parts of it to her to see if she liked them, but she didn't like anything.

MGP: How strange that she got angry.

EP: Afterward, when she'd seen it in print and when she saw that I'd put the Niñito de Atocha [Baby Jesus of Atocha] on the cover (she had that saint in her room), she liked it. I remember that one day I saw a Niñito de Atocha in the street, next to those street vendors who sell saints. I bought it and said to myself, If I put this on the cover, she'll like it. That's why I did it. And that's where the book cover came from.

✣ ✣ ✣

People say he speaks ever so nicely, ever so beautiful; that he sends his regard and says I shouldn't forget him; he's watching out for me because he's responsible to the man who entrusted me to him. That is why he still takes care of me, along with his entire caravan. How many thousands of years will have gone by, and still he won't leave me without his protection! But I don't actually see him anymore through revelation, though I see his color portrait in the chapel on Luis Moya Street, which is what the wide street used to be called. It is in a painting this big, and the eyes are open; they're black, black as coal, as black as black diamonds. He wears a turban wound around his head, and in the center gleams a white pearl-and-diamond cluster; and out of the jewels spurt tiny little plumes [*From* Hasta no verte, Jesús mío].

✣ ✣ ✣

MGP: How did Jesusa react?

EP: I felt she liked it, but she didn't say anything to me. Afterward, she asked me for twenty copies to give to the people with whom she worked. So I took them to her.

MGP: Why do you think she resisted it?

EP: I don't know. I don't know what she thought.

MGP: The character in the novel definitely recreates Jesusa's hermetic quality. What made you decide to talk with her?

EP: I think it has something to do with my childhood. After I finished school in Mexico, I went to Eden Hall, the Convent of the Sacred Heart in Philadelphia. The school's claim to fame was that it had played hockey with Grace Kelly's school. Eden Hall won the game, and they made quite a fuss over the romance between Prince Rainier and Grace Kelly. Those were the days of Clark Gable and Gregory Peck, Tyrone Power and Vivien Leigh. We all wanted to be like them. I remember Jennifer Jones. I thought they were all wonderful. I personally liked Cary Grant, and my sister said she was going to marry Tyrone Power.

MGP: How old were you then?

EP: About sixteen or seventeen. Those days and those things stick in one's memory. And I remember that we used to sing "Somewhere over the rainbow, way up high," Judy Garland's song in *The Wizard of Oz*.

MGP: Would that be in the fifties?

EP: Mid-fifties. Yes, because I began to do journalism very soon after I came back from the convent. Even though Jesusa happened many years later, she got me to try to recover the childhood the convent made me lose, perhaps.

MGP: Jesusa's world has nothing to do with yours. They don't even connect.

EP: I've always done books—except for *De noche vienes*—that have nothing to do with me, because neither the ones I've done nor the one about Tina Modotti that I'm working on now are related to my world. But I've started, and I'm going to do a book.

MGP: Let's go back to your youth for a moment. You went to high school in Mexico.

EP: Yes, but never to Spanish schools. When I finished the English school, I went to the Liceo Franco-Mexicano [French-Mexican lycée] for a year and then to Eden Hall, the Convent of the Sacred Heart. I never studied Spanish. I learned Spanish from the servants. In fact, until recently I still used certain expressions used by less educated people.

MGP: You used to speak like Jesusa.

EP: Yes, so I understand it very well. That's the Spanish I know. If you speak to me in the language of *Platero y yo* or Cervantes, that Spanish is utterly unfamiliar to me.

MGP: Have you ever written in other languages?

EP: Yes, I've written in English. I was treasurer of *The Current Literary Coin,* a magazine put out by the students at Eden Hall. We wrote things like "I am Joan of Arc," "I am Napoleon," "Nothing to Wear," and other such creative pieces. A number of different things.

MGP: What did you feel like in those days? Was it a convent or a high school?

EP: It was a high school, but they overemphasized religion. We spent too many hours in church. On your birthday, your friends would give you a "spiritual bouquet" as a gift, which meant attending thirty masses and saying four hundred prayers, "God bless XXX." Each girl would make a pile of little cards, write a little affectionate message, and list all the sacrifices she'd offered. It was the most religious atmosphere you could imagine. You had to be a "Child of Mary" or "Blue Ribbon." I was all those things. I was a little reserved during the first few months, but then I grew to like it because I enjoyed making sacrifices—all those slightly masochistic things they'd make you do. I washed all the dishes. I helped the sisters. This was a racist school. There were the "sisters" who were the servants and the "mothers" who were the teachers. The mother superior was a French nun, and there was another named Saint Margaret Allicot. They were swathed in wimples and veils. We also had numerous crushes: "Oh, we love Mother Heisler. Oh, we love Mother X." We fell in love with the best-looking "mothers." During Lent they'd all be in a terrible mood because they did so many penances and wouldn't eat enough. I made many good friends, and, yes, I got along well with people. Also, the daughters of South American dictators went there; for example, Somoza's niece's daughter, Liana Debayle Somoza; someone else from Cuba; and all the rich girls from Monterrey. There were a lot of Irish girls with red hair and freckles, because the Irish are strongly inclined to Catholicism. I liked it. There were many opportunities there to do things that I thought were very interesting, like making sacrifices.

MGP: Besides making sacrifices, did you ever read?

EP: Not very much. Our curriculum was terrible. We had to memorize the Old Testament and the New Testament. We recited it from memory. It was the kind of old-fashioned education that wasn't designed for thinking.

MGP: What were you educated for?

EP: They told me I had to be a child of Mary, of God, or of the Holy Spirit. Then, some unknown being would come and take me to heaven. They'd tell you that "at cocktail parties, you shouldn't get drunk; you shouldn't neck." It was funny and, in a certain way, very tender. Later on, I think that they got much more modern. Besides, there wasn't anything else to do. Despite all this, I remember that one girl got pregnant and would exercise all the time so her belly would disappear—until they ran her out of school.

MGP: What did you do after you finished school in Philadelphia?

EP: I got a scholarship to Manhattanville College. Then I came back here, and they told me I could be a trilingual secretary. I stayed in Mexico to do nothing. Well, I learned shorthand.

MGP: Did you continue your studies at the university?

EP: No. I went to an academy in San Juan de Letrán to learn shorthand and typing, which didn't do me any good because I only remember four things from that system today. At this time, I began to do interviews because my grandfather knew a lot of people. You know, I've never made a decision in my life. I didn't decide to be a journalist. I thought I could be a journalist, but I could also play the guitar, or I could sing. . . . I didn't have the drive to do anything in particular. But today my vocation is so clear and strong that I would write on walls if I had to. It's not that I *had* to write whenever I had a problem, though I did keep a journal and I used to copy fragments from books I liked. But it wasn't a vocation the way other writers describe it.

One day, my mother took me to a cocktail party for the U.S. ambassador. The next day, I interviewed him. It was a big break for me because this man hadn't even held a press conference until I interviewed him. Furthermore, *Excelsior,* one of the major newspapers in Mexico City, was pro-American at that time. With what was a stroke of luck, they published my interview. And they asked me to do another. I didn't know who to interview. *Excelsior* was located near the Hotel del Prado. I saw that a singer, Amalia Rodrigues, who sang Portuguese *fados,* was staying there. I went to her room to see her, she let me in, I did the interview, and that's how I got started. It's been almost thirty years since I've been doing journalism, thirty years with a lot of luck, a lot of continuity, and much tenacity. I cling to my typewriter as if it were an anchor, and even though it might sink me to the bottom of the sea someday, for now it's, if you will, my way of being, my way of living. Sometimes I tell myself I'm going to give it all up. Perhaps I'll paint or do something else. I say to myself, There's a nursing home here, I'll see if I can take care of the old ones. I ask myself why I do this so much. Sometimes, one wants to break the routine, right? Doesn't that happen to you?

Besides, I'm very given to depression. I think those years in the convent when I was washing so many dishes and performing so many good acts left me with a tendency to depression.

MGP: When did you go back to France?

EP: In 1955 my son Mane was born there, my older son, but I didn't get married. Then I went back to Mexico and journalism. And once I got started, I did it very seriously.

I'd already published a short novel, *Lilus Kikus,* which was the beginning of a book series entitled Los Presentes, a collection edited by Juan José Arreola.

✣ ✣ ✣

One day Lilus Kikus' mother decided to take her to a concert in the Fine Arts Hall. That white building, encrusted with turrets and bulging balconies, somewhat gilded and quite a bit sunk into the ground.

Lilus had three record albums she played all the time. Since she had a flare for the dramatic, she would laugh and cry to the music. Even at The Passion According to Saint Matthew *she would find a reason to make faces, smile, and pull her hair. . . . She'd undo her braids, stretch out on the bed, fan herself with a piece of cardboard, and smoke her father's Oriental pipe. . . . No one paid much attention to Lilus' readings, and one day she came upon this paragraph: "Nothing expresses man's feelings, his passions, his anger, his good disposition, his ingenuity, his sadness better than music. You will find in it the conflicts within your own heart. It's like a clash between desires and needs; the desire for purity and the need to know."*

So when her mother announced she was taking her to the concert, Lilus adopted an explorer's expression in her face, and off the two of them went [*From "El concierto" in* Lilus Kikus].

✣ ✣ ✣

Carlos Fuentes published his first book, *Los días enmascarados* [*The Masked Days*] in the same collection, as did José Emilio Pacheco and a number of other writers. Then I wrote a satire on intellectuals taken from *Meles y Peleo,* two Greek characters, which I entitled *Me lees y te leo* [You read me and I read you], a play on words in Spanish. It has one hundred and seventy scenes. They go back to the Stone Age and end up hitting each other on the head. Then I published *Palabras cruzadas* [Crossword puzzle] with Editorial Era—their second book—a series of interviews chosen by Vicente Rojo.

MGP: Who were the interviews with?

EP: Sabattini, François Mauriac, Luis Buñuel, Lázaro Cárdenas, Fidel Castro, all in 1959. Then the second edition of *Lilus Kikus* came out with some new stories. Then *Todo empezó el domingo* [Everything started on Sunday], which is about what poor people do on Sunday, with drawings by Alberto Beltran. Starting in 1969, I published *Hasta no verte, Jesús mío, La noche de Tlatelolco* [*Massacre in Mexico*], *Querido Diego, te abraza Quiela* [*Dear Diego*], *Fuerte es el silencio* [Silence is strong], *El último guajolote* [The last fool], *El domingo siete* [Sunday the seventh], and *La casa en la tierra* [House on Earth], which is a book of photographs and text about the very poor peasant houses.

MGP: What are you working on now?

EP: I've done a very long prologue to a book about the lives of women who are domestic servants, which is called "Se necesita muchacha" [Maid wanted], but it's almost a book in itself because the prologue is 170 pages long. Carlos Monsiváis told me that the prologue about the maids is an unwitting feminist summation.

✣ ✣ ✣

I am the handmaid of the Lord

In general, men and women tend to forget humiliation and unhappiness as soon as they take leave of them, and in the case of servants, forgetting is an almost irresistible temptation. They get used to things going badly, and no matter how bad their situation is, there's always another that's worse. Or, as Rosario Castellanos says, We have received so little, we are

> *so small, that we also console ourselves with very little. Rosario cries out: "We console ourselves with so little!" Thus, we women DON'T ask for anything, and if we do, it's in such a low voice, with such shyness, such fear of displeasure, that our very attitude invalidates whatever is good about our intentions. Less fortunate women have also acted as maids to their mates, just as they have to God: "I am the handmaid of the Lord." Their previous situations have always been worse, so that just as soon as they stop suffering (and that doesn't mean they're doing well, just that they're not suffering), they forget the terrible experience they have been through and they fall into the temptation of nirvana. Few are the women who remember the pain of giving birth and speak about it. Only a new birth revives the pain, and that's when they open up a line of communication and want or are able to speak. But if not, they pass into a state of unconsciousness and thus affirm: "Listen, Elena, I've just about forgotten that." They are so used to the pain that protesting seems immodest. Furthermore, long years of Christian tradition have imbued them with resignation, and among all the lessons, this one was learned at such a high price that they'll never forget it. For that very reason, what is notable about these stories—that they shake loose memories, wake them up, and bring them to light—is that they break the servant's isolation, and her cry is the call: "You who are confined in the house of the wealthy, you are not alone. There are others like you in the same situation! Let us unite!"* [*From* "Se necesita muchacha"].

✣ ✣ ✣

MGP: Did you say you're working on a new project?

EP: Yes, it's about Tina Modotti, but I put it aside because it wasn't coming out right. I put it down, got very depressed, and went back to journalism. But before the book came out, I was severely criticized.

MGP: Why?

EP: Because I called the book *Tinísima* and then Octavio Paz came out with an article called "Esta Linísima." I'm writing a novel. I'm not making a saint out of Tina Modotti. I didn't choose her. It's another one of those things that just happen to me. I was once asked to do a movie script about Tina Modotti. I started my research by reading a book by Mildred Konstantin called *Fragile Life*. When they told me that I had to do it in a month and a half, they might as well have said they needed it yesterday. I told them that what I could do was copy everything Mildred Konstantin said about her, but that I didn't know anything about the woman, that I had to do research. That's how I began to do interviews. And time went on and I didn't do the script, which is something I don't really have the talent for, anyway. I decided that with so much research, it would be better to do a novel. She's an interesting character, a photographer during the 1930s. She was an Italian peasant woman who came to Mexico with Edward Weston, an American photographer. She did photography. She was his disciple. Then she had various lovers. One of them was Julio Antonio Mella, the Cuban revolutionary who was killed when they were marching together in a demonstration. Her last lover was either Víctor Vidal or Carlos Contreras, the commander of the Fifth Regiment of the Spanish Civil War. He was one of the defenders of Madrid. She was a nurse in Spain. Her life is like a novel. I would have liked to have done something more accurate, which is quite difficult. So I'm doing a novel with the most realistic information possible.

MGP: In a way, the Tina Modotti project resembles the one you started in order to write *Hasta no verte, Jesús mío,* but it involves another type of search.

EP: Much more difficult, because with *Hasta no verte, Jesús mío* we were only dealing with one character. Here I have a thousand pages of interviews with people who knew Tina Modotti. It's turned out to be a very extensive work and much more complete, since Jesusa was only one voice and I never tried to check whether her anecdotes were true. The Modotti project is more complex because of the number of people who come into it. The task of reconstruction is much more difficult.

MGP: It's a novelistic biography in the style of André Maurois.

EP: Yes, like *Ariel ou la vie de Shelley* [*Ariel: The Life of Shelley*] by André Maurois, or the Brontë sisters. But I don't think it's quite that biographical. I think it's more novelistic.

MGP: What else have you written?

EP: *Gaby Brimmer,* which was published by Grijalbo. It's about a little girl who has cerebral palsy. The other is *De noche vienes* by Alianza Editorial. *Hasta no verte, Jesús mío* is in its twenty-first printing, and *La noche de Tlatelolco* is in its forty-fourth.

MGP: I think the book about Jesusa is wonderful.

EP: But now it seems to me that there are some things that could have been deleted and others that could have been worked on more, things about her inner life, not so many anecdotes or adventures. I liked the anecdotes so much: "And now I broke the dishes . . . and now I got up on the horse . . . and now. . . ." One anecdote after the other. There are people who think it's like a picaresque novel, like *La pícara Justina* [*The Spanish Jilt*].

MGP: That reading of *Hasta no verte, Jesús mío* seems right to me, because in picaresque works the protagonist is a young adventurer or adventuress—egotistical, quite lazy, a scoundrel and a cynic—who gets by on tricks and his or her wits. That's not the case with Jesusa Palancares, who is trying to find a place in society. The only thing they would have in common would be the representation of a certain social level.

EP: I do feel that I should have fleshed out her inner life. But I'm always afraid that people will get bored, so I think I should have a lot going on. What isn't there is also a reflection of what she *is*, isn't it?

MGP: I think that it filters through in Jesusa's interest in Spiritual Work. What does this spiritualist ritual mean in Mexico?

EP: It's very interesting. You've certainly heard of spiritualism. In Mexico, Spiritual Work is a spiritualistic sect that has quite a few temples. It tries to communicate with the "other side." People shut their eyes and go into a trance as though they were entering a special place. The most interesting thing is that women are the priests. Furthermore, it's a kind of poor people's psychoanalysis, because they can be possessed by the Supreme Being, who is Roque Rojas. He takes possession of them, enters their bodies, possesses them, and at that moment it's not them talking anymore, but their protector, the Divine Being. This situation allows them to say things like "Last night my husband didn't come home and he's cheating on me and going around with this one and that one." It's a cathartic process. "My daughter did this to me and the lady at the house where I work did—" They tell you a series of things and end up crying and crying—a true catharsis. Then they put on a lotion called Siete Machos on the napes of their necks and then shake themselves. It's real therapy.

MGP: It's similar to certain rites that blacks perform in Brazil and also in the Caribbean, I think. Could it be at all connected with voodoo?

EP: Yes, because they stamp and sway back and forth. Each one's protector possesses her in a different way. It's when they begin to speak—"My brothers"—that they begin to go crazy, to rant and rave and say all kinds of things and unburden themselves completely. Furthermore, because it's not really them talking since they're possessed, there's no possibility of fear or shame.

MGP: And do these communities attract many women?

EP: There are men and women, but the women are regarded more highly because they are priestesses. They operate on your body. If you say you're sick, they do a spiritual operation on you, but to you it seems like they're removing your appendix, for example.

MGP: Like Sister Sebastiana in *Hasta no verte, Jesús mío* who was completely rotten inside—

EP: All of that. Jesusa would tell you all these things and maybe I'd get bored and wouldn't give it much emphasis. A little French logic.

MGP: The other interesting aspect is the principle of reincarnation.

EP: Yes. That's very nice. Sooner or later you'll have to pay. Because your suffering is justified, maybe in your next incarnation you'll come back as a queen. Although *she* says that she was a queen before because she had previously been a very bad man, so that she's paying for it now and that's why she has such a hard life.

✣ ✣ ✣

This is the third time I've come back to earth, but I've suffered more in this reincarnation, because in the one before I was the queen. I know, because I had a vision and saw myself in a long train. I was in a beauty salon where there were enormous mirrors, from the floor to the ceiling, and in one of them I could see myself dressed in a gown.

. . . .

I told them about my revelation when I went to Spiritual Work, and they said that all those white clothes were the habit I'd have to wear at the hour of judgment, and that the Lord had decided to contemplate me exactly as I'd looked during one of the three times I'd come to earth [*From* Hasta no verte, Jesús mío].

✣ ✣ ✣

MGP: It's a way of explaining suffering. Does that work in such low levels of society?

EP: Well, it really does. If you go to Dolores, you'll find some followers. In Mexico, there are some spiritualists who work in the downtown area. Did you know that Francisco I. Madero was a spiritualist and that President López Portillo's sister, Margarita López Portillo, was too? She says she communicates with the "other side."

Francisco Madero, a member of what could be called an upper level of culture, always consulted the spirits. At Jesusa's level, I don't know where the belief comes from. But it gave her more satisfaction than the Catholic Church did, for example.

MGP: Jesusa criticizes the Church severely. Going on to another aspect of your work, what motivated you to do the series of interviews that make up the texts of *La noche de Tlatelolco,* for example?

EP: I think it's a way of acquiring knowledge. Think about the fact that my studies were so useless and that I have no academic formation.

MGP: But you're quite a reader.

EP: Don't you believe it. I don't read all that much. I read about particular topics, and I do read the Mexican writers who are working on whatever subject I'm working on. I read French writers like Michel Tournier or some American writers like Patricia Highsmith and Germaine Greer, and feminists, but I'm not a fanatic about reading.

MGP: When you were young, did you read much?

EP: Yes, I did.

MGP: And why did you do the interviews?

EP: It was a way of acquiring knowledge, because when I had to interview writers or painters, I had to read them or about them. It was my way of getting the academic background I didn't have. I'm so used to that method now that I can't undertake any project that isn't based on interviews.

MGP: It's your genre.

EP: After the novel about Tina Modotti, I have to do one about a railroad employees' worker named Demetrio Vallejo. It's another assignment. Then I'll do a novel about my world, which is the reactionary side, of course. I'll do it with interviews but using another type of research.

MGP: One aspect of your work and your public persona that stands out is how someone from your social background and with your education should have gotten interested in the fate of Mexico's lowest classes—in what happens in Tlatelolco—socially and politically. It's also evident that you have a very well-defined political position.

EP: People call me a Communist here. There's a strong political drive. But it's absurd to think that someone is interested in lost causes because of personal desires.

MGP: What got you interested in this subject?

EP: The guilt feeling of the bourgeoisie. Victorio Vidali, the Communist Party senator, asked me how I'd categorize myself politically. I told him that I'm a reactionary romantic, that I couldn't say I'm a Communist or a socialist. I would like to be or aspire to become one—

MGP: But it's very marked in your books. Being a feminist, furthermore, implies a radical line.

EP: I'm a feminist. But I see all these things not in spite of myself nor against myself, but rather by being a little ignorant of myself, you know? Not to play innocent, but I'm someone who follows what she believes. That's why I'm a feminist, a socialist—from a zeal that comes from somewhere else, that comes from much farther away, but that has nothing to do with indoctrination or initiation. I've never even tried to read Marx. I may have read some excerpts in French, but I've never had the slightest desire to do so, nor do I think I'm going to. But, of course, if you say Rosa Luxembourg to me, I'm interested in Rosa Luxembourg. If you say Rosario Ibarra de Piedra, I'm very interested in Rosario Ibarra de Piedra. I'm more interested in real people, attracted by a major event and people than by an idea. Ideas come later.

MGP: At any rate, your writings clearly reflect the preoccupation you have with certain problems.

EP: And with certain injustices and certain conditions. I come back, I'm rejected and ostracized, and many people tend to typecast me.

MGP: Do people in Mexico fight against you much?

EP: No, they don't. But there are a lot of things I can't have any influence over, and I already know it.

MGP: Could you give me an example?

EP: Television, where I'd never want to appear, but they go after me anyway. One has no forum on television, but I don't want one. They wouldn't call me because they'd say, "She's a Communist" or "She's going to say what she's used to saying" or "She'll defend what she always defends."

MGP: It's evident that what you say bothers some of the Mexican intelligentsia.

EP: Yes. Besides, they don't consider me a journalist.

MGP: Do they consider you a second-rate journalist?

EP: Actually, that's not true. Maybe I'm fishing for compliments in telling you this or not being very honest, because in any case I've had many very honest replies and written critiques from very highly regarded people, such as Carlos Monsiváis, Octavio Paz, José Joaquin Blanco, and Héctor Aguilar Camini. Maybe I'm telling a lie, but perhaps other writers do think I'm a journalist.

MGP: And who are your intellectual relationships in Mexico with?

EP: I'm friends with Carlos Monsiváis. I see José Joaquin Blanco and Aguilar Camini. Among women, I've developed deep friendship and solidarity, which I find very appealing and important for all of us, with Margo Glantz, María Luisa Puga, Sylvia Molina. I feel that we have a friendship, a loyalty, an interest in each other, partly because of feminism and perhaps partly because we protect each other.

When Elena Urrutia and Margo Glantz organized a conference on women writers here in Mexico City, I also felt the solidarity of those present. I think it's a very new and beautiful thing. Also, women writers in other countries are also very interested in women's activities. Whenever I've been invited to the United States, it's been by other women writers, and they've come here. That's not because Octavio Paz or Carlos Monsivais or whoever invited them, but because other women writers wanted to bring another woman writer. Of course, when Susan Sontag came, for example, she was invited directly by the university. I think women are quite open to helping each other. And I say that not only because I'm on the staff of *Fem* but also because that's how I think in general. Don't you?

MGP: Yes. I think you're right. There's a sort of agreement among us to help each other, to support each other in our projects, to get to know the huge number of women who are doing wonderful work in the field of culture. I agree with you. How did *Fem* get started?

EP: It got started as a result of the friendship between Alaide Foppa, who disappeared, as you know, and Margarita García Flores, who was the director of Universitarios and Prensa and of the Universidad Nacional Autónoma de México publications. They got the idea of starting a magazine for women, which came out of a long trip they made to Uruapán, Irapuato, to give a lecture. Alaide went on that trip instead of me. They became friends there, and the possibility of a magazine was born. They asked other writers to contribute. Margarita Peña, who's no longer with *Fem*, and Elena Urrutia, also were part of the first group that put out *Fem*. Then the magazine took a specific direction. First, the disappearance and then death of Alaide Foppa gave it an extremely political and very dramatic twist. Quite recently, some women from Guadalajara have been talking to me about starting a magazine.

MGP: You consider yourself a feminist?

EP: Yes. I feel considerable solidarity with women, and I want women to have the same opportunities men have with their bodies and with their work, as well as equality of salaries and the same possibilities for advancement.

MGP: And this will come about only with a combined and constant effort by women, won't it?

EP: I feel a great deal of solidarity with women, but then I've always cared about women. I remember, ever since I was very young, that while other women said they felt conflict whenever they were with women, I always felt I liked them. It must be because of the convent, where I was with women for two years, day and night, all the time. You can also fall in love with women. I had a crush on a volleyball player. It was the most innocent thing, but I died with admiration for that girl. I think I've always had great affection, great fondness, for women, great admiration for women's sensibilities. I think that the things that have been invented to separate us are things that, at the core, are fictitious, such as competition. There isn't much possibility of competition among Mexican women writers. It's not possible because each one does different things. I couldn't do what Margo does; Margo couldn't do what I do. I can't do what another writer does. If there's competition, it's healthy competition. I'm sure they all know that if one of us triumphs, everyone does, because it raises the possibility that bigger doors will open for all of us.

MGP: One function of the feminist movement is to promote solidarity among women and thus to destroy the suspicion, the envy, the lack of confidence that has grown up among us.

EP: And even within our households, we can exchange chores so that one can support the other.

KPL·90

✤ ✤ ✤

Marta Traba

✤ ✤ ✤

MGP: To begin this dialogue, I'd like you to tell me something about where you were born and about your childhood. What do you remember about your family? Where did you go to school? Do you remember the first things you read?

MT: I was born in Buenos Aires in 1930. My father was an alcoholic bohemian journalist, who was secretary of *Caras y Caretas,* an Argentine literary magazine, for a time. This connection provided for a varied library, but most of it wasn't very good. The books were gifts for the editorial board's secretary, the kinds of things published by Capdevila and Company, a house that published best-sellers. My mother was devoted to my father. I remember most that we were always getting evicted for not paying the rent, like in Russian novels. When I was ten or eleven, I came across *Leoplán,* a weekly magazine that published the world's most famous novels in two columns. I owe my entire sense of literary refinement, my passion for novels, and my astigmatism to that magazine. I devoured all of Tolstoy, Dostoyevski, Turgenev, Goncharov, Dickens, and Victor Hugo. I read Gorky's *La madre* [*The Mother*] aloud to my mother while she was ironing or cooking. We'd cry our eyes out. When I was twelve, I began reading books published by Tor, another company that published inexpensive books, and I learned to idolize Panait Istrati and found out about the injustice in the world. I always read by myself, and when I was fifteen, I discovered that the libraries had other books besides the popular ones I was reading. That's how I learned about English literature, and that's where my passion for Conrad and the Brontë sisters came from. Henry James introduced me to another world, which he shared with Melville. The first time I read English literature, everything else paled in comparison. Even today. Only German literature, particularly Broch and Döblin, approach that level for me.

MGP: Is there a group of male or female writers who have influenced you in any special way?

MT: I'm not too sure I've had "influences." I'd rather call them "preferences"—preferences and affinities. I feel I *share* my literary work with, for example, Carson McCullers, Sylvia Plath, Jean Rhys, Djuna Barnes, and Flannery O'Connor. Sometimes with Doris Lessing—her Africa books, not the current ones. I have nothing in common with Virginia Woolf, and I only feel an affinity with male writers when they have a feminine nature. That's why I'm a full-time Proustian.

MGP: How did you get involved in art criticism? Do you think your work combines criticism and fiction?

MT: For many years, it was both research and analysis. My first book about art, *El museo vacío* [The empty museum], was published by Mito in 1952, when Jorge Gaitán Durán was the editor of a magazine in Bogotá called *El museo vacío.* It was an attempt at being Croccian. I tried to do more than I was capable of, really. In Colombia, I began to study Latin American art more systematically. In 1961 I published a little book that was very incomplete but was the first attempt to give an overall view of Latin American painting, which established values of its own, values that were different from European and North American values. The book was called *La pintura nueva en latinoamérica* [New painting in Latin America], and it was published by Librería Central in Bogotá. The text consisted of a series of lectures I gave in Colombia. After that, I proceeded to specialize in Latin American art, though being a professor at the University of the Andes also meant I had to revise the entire art history curriculum and develop new courses, like the 1953 course on North American abstract expressionism. In 1973, with the help of a Guggenheim fellowship I won in 1968, I wrote another overview called *Dos décadas vulnerables en las artes plásticas latinoamericanas, 1950–1970* [Two vulnerable decades in Latin American plastic arts, 1950–1970], published in Mexico by Siglo XXI. I also published several articles about Colombian art. The increasingly strong relationship between critical text and literary text became clear to me when I wrote *Los cuatro monstruos cardinales* [The four cardinal monsters], which was published in Mexico by Era in 1964. It was a literary text more than an interpretation or analysis.

Two years later, in 1966, I wrote—all at once—*Las ceremonias del verano* [Ceremonies of summer] and sent it to the Casa de las Américas, which at that time sponsored the most prestigious literary contest on the continent. The judges were the Cuban writer Alejo Carpentier, the Chilean novelist Manuel Rojas, and the Mexican writer Juan García Ponce. My novel won the prize and the edition appeared with an extremely favorable introductory essay by Mario Benedetti, the Uruguayan writer and critic.

✣ ✣ ✣

I can barely recognize my own reflection in the murky, gilded mirror formed by the shiny pots and pans hanging in the kitchen. But my face does get distorted. It goes away and comes back. Here I am, making faces with a meaningless face, my hair limp and matted from the heat, and I can no longer stay calm because my aunt saw, naturally, the yellow stains on my dress and began to shout. She said, "Child, for goodness' sake, you don't pay attention to anything!" Her Castilian pronunciation always startled me, the way she'd pronounce certain sounds with a strong emphasis, not the way I would. Sometimes she seemed to be pretending, and sometimes I would get nostalgic imagining her on a river bank with a scarf around her head, sighing deep soul-shattering sighs, like a frightened ox panting on its way to the slaughterhouse. She and the grandmother I never knew. They're like beings from another world to me, seductive and disturbing at the same time, something in the middle of an unusual landscape, so solitary, like the MiKinito desert [*From* Las ceremonias del verano].

✣ ✣ ✣

This late foray into literature made me so enthusiastic that I felt inspired to write things I'd never dared to write until then. I was very lucky that Victor Seix came across my second novel, *Los laberintos insolados* [The sun-soaked labyrinths], when he was in Bogotá. I never had a more enthusiastic or attentive editor, not to mention one who corrected my work so harshly. *Los laberintos* was published by Seix Barral and got excellent reviews in Spain. My third novel, *La jugada del sexto día* [The sixth-day gambit], also had two extraordinary godparents in Juan García Ponce and Pedro Lastra. Lastra got the book published at the University Press of Santiago, but it got lost in the political chaos in Chile. Almost at the same time, Angel Rama published *Pasó así* [It happened like this], my only short story collection, at Arca Press in Montevideo. That's where I ended the marathon. For many years, I concentrated on the book that's most important to me, *Homérica latina* [A Latin Homeric].

✣ ✣ ✣

First chronicle

They informed them too late exactly when the Pope was coming, so they couldn't round people up until the last minute. What a disaster! The women had never seen such a spectacle: abandoned and neglected on the doorsteps, inside cardboard boxes or wrapped in layers of newspapers, they weren't as immodestly visible as they are now, one behind the other in that long line. The organizers' comments were almost always the same. They couldn't stop talking about the surprising layer of grime that had kept them from seeing even one of the gamines' faces until that moment. With morbid curiosity, they calculated how long it should take to become so encrusted with filth. Two years, three, one, without ever looking at soap or water. Opinions varied [*From* Homérica latina].

✣ ✣ ✣

But potential publishers didn't share my opinion about this enormous text, which they always thought was too long. Valencia Editores finally got up the nerve to publish it in Bogotá, but the book didn't do well in Latin America but, paradoxically, did very well in the United States, where it was studied in several university courses. My last novel, *Conversación al sur* [*Mothers and Shadows*], sold well, got good reviews, and penetrated other markets. Siglo XXI in Mexico showed great courage in publishing it. Swedish and Norwegian translations are about to come out, and German and French translations are under consideration. *Homérica latina* and *Conversación al sur* are texts written in desperation and rage. I'm no longer talking about myself, but about what's going on around me, what happened in our countries that was and is horrifying. I concur with the term *literature of the oppressed*, coined by Elena Poniatowska. Her praise has been my best reward.

Literature and criticism aren't divergent, at least in my case. To be a good critic, you must also be a good writer. And you can't be a great writer without having a critical stance. Both my theory about a distinguishable Latin American art that examines the profound peculiarities of our culture and my need to write, in literary narrative, about what's happening to us, are fed by the same concern for place: Latin America.

MGP: Do you think the concept of a distinguishable Latin American art can also be applied to literature?

MT: I think the literary text has gone through the same temptations and competitions as the plastic arts. At the beginning of this century, both sought to achieve representation or expression by subjecting the scientific method to a mediating process.

A literary text can only come out of a well-developed literary technique. I believe that the work of a fiction writer must be placed among the fragments of a world that exists without unity or coherence and that the writer's capacity for abstractness must be recognized in order to create a system or artificial solution that can organize chaos or express it as such, but in a distinct and systematic way.

MGP: Taking into account your experience as a writer, what is your understanding of what the writer must do with language?

MT: It's a very complex task that, first of all, dispenses with common language and that immediately comes face to face with the creation of autonomous semantic units that make up the embroidered canvas of a symbolic language. The more complex it becomes, the further language's space will be from everyday ideology, which is what's happened in this century as technique has been complicated by the desire to break with preceding models or by being anxious to know where and in what its autonomy takes root.

MGP: How does your political militancy relate to your fiction? Do you think your narrative has an intentional political presence?

MT: Strictly speaking, I haven't been a political militant. I firmly believe that good government cannot exist unless it is rooted deeply in socialist ideas, and I absolutely reject and hate any form of fascism, that is, any overwhelming abuse of power. My coming close to or pulling back from real political processes corresponds to that sympathy and hatred. The only political process I strongly supported was the Cuban revolution, from which I cut myself off in 1971, when there was no longer any doubt of Cuba's alignment—inevitable or not—with the U.S.S.R., where, I think, socialist ideals have been betrayed in the worst possible way. Nothing that is on the side of the U.S.S.R. is acceptable in my mind, the same way that nothing under the control and direction of the repressive mechanisms of North American systems—the Pentagon, the CIA, and the State Department—is acceptable to me. The most important theme of the *Homérica* and *Conversación al sur* is precisely the abuse of power and the desire for liberty underneath that crushing power.

MGP: How would you characterize literature written by women? Do you think there's a difference between masculine and feminine literature?

MT: I do think that there's a text, or a different feminine literature, which I understand as a difference from text to text, from writing to writing. This is the point of departure for a hypothesis I've developed.

In the first place, there's a difference in treatment. Literature written by women occupies little space compared with how much space literature written by men occupies in texts like Enrique Anderson Imbert's *Literatura hispanoamericana,* and those critics who do write about literary history periodically ignore feminine literature more often than not. In general, what women write is treated like a subliterature, somehow less valuable than what men write. A paper like the one the critic Jean Franco read not long ago, which was structured around three "conversations," is uncommon; *El beso de la mujer araña* [*Kiss of the Spider Woman*] by Manuel Puig, *Conversación en la catedral* [*Conversation in the Cathedral*] by Mario Vargas Llosa, and my last novel, *Conversación al sur.* Or the critic Angel Rama's special dedication to works by the Puerto Rican writer Rosario Ferré. Cases of late recognition make up a legion. The Caribbean-English writer Jean Rhys is a good example.

But the most important difference is to be found in the text itself, both in the writing and in the way of approaching it.

MGP: What aspects seem to characterize feminine literary discourse, according to your hypothesis?

MT: If we accept an emphasis on the producer-narrator as a constant characteristic of feminine literature, as in Doris Lessing or Jean Rhys, for example, and that feminine literature has an outward orientation toward the contact or channel of communication, these ideas can be applied to all literature written by women, and we'd have identified two characteristics of feminine discourse that have to do with the production of language.

Furthermore, if we think about the very elaboration of language, we can isolate some other factors that distinguish it. These texts tend to link facts, instead of elevating them to a symbolic level. They are more interested in explaining, rather than interpreting the world. Inés Arredondo's stories are a good example of the latter approach. Griselda Gambaro is a good example of the former. A third consideration is that in these texts the level of the real continuously interferes with the level of fiction, which tends to impoverish and eliminate metaphor and considerably shortens the distance between the signifier and the signified. I'm thinking of my own experience as a writer here, since for me this last point was constantly perceptible but unmodifiable in my last two novels, *Homérica latina* and especially *Conversación al sur,* where I continuously tried to have the narrative structure—its mirrorlike sonata form—outside language and inside historical time.

Finally, I'd add that the feminine text lives for detail, much like popular narrative does. This helps give it an expansiveness and a certain reach that self-referential literature doesn't have.

MGP: Who is the reading public for texts written by women?

MT: I think they're addressed to a larger, less literate audience. They don't have the segregated audiences or need the translators of hieroglyphics who have come about in recent decades. It is a marginal literature for marginal people, rather than a fetish literature for the initiated. This amply explains the near absence of feminine texts not only as a basis for literary theory, but also as integral parts of anthologies, which follow a masculine text model.

MGP: Do you find any connective link for feminine literature besides popular narrative?

MT: It's also somewhat related to structures found in oral literature, to its discursive devices, to the beautiful conclusions and explanatory digressions that explain the meaning of each story. Memorization and repetition, which are fundamental aspects of oral literature, are not only related to the structure of the text, but are especially important to its projection and reception. Oral literature is the basis for documentary literature, which in Mexico is expressed by the greatest figure working in this genre in Latin America: Elena Poniatowska.

The importance of dialogue in the texts of the Brazilian writer Lygia Fagundes Telles is also related to the preference for orality.

MGP: These ideas seem important to me, especially for our literature with its lack of theoretical propositions that might allow interpretation.

MT: There are still many important questions to be answered. For example, has this literary modality been capable of creating another model? Can we talk about a model that is closer to the analogies and images of the artistic sign than to the arbitrariness and homology of the linguistic sign? Has literary theory been incapable of establishing limits and specific qualities for a model of the feminine text simply because the men who write such codes think of women writers as subproducers of a single model? Do women who do literary theory fall into the same trap and accept the idea of a single model? These are some of the questions that must be looked into.

MGP: What is your position vis-à-vis the feminist movement? Do you feel or have any real contact with it?

MT: There are so many feminist movements that I prefer not to belong to any of them. I'm rather allergic to affiliations. The belligerent and aggressive feminist movement of the sixties makes me panic in a way, though I recognize that that attitude helped women achieve a great deal in the area of equal rights within a male-dominated society.

At that time, I was living in Colombia, where a very peculiar situation has come about—the culture there is run by women. Women are in charge of museums, television, theater, festivals, journalism, and cultural institutions. Men are involved also, of course, but they're the exceptions. People have to recognize that women were capable of organizing and developing all these aspects of Colombian culture, and they did it with indisputable competence. At popular levels, on the other hand, the Colombian woman, as are women in almost all our countries, is a victim, exploited and without any kind of legal recourse. In this area, which is a top priority, everything remains to be done.

MGP: What part did you play in Colombia's cultural development when you lived there?

MT: Ever since I came to Colombia, in 1952 or '53—I don't remember which—I've had terrific work opportunities. I was able to initiate many things: cultural television, which I consider very important because of the large audience; the art history professorship, especially my work in Latin American art; the art magazine *Prisma;* and the Museum of Modern Art. Colombia not only gave me the green light, which is quite unusual for a foreigner, but encouraged me and backed all my projects, which were all fully accomplished.

MGP: I want to get back to feminism, so you can go into a bit more detail about what you think of it. Do you think it's important for the future of professional women?

MT: I think feminism must be taken seriously. I have tremendous respect for the women who dedicate themselves to it completely and achieve real advances in labor, law, and socioeconomics. The degree to which women in the lower classes are abandoned to their fates is almost unimaginable if you compare it to their male peers, their employers, their own male children, the state, or other more favored social group. That's why full-time feminism, which looks to resolve these problems, is so admirable.

My own relationship with feminism is tangential, because I've dedicated myself to writing and teaching about very specific subjects, such as Latin American art. Most recently, I've dedicated myself almost completely to writing fiction. There isn't time for everything. But when an opportunity comes up, I don't hesitate to show my absolute solidarity.

MGP: How is this social vision reflected in your fiction? How can these minority groups assimilate without losing part of their identities? Do you think there's a danger of losing certain cultural characteristics in the process of assimilation?

MT: Everything I write, whether it's an essay or narrative, is imbued with that sort of social sympathy, nourished from a socialist perspective. Added to that, since I'm a woman, I can't help but write like a woman, which makes me feel like part of what the French sociologist Pierre Bourdieu correctly calls "counterculturalists," by which he means minority groups, ethnic groups, and also women. I write what Elena Poniatowska calls "literature of the oppressed." I write things that are probably true, that I feel an urgent need to communicate, and that carry a great burden of hate, of retaliatory rage toward the injustices and atrocities that surround us.

MGP: How do these ideas relate to feminine writing?

MT: Let's go back to the main problem, which is the problem of the text. The masculine text, in my opinion, corresponds exactly to the critics' and linguists' definitions of the literary text. There's a distance between the theme, cause, or perception of a fact, and the text—call it deconstruction, rationalization, metaphoric capacity, composition, structuring, whatever. That distance also implies a cooling off of the sharpness of perception—call it literary work, creation of the canvas of text to be embroidered upon. I don't see that kind of distance or cooling-off process in typical feminine writing; on the contrary, there's a kind of direct narration—reiterative, emotional, closer to oral tradition than masculine writing. Masculine literature is more speculative, more capable of setting up an overall panorama that includes details, more brash in confessing human relations, more sexual—in more recent times, of course. In a parallel fashion, feminine literature ends up being more emotional, better equipped to look at the details than the whole, more modest or romantic in telling a love story. It would rather, without a doubt, be erotic than pornographic.

MGP: Do you think we should follow the example of the American feminist movement in our cultural regions, or do you think we should look for a solution within our own context that focuses on our specific needs?

MT: We should definitely explore our context and live with both our own needs and wants.

MGP: Could you tell me, along the same lines as you've done in your sociological work, what you think about setting up a theoretical framework for analyzing literary works in our culture or cultures? Do you think we should adapt the models of literary analysis that have been proposed in more developed countries?

MT: Every theoretical framework we use to analyze literature—and also the plastic arts—has been formulated in Europe or in the United States, but that's not so bad as long as we know how to adapt it. We have to be modest enough to recognize that up to now we haven't been capable of elaborating theories, and we have to be discerning enough to try to adapt them and not apply them mechanically to creative material whose character and nature—like that produced in Latin America—is different.

MGP: Do you think avant-garde literature has given some sort of push to our desire to become independent of our intellectual mentors—Europe and the United States?

MT: First, we'd have to define what we mean by avant-garde literature, whether we think that our best literary figures—the Rulfos, the Onettis, the Carpentiers, the García Márquezes, the Vargas Llosas, the Fuenteses—write in an extremely or completely traditional style. Even Cortázar himself, who could be considered a bit more avant-garde. In the last Venice Biennale, people ended up saying that avant-gardes don't exist anymore. I think people have to distinguish between the avant-gardes that have and always will exist, that are elements of breaking with the past and are therefore fertile and creative, and the unfeeling stupidity of the meta-avant-gardists, the authors of little innocuous masturbation games that don't do anyone any good. The second group I mentioned doesn't have much to do with us, really; we've been saved by underdevelopment.

MGP: Between 1920 and 1930, a series of literary magazines with a certain nationalist emphasis were founded. At the same time, we see writers aiming for a broader literature, a literature without political borders. The best examples are the Chilean poet Vicente Huidobro, on the one hand, and Borges on the other.

MT: It's a good thing that the nationalistic movements, which tend to safeguard tradition, and the avant-gardists, which break with it, came into existence at the same time. It was interesting to see them collide, which is what happened sometimes in Buenos Aires, or to see them come together, which is what happened during Modern Art Week in São Paolo in 1922, definitely the most interesting moment for exploring new expressive possibilities that were also connected to national idiosyncracy.

MGP: What writers do you think are important? I'm going to start out with Victoria Ocampo.

MT: Victoria Ocampo is an important celebrity for Argentina because she created the literary magazine *Sur* and because she published great European literature in splendid translations. I'm no *ocampista*. The literary figures she reveres don't interest me very much, and her aristocratic upbringing interests me even less. There's a solid group of writers on the continent. I'll mention only a few: from Argentina, Griselda Gambaro, Elvira Orphée, Luisa Valenzuela, Liliana Hecker; from Mexico, Rosario Castellanos, Elena Poniatowska, Inés Arredondo, Luisa Josefina Hernández; Laura Antillano from Venezuela; Rosario Ferré from Puerto Rico; Julieta Campos from Cuba; Clarice Lispector—the greatest of all—and Lygia Fagundes Telles from Brazil; Armonía Somers and Cristina Peri Rossi from Uruguay; Fanny Buitrago in Colombia. Argentina has also produced writers who turn out best-sellers, cheap in every sense of the word, like Silvina Bullrich and Marta Lynch. Thank goodness that genre hasn't reproduced itself throughout the rest of the continent.

MGP: For poetry, who would you include?

MT: A number of wonderful poets, such as Blanca Varela from Peru and Antonia Palacios from Venezuela; and some splendid Uruguayan women, like Amanda Berenguer, Ida Vitale, Idea Vilariño, and Marosa de Giorgio; and Alejandra Pizarnik from Argentina.

MGP: Who reads feminine narrative? Whom do you think your public is?

MT: I don't know which public reads literature written by women. I know who my public is—mainly women, even though my *godparents,* as you've seen, are male. *Conversación al sur* has gotten enthusiastic reviews, but, at least as far as I've been able to tell, it's been women who've had the greatest emotional response to it.

✣ ✣ ✣

Luisa Valenzuela

✣ ✣ ✣

MGP: Besides Borges, who are your literary friends in Argentina?

LV: My literary friends are the people of my generation: Héctor Libertella, Jorge di Paola, Inés Malinov, and several poets like Hebe Solves and Ruth Fernández. Sara Gallardo is a very special person, and I like her very much. Alicia Dujovne Ortiz is a very good friend of mine and an excellent writer.

MGP: Were you in any kind of writers group then?

LV: No, I didn't really have to be, because I'd just get together with the people I liked. Sometimes we'd meet in bars, that kind of thing. Being eighteen was a lot of fun, because we had a theater group called the Teatro de Arte de Buenos Aires. We used to sell special coupons to earn money to go out drinking or to go dancing. Sometimes we'd put on a performance, but our big project was staging an *auto sacramental* on the front steps of the University of Buenos Aires Law School. The city lends itself to spectacle, and theatrical performances, such as summer theater, blossomed. It really was quite something. I remember when they took away all the streetcars. It was Buenos Aires' finest hour. I'm referring to when I was eighteen years old, but the city's ebullience lasted much longer. Most of all, I remember Illía's presidency in 1966, when they took away the streetcars and left only two lines (one of them was the Plaza de Francia line). A friend of mine managed them, Vicki Linares. She was married to the municipal director of cultural affairs of the city of Buenos Aires. As a result, some space became available for a folklore festival. It was wonderful because it was summertime, and the musicians sang in the middle of the plaza with a group of people around a bonfire, right in the middle of the city of Buenos Aires.

We organized a witches sabbath, or Halloween, which turned out to be dazzling. The idea spread like wildfire: Writers came to read their poems about witches, then painters showed up with witchlike things; people played strange music in the background. I Musicisti, which had formed not too long before, came for the first time, and they sang "Cantata de Laxante," which was brilliant. In addition, as if to help create some atmosphere, an ominous wind began to blow. In those days, we could do a lot of creative things that aren't possible anymore. Later the atmosphere began to fade, though not completely, because there were still a number of theaters.

MGP: There was still a lot of cultural activity during the Onganía military regime.

LV: Most of all in theater. We got together first with actors and actresses in the Bar Moderno, and then we'd go someplace else. We went from bar to bar, but those get-togethers couldn't be called a literary group. I never belonged to any group, though there were a number of them around, and they often invited me to join. I'm very independent of movements, because you have to fight a lot over the projects so that they come out right. I've worked for magazines, but I've never gone along with the management of any of them, and I've collaborated with most of the little magazines that were published then, for example.

MGP: When did you leave Buenos Aires?

LV: I traveled a lot after I left. But before that, when I was at *La Nación*, I traveled quite a bit because of the stories I was working on. That was a unique time, a sparkling era, when we did a series of stories called "Images from Inside Argentina." For two years, we covered the entire country. We traveled across all the provinces from top to bottom. Then Ambrosio Vecino, the editor of the magazine and the man who really taught me how to write, became ill. I spent a year in charge of that supplement. I learned so much from him. He'd gone to school with Cortázar and was a friend of his. He taught me innumerable stylistic details, very patiently, since I was very young then. There was a rigorous precision involved in writing for the paper, because we had to write very dense, concise stories. It required quite an effort and was very important for my development. I learned to do it very well. When Ambrosio Vecino came back, he told me he wanted to reward me for my efforts with a trip anywhere I wanted to go. So they sent me to the Amazon. It was 1967. I went everywhere following the river, from Bolivia to Peru to Brazil. That material resulted in a series of stories. In 1969 I was awarded a Fulbright, and I went to the United States to participate in the University of Iowa creative writing program. That place was bursting with writers. It was very interesting, and I got very lucky. My group was fantastic but neurotic: Juan Sánchez Peláez, Nestor Sánchez, Nicolás Escur, Carmen Naranjo, and Fernando del Paso. . . . Suddenly, after a long impasse, a miracle would happen, and we'd all start to write.

MGP: What kind of relationships developed in this type of writers group?

LV: The idea and intention of it was to give writers some time and space where they weren't obligated to do anything but write. Once a week someone in the group would give a talk. It was difficult to write in the beginning, but then you'd get used to the place and get started. And that's how I wrote almost all of *El gato eficaz* [The effective cat]. I only had to finish the last part by the time my fellowship was over, and I completed it in Mexico. This experience was amazing for me because it was exclusively creative. I wasn't doing anything else. Quite a few times we couldn't concentrate at all and did nothing but sit and argue about literature. Our schedule was all turned around. We'd go to bed at five or six in the morning. An Argentine schedule . . . Then we'd get up at two in the afternoon. And we'd force ourselves to go into town for lunch, walking through the frost. And we'd come back in a bitter mood. Afterward, at night, it was more fun. We'd put on music; we'd dance; we'd sing and talk. And one morning I woke up at dawn and felt I had to write. After an inner struggle, a brilliant idea occurred to me that worked itself out like a dream. At first I discarded it because it seemed to be like one of those dreams that you think are wonderful but very strange. And it was very strange, but eventually it became the beginning of *El gato eficaz*.

✣ ✣ ✣

How I like to wander about the village at dawn and spy on the garbage-can deathcats: They poke around crazyhungry in the trashcans until they find the garbage that can kill with a scratch once it's under their claws.

. . . .

I like to wander about the village with the first weak ray, while the sly unknown ones retrace their tracks to get back to the doorsteps and the deathcats bristle and turn into a pure current of sharp knives [*From* El gato eficaz].

✣ ✣ ✣

This text really surprised me. From that beginning, my writing started to flow like a fountain, filled with the idea of death that I was carefully resisting during the nighttime conversations with my friends in Iowa.

MGP: Could we talk a little more about that idea? Were there mutual influences in this group?

LV: Yes. Very important ones. And many. We used to read our stuff to each other, and it was a rich stimulus for us. That was when Fernando del Paso started writing *Palinuro de México* [Palinuro of Mexico]. We saw it being born.

Sánchez Peláez always talked about his poems as though they were fantasies. There was, in fact, a reciprocal influence. And unsolicited. We lived a very rich reality, richer than we ever could have believed. We saw ourselves as being isolated, cut off from reality, but actually we belonged to another very powerful reality. For me, the experience in Iowa was fundamental. It was a powerful shock, a surge of negative electricity. Nothing happens by itself. I felt a terrifying anxiety. I think it was partly due to the transition from a difficult age: we were all more or less thirty years old. We weren't mature enough to disentangle ourselves from nostalgia, but at any rate, it did me a lot of good.

MGP: Where did you go after Iowa?

LV: I went to Mexico, and I discovered a Mexico that I really didn't know.

MGP: Why did Mexico attract you?

LV: Because it's a magical world. There's a whole subworld there, an entirely hidden truth. There's a magic dimension, off to one side, that functions parallel to the culture, the mystery, the language of what is Mexico. Along with that, there is its indigenous world, buried, quite crushed, but at the same time very alive, and you can feel that. I went to live in a little village called Tepoztlán. You don't see anything, nothing happens, and yet many, many things are going on beneath the surface—but that's a question of skin. You can feel something through your skin and then try to transmit it to literature, but when you compare the two, it's flat, submerged again. It sounds like something out of Castaneda, but that's how it is. For example, one day a small procession passes; the next day you see a cross painted with lime in the street with a flower on it; then a strong wind comes, a tornado. My daughter and I would walk by an open door and see all those candles the Mexicans make out of wax pictures, hanging from the ceiling. We'd ask them if they were for sale, and they'd answer no because that night they were keeping a vigil over the candles. They invited us to come in. Everyone was seated as though they were in a wake, sitting around the room on wooden benches. They passed around a bowl of pomegranate punch ever so often. People were talking to each other, as in a wake. They sang all night, keeping a vigil for the candles that would be carried in a procession to the patron saint of the next village. Then they'd go out carrying the candles with thick wicks on long poles . . . without discussion. You can read many different possibilities into these things. It seems to be a superficial religious ritual, but underneath it is a magical, archaic world that you begin to discover little by little.

MGP: What are you seeking and what have you found at these events? Is there any particular reason why the magical, religious world interests you?

LV: It helps me establish a connection with Mexico that's important to me. For example, a year ago, some friends and I—four women in a Volkswagen—managed to get to northern Mexico for a meeting of dancers who wore feathered Indian costumes and danced some very simple, absurd dances. The dancers prayed while they danced. The purpose was to keep alive the idea of pre-Hispanic religions in a very simple way. They gathered in a remote place in northern Mexico, the land of the Huehuenches, in a place called El Llanito. It was marvelous. We joined in all the flower-bedecked processions. What's strange is the mixing of worlds. In a horrible place, a desert on the Mexican plain, you run into two little churches, one of them baroque. Then you go into the chapel and the sorcerer arrives to purify the area with some branches. People came from everywhere, very poor, very humble, to spend the New Year.

MGP: Wasn't your presence a disturbance in that place?

LV: No. All kinds of people belong to these secret societies. They come from many different places. You can think of it as a true pilgrimage.

MGP: After your stay in Mexico, did you go back to Buenos Aires?

LV: Yes, in 1970. In 1972 I went to Barcelona for a year. I kept writing newspaper articles while I was traveling around Europe.

MGP: Who were you writing for at that time?

LV: For *La Nación* and for some magazines, *Maribel,* for example. I did feature stories, and also I began to write *Como en la guerra* [*He Who Searches*]. It was one of the worst times of my life because I felt very much alone.

MGP: Whom did you see in Barcelona?

LV: Alberto Custe, Mauricio Barques, Cristina Peri Rossi a little, because she was traveling in another part of the country at the time. José Donoso was around at the time, but I didn't see much of him because he lived in Calaceites. I also met a lot of painters connected with the Galería Pecanins, which was where we'd meet. The atmosphere in Barcelona then wasn't very friendly. It was very alienating, so I ended up inventing the mythical Barcelona in which *Como en la guerra* takes place. I wrote a lot, which benefited me a great deal. Then I went to Paris, and from there I went to Scotland where Norman di Giovanni was going to translate my book of short stories, *Los heréticos* [The heretics]. We worked on the translation together. But it was never published, though the translation was very good. We had problems with Harcourt Brace, not very serious, but annoying enough to lose out on that translation. Then the stories were translated by other people.

From Scotland I went to Madrid, because the Instituto de Cultura Hispánica had given me a grant to write newspaper articles. Finally, in 1973 I went back to Argentina, when Perón was back in power.

MGP: Let's take up the idea of death again; it is central to *El gato eficaz,* and it seems to mark a turning point in your writing.

LV: This obsession with the idea of death wasn't mine. It was due to the fact that we were a bunch of writers shut up in this crowded Iowa residence, shall we say, and this sequestering generated a lot of anxiety. Every man and every woman had his or her own phantoms and obsessions, and suddenly, those phantoms and obsessions were unleashed in the hallways. Everyone talked about death, about airplanes, about vertigo, and I thought I was completely above such fears. I thought they didn't have anything to do with me. But suddenly I began to write *El gato eficaz,* a book about death, and suddenly all of us were imbued with that fear. I didn't recognize it as fear at the time, but that's precisely what it was. Recognizing fear can be beneficial, because I think fears are positive and stimulating—to the degree one recognizes them, can name them, can act on them. Otherwise, fear is paralyzing.

MGP: I thought you had a specific preoccupation, your own, an intimate one, with death.

LV: It was both a shared feeling among us at the time and a feeling of being enclosed, of being separated from our medium. I wasn't used to it. I'd never seen a North American university campus. I'd never lived in a small town. I'd never spent nine months in such a schizophrenic atmosphere, the atmosphere that only a group of international writers who don't know each other can generate. Truthfully, it was a long time to spend together during a very harsh winter, trapped by the snow.

MGP: It's what José Agustín talks about in his novel *Ciudades vacías* [Empty cities], the saga of the writers in the Iowa program.

LV: It ended up being a positive experience because Fernando del Paso started that long, wonderful novel, *Palinuro de México.* Everyone began to write important things.

MGP: In *El gato eficaz,* the deathcats are lying in wait for you, lying in wait for the narrator. What got you to work through that obsession?

LV: What began to stimulate me was the sight of New York. I was quite frightened of going there. I didn't want to go. And suddenly I found myself in the New York of the late sixties, a time of tremendous vitality and harshness, combined with the Vietnam War, people seemingly inclined to self-destruction. It touched me in many ways. But, really, people don't write about what happens to them on the outside; all that things from the outside do is wake up things that are inside. It's evidently an obsession of mine.

MGP: I see a tension in your texts, a search for something not very well defined.

LV: What happens is that you never know what's underneath. I think it's important to pursue your obsessions thoroughly because that's ultimately where we'll catch a glimpse of something. If you pursue your obsessions, there comes a moment when you corner them. We were talking about this the other day with Carlos Fuentes, because he's also a man of many obsessions. The books in which he pursues his obsessions are for me the most interesting ones—like *Terra nostra, Una familia lejana* [*Distant Relations*], or *Aura,* where the source of his obsessions is visible, but you don't know what's behind it. The important thing in writing is to surprise ourselves. It's the only reason to write. And to discover and unveil a little of what's inside of you, what there can be inside every human being. If I knew whether it was death or else the search for another truth, or another face of reality, perhaps I wouldn't write. Why write if I already know where I'm going?

MGP: And the cats, where do they come from? It's the animal that comes between the couple in *Hay que sonreír* [*Clara*]. The cat bothers the female character, climbs into her bed, shares her room, among other things. Cats have appeared in your fiction from the beginning.

LV: The cat is a very magical animal, very mysterious. I think I've had that feeling since childhood, because I always had cats. My mother also had a lot of cats, and all those cats appear in *El gato eficaz,* but they can appear as representations of something else—desire, evil with a seductive face. They are the household demons, familiar, charming.

MGP: And the mask you put in the photo that appears on the book jacket?

LV: That's the *gato eficaz.* When I finished writing the book, I was in Buenos Aires, but I already had a contract with Joaquín Mortiz and they were going to publish it in Mexico. The original title was "Los gatos de muerte, Salud!" [Deathcats, here's to you!] taken from "Al Gran Pueblo Argentino, Salud!" the first line of the Argentine national anthem. Díez Canedo told me that the Mexicans wouldn't understand the reference. I was looking everywhere for a title, and suddenly I hit upon what's called a *gato eficaz,* a scarecrow. Since I hadn't finished the book yet, I called one of the chapters "El gato eficaz." What I have as a mask is that *gato eficaz,* but it's another of those crucial obsessive points of mine because masks are another one of my obsessions. I believe that what you have to ultimately achieve is to become aware of the universe that obsesses you and surrounds you.

MGP: The mask idea has to have a connection with your interest in magic. And your interest in Mexico is related to magic in some way. You already referred to it in an anecdote—the trip around Mexico to observe religious ceremonies, which certainly has a magic component. This obviously interests you. Now, I say that it's possible that we believe an exotic component exists in places where we don't belong, that the exotic for the outsider is a natural part of the culture of certain groups of Mexican society, the people that have most strongly preserved its tradition. The same is true, for example, with the *coyas* in Salta, which is what we call rural people in northern Argentina. In other words, we label exotic that which is marginal from the dominating cultural center.

LV: I think it's the other way around. My quest in that area shows it's completely the other way around. The point is that it's not that we don't belong. We do belong, but we deny it. I think Argentines are infinitely more Latin American than we'd ever let ourselves believe or were allowed to believe, so that on the one hand, that world *is* our world. Furthermore, that world is not only the Argentine or Latin American world, it's the entire structure of magical thought. What I found in Mexico, or with the *coyas* in the most primitive villages, is the flowering of another reality, of another way of thinking, of lateral thinking. It's inside everything, but we deny it. Intuition, the magical thinking in the right hemisphere of the brain, is quite visible in these places. I'm talking about very complex things that can be scientifically demonstrated. Science is discovering and reconstructing certain aspects of behavior that appear to be ritualistic but actually reflect very closely the workings of nature, natural truth. That's what interests me. Besides the tremendous poetic and artistic implications, I'm interested in the relationship with art, the relationship with fervor man has for the natural world in these places. I don't know where that comes from. But from the time I was very young, about twelve or thirteen, one of the books that most fascinated me was *Historia de las religiones* by René Guénon.

MGP: That primitive and magical element isn't readily apparent in your work.

LV: In *Donde viven las águilas* [Where the eagles live], my last book of short stories, which was published in Buenos Aires, there are many of these elements. The primitive, which is a particular cosmogony, is a complete restructuring. All this rationalization is totally a posteriori. It's not what I thought I'd do when I wrote those stories, but there is a restructuring, a re-creation of myth. All mythopoetic elements interest me a lot. The primitive allows us to pull out threads and embroider myths. That seems a real marvel to me. These cultures are constantly giving us things like this.

✣ ✣ ✣

The secret city. I don't know its exact location, but I know everything that relates to it, or maybe I suspect it. I know it should be the same as this humble hamlet where we live, a faithful replica, with an equal number of bodies, as long as when a new one dies, the oldest mummy gets thrown into the void. There is a great deal of noise in the secret city; the noise should announce it and is absolutely necessary: all kinds of tin cans hang from the rafters of the huts to frighten away the vultures. It's the only thing that moves in the secret city—those cans to frighten away the buzzards—the only thing that moves and makes a sound, and on certain very clear nights the wind carries the sound to where the living inhabit, and then they meet in the plaza and dance [*From* Donde viven las águilas].

✣ ✣ ✣

MGP: Are you interested in Greek mythology?

LV: It interests me, but not as much as other things, mainly because it's already been exploited. Those are the frozen myths, the archetypes. The idea of Latin American myths, in a certain sense, is less structured. They're more workable and give rise to other myths; that is, suddenly, for us, they're mythopoetic myths, while the others are already archetypal.

MGP: Rosario Ferré, for example, who in her text *Fábulas de la garza desangrada* [Fables of the bleeding heron] reworks myth, rewriting it, going through the original logocentrism again and again. Rewriting myths is doubtlessly a source of enormous possibilities for literature, as is illustrated throughout Western literature. But what's more interesting at this time is the possibility, with the help of new versions, of turning around the emphasis on the male, and in that case, Greek myth begins to thaw out.

LV: It's what Anne Sexton does to children's stories in *Transformations*—Sleeping Beauty, Cinderella, and others. She goes through them over and over again to delete the things that are antifeminine.

I prefer to invent new myths. That's where I see it most clearly how to use certain aspects of reality in different ways—that impressed me. And from there, go on to create a world, invent an anthropological background. In *Como en la guerra,* certain elements appear, one of which is the *temazcal,* the purification bath that is practiced in Tepoztlán.

✣ ✣ ✣

The hour for his first purification has come and perhaps the women will be able to make him understand this by speaking in Nahuatl. Or perhaps they will do it by trying something a bit more obscure, like making him drowsy or getting him to submit by using an unspecified form of hypnosis. In any event, he gives in, and they undress him, without curiosity, without haste. Once he is naked they lead him through the tiny door of the mortuary chapel of demons, which is what he has come to call this rectangular adobe structure, six feet high and six and a half feet wide with a very low ceiling of matted, sooty straw.

Inside, the smoke and the suffocating heat make his eyes burn. Only by lying on the floor does he manage to breathe a little, with his legs raised against the wooden beams of the ceiling because there isn't room for him to stretch out full length, with a flat stone under his head, trying to remember that he shouldn't ask himself the where much less the why [*From "El temazcal" in* Como en la guerra].

✣ ✣ ✣

There the mountain and the rock are like part of the voyage. In *Donde viven las águilas* there's also a story called "El fontanero azul" [The blue plumber] that takes place in Tepoztlán. I was writing the story as it was happening in front of me, though I did develop the background because I can't write about a cut-and-dried reality. While the Holy Week ceremonies were taking place, I was writing the story in "El fontanero azul." It was a wonderful experience because I had the feeling that this complex story was structuring itself, as it were. It is a story centered on an anecdote that is not real, that I invented. Nonetheless, the narration is set at the same time, when the last Easter religious rituals are taking place.

✣ ✣ ✣

Stillness throughout the village and throughout my life. Only the pipe-layer's left hand, his face, and one testicle remain flesh-colored. The rest is already the color of indigo, and I can't figure out why. Only the children are about in the village, and the dogs, like dried-out, tethered hides on four legs. From my window, I saw the wagon arrive with the Judas. Our Judas is blue. We're terribly afraid of him. He's not papier mâché; he's not hollow inside: his innermost organs are evil.

I also saw without looking too closely how each puppet had rockets nailed in his belly, how their necks were perforated by a row of rockets, and fuses were left in their sides. (But it's one thing to see and entirely another thing to apply what you've seen.)

(All of them saw it. They've known it for four centuries, much better than I, who arrived from so far away. Even I am a believer in the cause. I swear it wasn't I. Don't fall into the eternal error: pointing out what doesn't belong even while making a sound of benediction) [From *"Sábado de pasión"*].

✣ ✣ ✣

"Donde viven las águilas" takes place in Huautla, Oaxaca, a marvelous place in Mexico. It's where María Sabina lived, and hallucinogenic mushrooms are part of the native culture—that also appears in *Como en la guerra*. There's one part, a story about Lake Titicaca, which also appears in *El gato eficaz*. These places have marked me deeply. They're fabulous places, so incredible that I intend to keep going back.

MGP: Where was your first trip as a journalist for *La Nación*?

LV: That was when I went to Salta and Jujuy. Afterwards, I traveled by myself from La Quiaca to La Paz. I arrived in Cochabamba, Bolivia, as a reporter, and I insisted that the director of tourism in La Paz invite me to one of the official functions. We went to the mayor of Copacabana's swearing-in, which was something in between the rational and the magical. Everything was on the borderline—the speeches, the oaths—and we stood for the important characters. Next to us, behind the serious, well-dressed public stood all the *coyas*. They were quiet, with their heads bowed. When the ceremonies were over, they began to sing and throw confetti all over the mayor. All this can be read several ways, of course.

MGP: If you had some purpose in putting all this material into your narrative, what do you think it was?

LV: If there were a purpose—but I never believed there was one—it would be to understand ourselves, to understand our world. That world is much easier to understand. I think we comprehend the tremendous world of dominating civilization through this other world, in constant comprehension of this other world. If we human beings cut ourselves off from the world of nature, we are lost. Then it's a matter of rescuing this other world, and that world is rescued, even though it's beginning to die. It's about rescuing us from ourselves. I want to rescue myself, ultimately, from this thing that consumes me. Besides, I love all these things very much. There are photos that suddenly awaken entire sets of associations inside me. Once I saw a photo of an abandoned village—all red—of Indians in Arizona. The mountains were red and the village, built of adobe made of the soil from nearby mountains, was also red. Everything looked the same. It seemed like the village was trying to imitate the land, like protective coloring. From that came a short story called "Crónicas de Pueblorrojo" [Chronicles of Redtown], which awakens very ancient resonances inside me.

✣ ✣ ✣

They chose the most appropriate hue of stone for each house. The stones for the officials' houses were red. The more pink-colored stones were reserved for the brothels. The hue of their house was almost purple, and Pocaspulgas slowly began to recuperate all her features, including the arch of her eyebrows. Pocayerba was giving them back to her without feeling bad, in the same way she had yielded her own features to her before. She thus discovered that the role of a living but inactive God turned out to be much more comfortable than the role of a sorcerer [From "Crónicas de Pueblorrojo" in Donde viven las águilas].

✣ ✣ ✣

MGP: Politics is another theme in your texts and has appeared in a number of your stories and novels.

LV: That's right. Politics has left its mark on us. It shows up in *Aquí pasan cosas raras* [*Strange Things Happen Here*], in *Como en la guerra,* and in my last novel, *Cola de lagartija* [*The Lizard's Tail*]. Because there comes a time when you can't break away from it, when the horror becomes so great that silencing it is worse.

Finally, when you talk about purpose, one writes to understand. Octavio Paz says it is to put the world in order, and in some ways it's like that; but it's both to put the world in order and clarify something. To write about politics or, more specifically, about the horror of deliberate killings, of disappearances, is really to ask the *why* of this cruelty, the *why* of this horror, and to take it unto yourself and recognize it. That is the narrator's function as *the one who names.* There is a way of recognizing, of not denying reality, and it takes a lot out of people to do it. I think that it's one of the most difficult aspects of writing, and yet it's the only thing we can do. That is, to keep that memory of pain alive so that it never happens again or at least to try to keep it from happening again.

MGP: What personal relationship do you have with all these things?

LV: In *Cambio de armas* [*Other Weapons*], the relationship is quite explicit. My personal commitment was very strong because I was deeply involved with socialists and leftists, with Chilean exiles, with the embassy that appears in the book, and with trying to help the exiles. The background of one of the stories—"Cuarta versión" [Fourth version]—is somewhat of a novella itself, set more or less in 1976 and 1977, after the military takeover in Argentina but at the beginning of the regime, when the violence was at its worst.

MGP: During the Videla regime.

LV: That's right. I had a lot of friends who were arrested. I was working at the magazine *Crisis* at the time when it was being attacked fairly often, so I was dedicated to its defense. My involvement wasn't all that direct, because I never believed in solutions that were too simplistic. But I was very much against what was going on, and I was trying to protect people. The important thing at that time was the possibility of protecting people. Two or three disappeared from *Crisis.* It fell to the daily newspapers to get mobilized and warn people because papers could still publish that someone had disappeared.

I felt moved by that, and then by my experiences trying to get people who were being persecuted into an embassy, whose name I prefer not to mention, where I had some connections. Then in 1976 I came here because *Aquí pasan cosas raras* was published in English. I'd planned to come to the United States on May 20, but I got a cable asking me to come sooner. I left a week before I'd planned, and three days later the police came looking for me. It was fate. They advised me not to come back. I work through it all in that story. I went back later on because I thought it couldn't be that dangerous, that we shouldn't be consumed by paranoia. I was very lucky that way—first, because the police really did come looking for me, and then because a judge who was a friend of mine took my case off the docket. So it was as though everything had been erased. Things began to get much more difficult right after that, but I stayed in Buenos Aires until 1979. They were afraid because I was taking documents out. Those were the first documents to circulate about all the torture. When I left for a trip to Peru and Colombia, someone had to get the accusations out of the country, and so I did it.

MGP: You said you had a book that you had difficulty getting published.

LV: *Cambio de armas* and *Donde viven las águilas* were one volume. I split it up and added some stories to each book. What was originally part of *Cambio de armas* and some of the stories of *Donde viven las águilas* were published in Argentina by Sudamericana. Then when fear began spreading, I withdrew the book because I didn't want to get the publishing house into trouble. The short story "Cambio de armas" was published by Gustavo Sainz in an anthology, and then it came out in English in an anthology called *The Web*. The book *Cambio de armas* was published in the United States by Ediciones del Norte in 1982.

MGP: Why did you leave Buenos Aires again?

LV: Because I was invited to be writer in residence at Columbia University, and by then I thought I'd come to the United States and stay for a long time. It was already very difficult to live in Buenos Aires. There was no freedom left; you couldn't do anything. We couldn't collaborate. It was impossible because the repression was ferocious and penetrated everything. And you never knew where the next blow was coming from. At first it was open, and you could always see it coming. But then came the paramilitary groups, the para-police, the gangs hired to incite violence, and I didn't think I'd be able to write anymore if I stayed. I felt asphyxiated. Besides, something very strange happened. People began to acknowledge and justify the situation, saying it was a dirty war. You couldn't talk to anyone. If you said someone had disappeared, they'd tell you the person must have done something. But later, when people began to speak out, they began to acknowledge it. Lists of *desaparecidos* [people who had disappeared] came out in the papers, in *La Voz*, for example. They reported the secret jokes. People couldn't deny a very ugly reality. The situation became quite serious, because the shocks were constant.

When I went back in April 1983, the *apertura* [opening up] was already fantastic. There were demonstrations, and there was also a strike in which 80 percent of the workers participated. The demonstrations by mothers demanding the return of their *desaparecidos* were very moving. I think they'd lost their fear. Even though it might return, it wouldn't be as bad as that paralyzing fear that makes you deny everything that's happening around you. That won't happen again; it won't come back. Everything finally surfaced when the corpses appeared. It is a metaphor made bones.

MGP: Do you want to go back to Buenos Aires now?

LV: When I was there that April, I felt like staying, but I don't anymore. I prefer to keep a certain distance. Distance is important to me. I need it. Buenos Aires is a place where I can see myself getting trapped in situations I don't want to be in. It has nothing to do with anything that's going on right now. I see myself getting trapped in something asphyxiating. I prefer to look at things from the outside, and I'm afraid to have a book come out there. Don't think I take this all very calmly, because *Cola de lagartija* is a very political book, extremely ferocious, and very critical of everyone, of the whole world, of the right, the left, the center, the Peronists, of me myself. It's a book that is very critical of my country's fascination with the Peronists, of the need of a father and a mother, that childish something that is deeply rooted within the people of Argentina, and also their fascination with dogma and doctrine—the pillars of Peronism. And the religious element as well, because there's a death cult in the novel that is quite amusing, but much of it has to do with *difunta* Correa, an Argentine popular cult, and with the death we already know about, which is the ultimate death in the novel. The book is an elaboration of this religious-pagan and quite stifling side of Argentina. It becomes a kind of necrophilia, the fascination with death.

It's time people opened their eyes and realized what was going on there. I work through that a lot in this novel—the mythical aspect. *Cola de lagartija* is one enormous metaphor. It's the only way to say what one wants to say. Through metaphor, you're saying much more than you already know, you express extremely profound truths that you yourself aren't aware of. It all works together. The Sorcerer Red Ant has three testicles, and the middle one is his sister Estrella. It's an embryonic cyst. Everything seems magical, yet it's real. The Sorcerer wants to rule the world. He's the adviser to the military government that is currently in power, and he lives in the salt marshes, which are called the Marshes of Iberá. During the time he is adviser to the government and the ministers come to consult him in secret, he lives half underground in a gigantic anthill. What he wants is to fertilize his own sister with his own testicle and have a son born of himself, the son he's going to name I. That's how he'll come to rule the world. All the two-faced intrigue that's going on in the capital through this character's scheming, this character who is the Sorcerer but will remain nameless, who through his own autogestation hopes to rule the world, is inscribed with the prophecy of Don Bosco: "There will flow a river of blood and then will come twenty years of peace." This character doesn't want peace because it will paralyze him. He is eternal as long as the river of blood flows.

MGP: The situation in Argentina is a fundamental part of this theme, then.

LV: At this time, life in Argentina centers around a disastrous political situation. I think that when political life is more or less under control, this kind of theme will be obliterated. The moment politics becomes threatening and disastrous is when you have a political consciousness.

That's what's happening now in the United States with the question of Central America. People are beginning to have a political consciousness.

MGP: There is also a displacement of the function of literature. When there is no dislocation in the political order, literary creation addresses other areas. That's why there is a literature of accusation in Latin America.

LV: The function of literature is to open people's eyes. Right now, the theme of politics is consuming us. There are other themes, but they also have a political cast. I can't escape this problem because it's such a lacerating truth.

MGP: Do you think literature can create a new consciousness?

LV: No, but it can awaken some new echoes, because ultimately we're not very well read. In Latin America especially, few people read. It may be that literature is a game of reflections. This kind of literature can eventually be reflected in another author who will come up with another aspect that in turn will be reflected by others, that is, open up more people's consciousness a bit. This isn't the way major change occurs in the world. But if you think of the situation as one of facing mirrors, it's another matter. What the writer wants is to disconcert readers—make them think in a different way to keep them from following the paths they already know, from returning to familiar prejudices and to break with them.

MGP: Who are your readers? Are you conscious of who your public is?

LV: One has some idea of the public one writes for. I have an idea that they're people like you who come to see me and ask things, but that huge public, that invisible being that no one knows, of that I have no idea. Those are the people I want to move in some strange way, to show them there are shadings, shadows and luminous places where they are least expected. But how people respond to my work, I don't know. The responses are very mixed; for example, critics get excited about things that don't interest you much.

But that's all right. These are all openings, and ambiguity arouses varied and multiple responses.

MGP: A writer needs a public to complete the circuit of communication. I wonder what kind of imaginary relationship is established. What do you think about when you're writing? Many people say what you've just said, that they have no idea who their reader is. I imagine, nevertheless, that writers engage in some sort of speculation.

LV: I surprise myself because I put myself in the reader's place instead of the writer's place, and I read with amazement. What I read, I read with the wonder of someone beginning to discover something new. The more wonder I feel, the better I think the work is. When I already know what I'm going to write, when I get to a fixed point or stay on a fixed course and it doesn't seem to be working out, I don't use it. So deep down, I am my ideal reader. Then comes the criticism that amazes you, that is very intelligent.

MGP: What kind of circulation does your work have?

LV: In this country, in the United States, it's quite large, which I find astounding.

MGP: And in Latin America?

LV: In Buenos Aires and in Mexico I have a loyal public, but you don't know any individual readers unless you bump into them on the street and they recognize you. That's happened to me a few times. The people who have the courage to break through the barrier are the ones who are involved with literature.

MGP: But in concrete figures, in numbers?

LV: I have more readers in the United States than anywhere else, but my circulation in Argentina and Mexico is respectable, even in spite of the fact that in Argentina I'm on the margin of the established trends, a little strange somehow. They know me, but they can't place me. People on the right put me on the left; those on the left have me on the right. There's no one place for me. I'm not looking for a center in any way because it's part of my rebellion, but it's annoying. The left—those who don't know me, of course—associates me with *La Nación*, with my mother, with that world. Those on the right think I'm a leftist.

MGP: What kinds of things do you try to do in Buenos Aires to gain a definite identity for yourself?

LV: During my 1983 trip, I gave talks and participated in a roundtable about censorship that was very important. Even though you're quoted out of context afterwards. Women—this is the first time in my life I've felt this way, and I don't know if it's because the situation is more acute or if it's just that I've gotten more sensitive—are pushed aside. As a woman, I was furious to be treated this way, because I was touching on subjects that many men don't have the courage to discuss.

MGP: How many women participated in the roundtable?

LV: I was the only one, and, besides, how many women are there right now in Argentina who have the courage to speak out? I don't know. Except Marta Lynch, who was very feisty and involved in everything, so they respected her a little because they were afraid of her.

MGP: Who arranged the roundtable?

LV: Editorial Bruguera [a publishing house]. The participants were Osvaldo Soriano; Isidoro Bleistein; Bernardo Cordón; Jorge Laforgue; Enrique Medina; and Ulises Petit de Murat, who was the coordinator. These men all acted as if they wanted to leave me by the wayside. Pure machismo.

MGP: Among the writers who are working in Buenos Aires, whom did you see?

LV: A lot of them. I discovered new people. I met Griselda Gambaro, Marta Mercader, who is a best-selling author. Things are going very well for her because she deals with subjects that are very much a part of women's lives. She doesn't deal with subjects that people think women shouldn't deal with. Also, she handles them very well. But she stays within the prescribed limits.

There were some very fine poets—Cato Molinari, who is probably about my age; Cristina Villanueva; Ruth Fernández. They put together writers' workshops. They invited me to speak about masks with a woman who makes them.

MGP: Has there really been an *apertura*?

LV: Yes, with many victories, and at the same time, considerable discouragement.

MGP: What other things happened in Buenos Aires with you and your books?

LV: It was wonderful because *Cola de lagartija* came out and because three of us women appeared in a new short story collection. That was another marvelous thing, incidentally, the fact that this new publishing company, Celtia, came out with a short story collection. It takes great courage to publish short stories, because they sell the least, as we all know. And they brought out three books by three women: Inés Malinov, Alicia Steimberg, and me. But the most thrilling of all was the 1983 Buenos Aires Book Fair, because that's where the roundtable on censorship was. We had to move to another room because so many people were waiting to hear the discussion. Nevertheless, most of the panelists treated censorship as a joke and spoke in a humorous vein. Soriano, Lafourcade, and I were the hardliners. I have the feeling that this proves what I was saying before. When you're immersed in rigid censorship, you end up not seeing the truth. You lose your sense of perception. Because the danger is so great, the Freudian repression is enormous. You don't permit the truth inside you to come to the surface and be recognized. People are not forced to acknowledge all the things they were discouraged from recognizing before. For example, everything they had to swallow simply in order to survive. María Ester de Miguel said something to me that was very moving, lucid and terrible: "What are the ones who come back going to think of us?" This having to keep justifying and distorting reality operates almost on a subconscious level.

MGP: Censorship has generated a new kind of self-censorship. And you said at one point that part of the reason you left your country had been to escape self-censorship.

LV: The government created a system of censorship to enforce a self-censorship born out of irrational fear. Suddenly people were persecuted and killed, along with their families, for things they'd said, and they weren't even sure what they were. Fear provokes a self-censorship much stricter than the censorship imposed by the government.

MGP: It's an evil that afflicts our societies.

LV: What these repressive right-wing governments have succeeded in is creating diffuse fear, because totalitarian governments ultimately have a structural kind of censorship. In countries with democratic governments, you know what you can and can't do. There is a possibility of playing one side against the other. In countries with dictatorial governments, since you have no idea what you can't say, fear makes you keep everything back.

MGP: What new projects are you working on?

LV: I'm working on a book of short poems and prose poems that has been on the back burner for awhile, "Los deseos oscuros y los otros" [Obscure desires and the others]. It's coming along very well. I'm still working with the mask theme, which is very important, but in Argentina this theme can overlap with others.

MGP: How did each of your books get published? What kinds of revisions did they go through? How do you see your work changing? What subjects make you write?

LV: I started writing a poem when I was six. I dictated it to my mother, because I didn't know how to write. That little poem already included the theme of death. The poem ends, though it's very silly, "and a bird came to the window / and it said to you / death is coming toward you." That poem appeared in my life several times because my mother wrote it down in a huge notebook and it kept turning up.

Then I wrote one or two things when I was in grade school. But the first real story I wrote was one I called "Ese canto" [That song], but is now called "Ciudad ajena" [Alien city]. It came out in the magazine *Ficción* when I was eighteen. Juan Goytisolo, the Spanish author who, besides being a great writer, was the editor of the magazine, told me I had to write novels. At eighteen, that seemed impossible to me. I wrote one or two more stories, and then when I was twenty I got married. I immediately went to live in France. My intention was to write short stories. One day an idea popped up—because these things are born slowly, but these unconscious associations suddenly pull themselves together—of this woman who works as Flor Azteca [a character in Aztec mythology], but who is going to be beheaded. The idea grew richer from the constant presence of the prostitutes I could see from the window of my Paris apartment in the sixth arrondissement. They used to walk by with heels clicking, pick up men, and set out for the Bois de Boulogne. To me, it seemed very brave of them to get in a car with someone they didn't know—it was the ultimate in courage. We used to look at each other and say hello. Prostitution became a part of the story through that and through my whole fascination with the lower-class neighborhoods in Buenos Aires. I went on gathering the experience of my Buenos Aires life, of my frequent wanderings in the Parque del Retiro, down by the port neighborhoods (I was married to a navy officer at the time). That's how I began to write what I thought was a short story. It grew by itself, and almost without my realizing it, it moved into that wonderful zone of the novel, in which one phrase leads to a second situation that becomes entwined in still another. This novel and these characters came to life and began to live in spite of me. They began to do their own thing. That's how, in 1961, when I was twenty-one I came to write the novel *Hay que sonreír.*

I identified a lot with the character in *Hay que sonreír* because in Paris I felt a bit like a country bumpkin. There's a certain innocence in that book. I returned to Buenos Aires, and I put the manuscript in a safe deposit box because I thought it had no humor. I didn't want to write works without humor. And there it stayed, until I rescued it six years later. I laughed my head off and realized that it *did* have humor, though what the book did was to so greatly exacerbate the sordidness of the situation that it ended up being funny.

The characters were archetypes. Meanwhile, I was beginning to write stories that centered around the theme that finally gave the book its title: *Los heréticos*. My obsession with the theme of religion had been nourished by my many hours of reading about the history of religions. True religious feeling, what people think is true religious feeling, is heretical because it takes religion as something material and physical. The Virgin has to perform miracles and become the intercessor for our prayers, a deity before whom one can bow in penitence and from whom one can receive punishment.

✣ ✣ ✣

As you can imagine, I'm seeking total absolution of my sins. That's not something new. No, it's been that way with me since I was a boy, since I was eleven and robbed a cap full of coins from a blind beggar. I did it so I could buy myself a medal, and of course I had figured things out very carefully: the medal had the Sacred Heart on one side and on the other an inscription offering nine hundred days of indulgence to anyone who said an Our Father before the image. If my calculations were right, four Our Fathers were enough to get Heaven to forgive me for the theft. The time left over turned out to be clear profit: nine hundred days in itself isn't an eternity, but a series of nine hundred days, one after another, adds up to a holiday in Paradise. Now, that's a pleasure worth contemplating [*From "Nihil Obstat" in* Los heréticos].

✣ ✣ ✣

The prostitute appears in another story in *Los heréticos* ["Una familia para Clotilde" ("A Family for Clotilde")] along with anthropological stories (or stories set in Brittany)—"Los menestrales" ["The Minstrels"] and "El hijo de Kermaria" ["The Son of Kermaria"]. Through these themes enters the other source of my interest in short stories.

MGP: Where do the stories from Brittany come from?

LV: There are certain landscapes that move me very much, that are very strong. Brittany, in all of France, where I did a lot of traveling, seemed magical to me, closed, very mysterious, with a very powerful landscape. These stories are bound up with religion, too. The Kermaria church is an absolute marvel. Those places attract their own characters, their own world.

✣ ✣ ✣

> *Little by little, the chapel of Kermaria would take on a halo of cleanliness, and the sky set free a soft, steady rain to wash its sides. The children worshiped the grandfather at this time, because they felt they were losing the chapel and they thought he was the only person who could bring it back. Covered with mud, they would sit on the wet floor on rainy afternoons and listen to him talk, as if he were a prophet of Kermaria, which for them was alive and had a soul [From "El hijo de Kermaria" in* Los heréticos*].*

✣ ✣ ✣

Then I wrote a novel that hasn't been published and never will be. It's called *Cuidado con el tigre* [Beware of the tiger]. Losada was going to publish it, but I took it back to make some revisions and never returned it. There I began the theme of politics, but it didn't come out the way I wanted. It could be read two ways, and one was the opposite of what I meant. Also, it wouldn't matter to me now. You have to say things but not be a pamphleteer, not try to impose a certain truth on someone. At the time, I didn't think it was well realized from a literary point of view, which is what is most important, and there it stayed.

When I arrived in Iowa, I continued to write short stories because I always write. I also continued working on journalistic assignments, and I had plenty of work. That's where *El gato eficaz* was born, as I told you before. Until that moment, my narration was very linear. I was repeating myself. It was a time of change in Latin American literature, and I wanted to get into the trend and change my voice at the same time, because it had become monotonous and a little plaintive. When the idea for that novel, *El gato eficaz,* came up, my narrative voice suddenly took off in an intense flight that gave shape to another rhythm. That's the origin of the multiple narrators, of the decentralized narration. It's a book that breaks with established tradition, as well as other things.

MGP: Do you think it was the atmosphere in Iowa that provoked the change?

LV: No. It was being confined in such a secluded place and then being confronted with the activity of New York.

With my next book, *Como en la guerra,* something different happened. I was reading Lacan. I understood both what I could and what I wanted to understand. I was also reading about Tibetan Buddhism and the nonexistence of the "I." I tried to understand and visualize the notion of a nonexistent "I." They say the essence of the "I" isn't anywhere. That's the start of the structure in *Como en la guerra.* In that text, it reaches the point where the disintegration of the character's "I" is so strong that it took too much for me to follow it. I couldn't go on writing. I had to break it off and do something else. I was working this out in Barcelona, where the novel takes place, in a very closed, very secret Barcelona that I was making up for myself while I was there. It was as though I were in a set of Chinese boxes, each fitting inside the next, set down inside an inner Barcelona where I felt very alone and isolated. I created that nighttime world all over again, and I also wrote my book at night. In other words, the novel was beginning to create its own resonance. When I went back to Buenos Aires a year later, I had half the novel written. To motivate myself back, I made a clean copy of it, but when I got to the part about the great destruction of the "I," where I'd stopped before, I couldn't go on with it. A terrible fear possessed me. I was afraid. I couldn't go on. I was in the Buenos Aires of terrible violence.

✤ ✤ ✤

Where is the door to madness or to some other pathological framework where I can enclose myself? I'm afraid of falling apart, of not knowing how to diagnose my illness. I'm afraid of exploding and spattering all four walls, afraid that a part of me, only a part, may reach her in her image. I'm afraid of becoming one with her in this room and yet I remain. Little by little I melt, and I feel that this liquefaction of my person answers imperious needs of the species and I cannot contain it yet at the same time I would like to put myself back together again, to get out of here and forget her [*From* Como en la guerra].

✤ ✤ ✤

So I put the novel aside and, over a period of a month, began to write a book about this violent Buenos Aires, to try to understand the reality of the city of López Rega, of the police sirens, of what was happening in the streets. That's how, in one month, I wrote the stories of *Aquí pasan cosas raras.* Of course, cleaning it up afterward and revising it took time. I finished those stories and went back to the novel, which began to work itself out on another level. It became the character's arrival in Buenos Aires, the queues of death.

✤ ✤ ✤

Down the streets lined with closed shops and shuttered houses floats the word holy *(not the Holy Word) as in an aquarium. He knows it is on account of that that he must continue running toward the same unknown point that the lines of people are approaching. Luckily the cops don't see dreams and if one spots him it's with the other eye, the eye that records and then lets him go ahead, not interfering with his advance which scorns preestablished order* [*From* Aquí pasan cosas raras].

✣ ✣ ✣

Aquí pasan cosas raras came out first, and then *Como en la guerra*. As part of the censorship imposed by Rodríguez, minister of economics under Isabel Perón, we had to polish up the novel because it began with a torture session. Alberto Girri helped with this. Those pages didn't reflect history. The pages that came later did. They depicted a torture completely subsequent to the character, subsequent in every way, but having to do with the mystical initiation of torture with all its possibilities, or almost all of them, that is, the shamanic disintegration of the body followed by that of the "I."

After this, I managed to put aside the political subjects. I think I fulfilled the need to talk about the violence in Buenos Aires, and I went back to the anthropological stories.

And so a life filled with political implications began. That was when the story of the embassy occurred, that we discussed before. I wrote about all that. That was in the novel I never published. I added things before it, in the middle, but I didn't finish anything.

MGP: What text is that?

LV: What would later be "Cuarta versión" (the first story in *Cambio de armas*).

Then came 1978, along with an invitation to be writer-in-residence at Columbia University. I started to do something really crazy. I decided to create a traveling library. I began by taking the few novels that interested me. Then I tore out the pages I needed from my essay collections, vandalizing my library. I had a strange sensation of being cut loose from my books, of casting off, a sense almost of desperation. At the same time, I collected all my notebooks and found I had a score of them.

From these notebooks, I began to extract brief sketches, texts, and longer stories that later formed *Libro que no muerde* [The book that doesn't bite]. Meanwhile, I continued writing a novel that went backward instead of forward. I also began another text, "La crónica de los demonios" [Chronicle of the demons].

In 1980 I went back to Mexico and wrote another chapter. I'm always writing first chapters, as in Italo Calvino's book. After several tries, I decided I didn't know how to write, that I should forget it. Meanwhile, I wrote short essays and lectures. Also, that's when my experience with teaching literature began, which was something I'd never done before. That's when I told myself I had two professions, journalism and teaching. My creative life was over. Then I remembered Darcy Ribeyro, who said that you have to change professions every four years. So I decided to change lives, and I made one last attempt. I gave myself an ultimatum. If by the next day nothing happened or nothing occurred to me, that would be the end of my writing. Of course, the next day I woke up in a state of enlightenment.

From that experience was born *Cola de lagartija*, which at the time was entitled "El Brujo Hormiga Roja, Señor de Tacurú" [Sorcerer Red Ant, Lord of Tacurú].

MGP: But you already had some ideas along those lines, didn't you?

LV: A few scattered ones. López Rega as a New York transvestite, dressed up as a fairy. And the other one about the men with three balls, who are more brave, of course.

These ideas weren't very coherent. Then all of a sudden, before the despair, the first chapter was born. Also, I was talking with Luis Mario Schneider and Margo Glantz about my experience with the red ants in Corrientes [the northeastern province of Argentina]. When I was two—my first literary experience—I sat down on an enormous anthill, or *tacurú* [Guaraní for *anthill*], and they found me covered with red ants; but none of them had stung me. So I began to write about the other landscape that moved me so much—the Marshes of Iberá, which brings out the Corrientes side of me that was always suppressed.

MGP: Why Corrientes?

LV: My father is from Corrientes. Everything on my father's side was suppressed. And after the red ants, I never went back to that land until I went back as a journalist to the Marshes of Iberá, which is a very lovely place.

Getting back to the novel, I wrote a good part of it in Mexico and then finished it in New York. I wrote it in a single burst of energy over nine months. With a lot of imagination. It was wonderful.

Later on, publishing companies in Argentina and Ediciones del Norte in the United States asked me for more short stories. So I decided to split up the novel and write enough stories for two volumes. Then I took up the original novel and saw what I hadn't said, what I'd skipped over, and that appeared in the stories "Cuarta versión" and "Ceremonias de rechazo" [Ceremonies of rejection]. I also rescued other texts that I'd forgotten about and was able to finish one, the one entitled "Donde viven las águilas."

I wrote poems, too. I always wanted to elaborate on the man-woman relationship in "Cambio de armas" ["Change of Guard"]. In poems and short vignettes: *Los deseos oscuros y los otros*. Margaret "Petch" Sayers Peden translated all of them for me and they began to appear in American literary magazines—*River Styx, Icon,* and others.

MGP: What do you think is your most important book?

LV: I think the short story "Cambio de armas" is the best thing I've written.

Cola de lagartija is also important. It's a very rich book, and I talk about everything in it. I touch on the themes of heresy and dogmatic blindness, which now interests me very much, religiosity without judgment, and how that all merges with political strategy. For the first time, I discussed the theme of power. Another theme that's very important to me is messianic madness and lust for power, the insanity of Nero and Caligula, of the blacks of Ethiopia. We see that insanity so often in the people of Africa, but it is also present, more veiled and less primitive, though at the same level of intensity, in our own military. That's why *El gato eficaz,* where some of these themes are initiated, is a text that breaks with tradition.

MGP: To begin winding things up, you've already mentioned your interest in the prostitute. What is your interpretation of this type of woman?

LV: I counterpose the prostitute with the virgin, that is, with masculine ideas about women: the whore versus the virgin. But the other conception of the prostitute, which we have a tendency to forget, is that for a long time, prostitutes were the only ones, among women, who had access to the world of intelligence and power.

MGP: The hetaerae—

LV: And sacred prostitution, which appears in *El banquete* [The banquet]. Prostitutes could accompany men, and they knew much more than other people did.

MGP: To what are you referring when you talk about sacred prostitution?

LV: In Hindu temples, women earned their money from men who came from far away, and they'd offer the money to the gods. It was the temple, particularly in India and in certain primitive African villages.

The prostitute acts much like a mirror for the man she has a relationship with. He tells her his life's story. He uses her as a confidante. She's the character who appears in *Como en la guerra,* that is, the call-girl, the "whore with a heart of gold" who listens and ultimately is more intelligent than the man. The identification with the other.

MGP: Prostitutes are connected with pornography in a number of ways. What do you think of pornography as literary material?

LV: Instead of pornography, I'd rather talk about eroticism. Pornography is the negation of literature, because it is the negation of metaphor and suggestion, of ambiguity. It is a material reaction within the reader, a direct sexual excitement. Eroticism, on the other hand, which can be tremendously bold and forceful, passes through the filter of metaphor and poetic language. Pornography doesn't enter into literary disquisition.

I think we women must rescue erotic language, because it ends up being dominated by men's fantasies. Everyone should speak his or her own truth, try to express the other's desire, because ultimately, all people want is to express desire.

MGP: What is artistic creation?

LV: I have a model: write what you don't know you know. Artistic creation is writing what you don't know about what you know, which is a phrase of Martin Buber's: "In creation, I discover." It is a path of discovery. You know what you don't know you know. Arriving at that point.

MGP: Language begins to unveil something new for you—

LV: Language begins to unveil a series of things for you—the unconscious. It's the muse. One minute we know what the unconscious is; then we say it's something else. It's what's inside one person that others don't know. What holds itself back. The unconscious is something very intelligent, a highly purified intelligence. It isn't the unconscious of the surrealists, that of automatic or oneiric writing. It has happened to every writer. It starts out with a phrase that leads you somewhere you don't know, and you continue pulling on the thread until an absolutely complete story emerges, very intricate, very intelligent. Theoretically, it has come out of nothingness. It has come out of an entire kind of unconscious machination, and that is fascinating.

Physikalische Karte
SÜD-AMERICA.

✣ ✣ ✣

Ida Vitale

✣ ✣ ✣

MGP: To start out, I'd like you to tell me a little about your childhood in Montevideo.

IV: I had a solitary childhood, without brothers or sisters, among uncles, my grandmother, my father, with adults who didn't have time for children. My childhood was full of magazines and books. That forced me to create my own world, to read. I suppose it's the same with children who have asthma. They create a world of their own because they can't exercise or go out and play with other children. That wasn't what happened with me, but my family was old-fashioned, eccentric, a family that didn't understand the need for friends. Besides, I didn't go to school until third grade. I studied at home. The reason was because I would have had to go to a school run by an aunt of mine who was a very well-known pedagogue, but whose school was so far from my house that getting there was too complicated. So school was at home, and a very precarious one at that. I don't know how I was able to fit in with the rest of the third graders later on.

MGP: Who was your teacher, your mother?

IV: No, no. My aunt, my father's sister. After she got back from school, she'd correct my assignments, and at the end of a full day of work, when I was already falling asleep, she'd do the actual teaching. I suppose she gave me something resembling instructions so that I ended up being somewhat self-taught.

MGP: It didn't make you react negatively?

IV: It gave me a wild desire to go to school, and when I did go, it was wonderful! I was miserable on Saturdays and Sundays because I didn't go to school. It was obviously a lot more fun to be with twenty children my own age and a teacher who took good care of us than to be at home inventing distractions for myself.

MGP: Why do you say your family was eccentric?

IV: Because they were. They were atheists and puritans. They didn't communicate much with each other, and I suppose they inhibited me. What happened to me with school was a bit odd, especially for cultured people such as they were. It's not very normal to keep a child isolated from other children, but it worked out very well for me. That's what I think now. I mean, I don't remember having a boring childhood. Sometimes boredom is the father of all virtue. If you get bored, you look for a way to avoid it, whether it is imagining, reading, or doing things.

MGP: What did you read? Do you remember?

IV: Oh, yes! How could I not remember if it was the most important thing in my life before I started going to school? That and a basement was the best part of my childhood, a dark basement they didn't let me go into often. It was full of trunks. In those days it was an adventure. The entire collection of *Ilustración* was there, including the special Christmas issues, which were very beautiful. I read the complete history of Tutankhamen for the first time there. You always need something you don't have to share with adults. I've just finished reading a wonderful book, *The Valley of Issa* by Milosz. It's about the main character's childhood. The story begins with a description of the valley, the village, the family, but the main part remains the little boy's childhood in the forest, his own world, where only he goes. Well, I didn't have a forest, but I did have a basement. I read books that were appropriate for my age—wonderful fairy tales by Andersen, d'Amicis, Poe—magazines—among them *Tit Bis,* which I'm sure isn't published anymore—translated from English, tabloid size, no illustrations, small type. My third-grade teacher gave me *Nils Holgersson* by Selma Lagerlöff, a book I adored. I'd read books over and over again. A friend of my family had a library in her house from which I could borrow books by my favorite writers; however, books by another of my cherished authors—a writer to whom I have remained faithful through the years—were in my house. That author is Fabre. At any rate, the fact that this woman would bring me books now and then made me look forward to her visits, but I would get upset when I had to return them. I was always waiting for her to come over. And sometimes she'd make up a story for me, which I always found fascinating.

MGP: Was an oral narrative?

IV: Yes, it was. Sometimes she was a bit sadistic. Once she brought me *Genoveva de Brabante,* and she asked me afterwards if I'd cried very much. Whether I cried or not, I liked everything. I accepted it as part of my own world.

MGP: Even though they wouldn't let you go down into the basement, did you go on your expeditions anyway?

IV: It's not that they wouldn't let me, but that I had to ask for the key, wait till someone went downstairs. Maybe there were spiders. . . . I remember a little about when I discovered humor, which was by reading Miguel Cané's *Juvenilia,* which I enjoyed very much, for example, the part about the dining room, where everyone had to eat quietly while someone read an episode from the life of a saint. I could read that funny description of the horrible food over and over, and it would always make me laugh. A little later I began to read things that weren't meant for someone my age, like *La guerra y la paz* [*War and Peace*]. But Natasha's love affairs didn't interest me. What would captivate me was Napoleon's and Alexander's strategy. I read *Werther* then, too, which seemed infinitely boring. Of course, years later I read it again.

MGP: How old were you then?

IV: Twelve. The Romantics didn't interest me then; I discovered them later, when I was already in high school. With Heine, for example, I discovered irony. When I read Bécquer in high school, I didn't like him much, but I adored Garcilaso. I rejected the Romantics more because I perceived them as weak, victimized. Taking oneself seriously, as a victim; maybe their spiritual complexity required a mature reader. But it's difficult to know years later exactly why you liked or disliked something. As far as adventures went, I adored Jules Verne.

MGP: Were you a Salgari reader?

IV: No, I wasn't a Salgari reader. But the age people are when they read him is somewhat left up to chance. Maybe at home they thought Verne was more constructive. You can imagine that in those days I didn't go out to buy books, and I didn't go to the library yet. This friend of the family brought me Dickens, and I cried over his books at the drop of a hat. At any rate, I always think of how much would be lost and how little of those books stayed within the voracious reader I was. But every reading implies, at any age, to lose something in order to gain something else. That's the terrible thing about literature. The reader never perceives everything. As time goes by and you reread certain works, you find another world. At any rate, what little I did pick up nourished me. They didn't force me to read, though they brought me books. They didn't impose them on me as an obligation.

MGP: Were you a docile little girl?

IV: I think so. I think I was very restless. I probably felt that children didn't have too many rights. That's something that modern pedagogy has changed. But in those days, I felt like I was on the other side of a certain frontier. You couldn't talk at mealtimes, you didn't answer, et cetera. Well, my grandfather was a Mason. My father, my uncles must have been branded by my grandfather, whom I never knew. I knew him through my father, who was a very strange person. He left Uruguay to make his fortune in the United States. And things went badly for him.

MGP: And did he come back?

IV: Yes, he went hungry and came back. In those days, people weren't used to the idea of people going away. He always kept to himself and didn't have much to do with the rest of the family. All of them were reserved. They didn't talk much, at least not about things I could understand. I got used to being reserved, too. That's why school was liberating for me. And that's where I began to discover friendship. I still have a friend from those days. I found out how much I needed it.

MGP: You discovered friendship, the most immediate relationship one can have with people.

IV: Yes, it was something that allowed me to act naturally, without inhibitions. There were also other problems. In Uruguay, there were two political parties, *Blancos* and *Colorados*. And one part of my family was *Blanca*, the other *Colorada*. I realized that when they talked about political matters, they'd get tense and argumentative. Then one day I said something about the national spirit. And it turned out that the *Blanco* party was also called the *Nacional* party. I said the word *nacional* and blushed. And I thought I'd made a mistake. . . . I felt that I was walking on territory where I didn't belong. I remember many times when I felt apprehensive because it was hard to understand the world of allusions, to master the language of adults. But today, now that I've gotten used to looking on the positive side, I think that kind of anguish was good for something. I watched the adults and realized that there are things one can say and other things one cannot say. There are obstacles, and then you get a desire to overcome those obstacles, to find out how adults manage in a world that seems too vast and unmanageable. That caused me terrible anguish, to feel that the world was something vast for me, especially that I was never going to be able to understand the world of literature, when I found allusions that everyone else doubtless understood. Hasn't that happened to you? There are books that fascinate me for precisely that reason. I come back to them time and again. A good example is *The Magic Mountain* by Thomas Mann, which made a tremendous impression on me, especially the conversations between Settembrini and Naphta. I discovered that authors can divide themselves in two; they can master two opposite positions, confront them, and talk about them—handle two different discourses. The same thing happened to me with Huxley's *Point Counterpoint,* which I thought was the height of intelligence. When I read it again, many, many years later, I wasn't so easily surprised anymore.

MGP: I think that kind of appreciation comes through reading and through learning to be a reader. The first text that's a little more difficult makes you uneasy. You think you'll never understand it. And then suddenly, it begins to clear up.

IV: But in that case it's different. You don't have to understand them.

MGP: But there's a logic—or antilogic— that has to be understood.

IV: But it's also good to learn to keep up a respectful relationship with the illogical. You don't have to try to understand everything.

MGP: You mean, readers find ways of entering a text.

IV: Yes, there are texts that don't seem that difficult, and then the subterranean communications start. When I couldn't follow them, every page was telling me how much I was missing.

MGP: That seems to happen a lot.

IV: Because I was constantly reading during my childhood and my adolescence, I'd get very upset at night when eight o'clock came around, and my book and the world it brought with it was over. I'd have to start another one that, right then, would feel completely foreign. Of course, I read a lot of novels in those days, but soon I was able to tell the difference between a good novel and a bad one, between what was literature and what was pulp. I realized that I had to be careful of the attraction and special appeal that bad novels hold for the adolescent. And poetry came much later than novels, a few minor twentieth-century Uruguayan poets. Although I did eventually discover María Eugenia Vaz Ferreira at that time, a poet who is little known outside of Uruguay, a contemporary and an opposite of Delmira Agustini. What I mean is that Delmira is formal luxury and verbal sensuality. Perfection of form. What happened with María Eugenia is very strange, because I think she deliberately looked for ways to express herself poorly. María Eugenia eludes the usual modernist forms. Her great poems, which are few—two or three—are very austere, very frugal, reticent. So while Delmira tells all and trusts in the word, María Eugenia doesn't. She resists. In that struggle with language, she wanted to look for a route that's different from Delmira's, or perhaps she wasn't as gifted as Delmira. What I find peculiar now is that María Eugenia was more important for me.

MGP: Why?

IV: Maybe for the same reason that I first liked Amado Nervo better than Rubén Darío, though this may be a literary absurdity. I felt there was a sort of nouveau riche manipulation of the language. So much imagery! So many metaphors! Naturally, I later discovered the other Darío, the incomparable late Darío, who loses the rococo in one of the many abysses where he took lessons.

MGP: I think it's a perception, or perhaps an impression, that people get of Darío, especially when he is read for the first time and there is not enough knowledge about poetry.

IV: That happens with some of the poems, as when you read for the first time poems like "La princesa está triste" [The princess is sorrowful] or "Era un aire suave" [It was a gentle breeze] or the reader encounters Princess Eulalia. María Eugenia seemed accessible to me; I was also attracted by Delmira's inexplicable wealth of expression.

MGP: What poets have been most valuable for your development as a poet? Besides the Latin Americans you've mentioned, are there any poets from Spain who have been important for your writing?

IV: Antonio Machado was the first, and I felt the affection he always arouses. But the admirable Machado is a poet whose influence can be dangerous, that of limiting oneself to simple experiences, deliberately looking for a simple register. The Machado I like best is the late Machado, where there is greater artifice in the best sense of the word. Maybe because he had deeper and terrible experience, and there's an element of secrecy in what he says, something he keeps to himself.

MGP: Have you read Gabriela Mistral's work? Do you think this Chilean poet's work is a major development in Spanish-American feminine poetry?

IV: Once I had to write down a poem by Gabriela when I was in school, and I didn't understand it. I didn't dare ask about what I didn't understand, or maybe I discovered my lacunae only after I had to memorize it. The poem I'm talking about goes like this:

✣ ✣ ✣

It is afternoon time,
when its blood is spread out over the mountain.
Someone is suffering in this hour;
this afternoon, one is losing, grief-stricken,
the only bosom she ever stretched out against

✣ ✣ ✣

et cetera. *One, someone,* too many indefinite words—I couldn't understand. But I went on remembering it, repeating it. One day, years later, I remembered it again, and that time I understood. Some writers have the great vice of wanting to say everything and have everything be understood, not allowing for any mystery. I don't mean that one must deliberately be mysterious or obscure. That either happens or it doesn't. Some poetry has to be crystal clear, and some tries to be. That's why I'm not at all interested in engagé poetry, the kind of poetry that has to have a message and give it in detail. Subtlety and ambiguity would be a disaster in this kind of poetic discourse, as it is in the case of a commercial. And I don't think poetry needs to compete with propaganda. Maybe that's when the idea became real for me. Gabriela is clear. She uses everyday words, but her syntax is new, rough, and of her own creation because she eliminates everything that doesn't seem essential. Her work is one of the poetic experiences that is wasted and undervalued in Spanish America. Few people have read her entire work. They read only *Desolación* and get lost in *Lagar* or *Tala* and the last poetic work, of which just a few poems have been published. The rest remains unpublished. Gabriela's song is so peculiar, as if she'd appropriated the hendecasyllable. We hear a hendecasyllable, and it sounds like Gabriela Mistral right away.

MGP: You said earlier that to change registers, you've resorted to English and German poetry.

IV: Among those poets, Whitman didn't interest me when I read him, in translation, of course. I abandoned Poe after a precocious and very biased experience when I was quite young and I'd imitated him. I think that the distance from the purely formal that reading poetry in translation compels—I read German poetry in wonderful French-German bilingual editions by Aubier—helped shake me out of excessive attachment to the Spanish tradition. This solidified when I read the Spanish surrealist Cernuda, who also tried to rid himself of the excess of influence from the Hispanic tradition by reading poetry in English. However, my relationship with Cernuda was contradictory. At first, I felt put off by Cernuda's last works. I found him too excessive and virulent. He seemed to be turning into a prose writer, but I didn't read him in vain. I could see his dryness, and he forced me to struggle and face the musical excess in an Alberti, for example. On the one hand, how could you not admire the skill with which the Golden Age Spaniards could handle form? But we've been taught not to repeat past experiences. Form implies a limit. It is accused of usurping the depth from meaning.

Then you realize that free verse isn't so easy. What we lose in abandoning rhyme and metaphor, we must gain somewhere else. That's where the big struggle is. Breaking with all forms hasn't always given memorable results.

MGP: Do you think beginning poets should deliberately do exercises in form at the beginning of their poetic practice?

IV: No, I don't think they necessarily have to write sonnets or *liras;* nevertheless, it helps to be able to overcome difficulties.

MGP: What was your own experience along those lines?

IV: I wrote four sonnets and published them. I'd discovered Gerardo Diego, who writes sonnets prodigiously and who did them in the midst of his avant-garde experience, and the poems by the young Vicente Aleixandre.

MGP: And Federico García Lorca?

IV: Everyone went crazy over *Romancero Gitano* because they became very popular. It never occurred to me to write romances. But it's hard to establish how they influenced me during that period of total eclecticism. The advantage of eclecticism is that you avoid being dragged along by one particular model. You choose influences, different elements from different writers, while you're always looking for your own voice.

MGP: Which eventually leads you to find your form.

IV: Well, either you find it or you don't. That's what you never know, whether you're repeating what others have done.

MGP: I know Juan Ramón Jiménez was important for you. When did you become acquainted with his poetry?

IV: In high school, with the sonnets. Then I read *Animal de fondo.* It was hard for me to get into that text. In those days, maybe I rejected what seemed too rhetorical. But what always happens with the great poets is that they're way ahead of us, and when we become acquainted with a certain poetic modality, it turns out that they are proposing another one that goes yet further. And this goes on and on. Then in *Espacio* the autobiographical is incorporated in a critical mode in poetic lines of remarkable modernity. While reading Juan Ramón Jiménez, the entire world passes through us. How else are we going to get to the world? And Juan Ramón didn't hide it; rather, he did it openly. Juan Ramón's experience is very complex. I think it includes the anguish of wanting to get to reach a most profound depth through a language that is always aware of its precarious nature. There's a new edition of his poetic work I still haven't had time to study in depth. There Juan Ramón reorders everything: he changes the titles of all the poems; he changes the place of each poem within each section and then shifts sections within books—all in the desperate search for the Oeuvre, with a capital *O*.

MGP: In Juan Ramón's poetry, redoing is part of his poetic practice, is it not?

IV: Yes, though it's disconcerting for the reader. First, one gets used to one poem. Then you have both the poem and its ghost. Besides, the titles change and the places of the poems change, and he organizes the books in a different way. It is like a topological chaos. It's an extreme of what Gonzalo Rojas does, an admired Gonzalo, who in his last book, *Del relámpago,* reorders the poems from *Oscuro* and inserts new ones between older poems. This implies that poetry should be considered as one poem, as a total unity, along with the poet's right or demand never to think of himself or herself as satisfied with what he or she has done already.

MGP: As is the case of Juan Ramón, who redid his texts constantly.

IV: Constantly, and that implies an obsessive preoccupation, perhaps understandable in his case. He is one of the very few privileged artists to be able to live exclusively for poetry, inside four walls, dedicated to it all day. I remember when he was in Montevideo, around 1948. I saw him several times. I brought a copy of *La estación total* for him to autograph. He opened the book, at random, to a poem, corrected a line and then opened it to another page and corrected another line. I never found out if he was so obsessive that he corrected something on each page or if he knew the book so well that he opened to the exact page he wanted and it only looked like chance.

MGP: Could you explain why Juan Ramón Jiménez is important to you? What did you learn from his poetry?

IV: Perhaps I haven't found anyone else who can transmit his spirit so faithfully through his presence, his gesture, his words. His poetic attitude is exemplary. His life was completely dedicated to poetry. For me, poetry is nothing more than a wound, a difficult goal to aspire to and to achieve. But poets should do what he did. In Juan Ramón's case, the circumstances allowed him to be totally dedicated to his task. Or did he create the circumstances? But in any case, although it may be difficult to dedicate one's life to poetry, Juan Ramón taught us nobility through his work. He taught us respect and awareness of what it demands of him. Even his practical advice for writers shouldn't be forgotten: don't take a poem as a finished work from one day to the next; leave it in a drawer for awhile and forget about it in order to see it from the outside. His way of working demands a critical attitude toward poetry, the conviction that one has never reached the end.

MGP: Isn't that usually the poet's experience?

IV: No, I don't think so. I think the world is full of people who are too satisfied. You must be conscious that you can always go farther. And above all, one mustn't accept that language can express everything. What is said is a specter, an illusion of something else.

MGP: Could you name another poet who is satisfied with his or her work?

IV: Among the good ones? How would I know? One only suspects. There's the general image of someone like Goethe, sure that everything he wrote was perfect. There's a story about the time Heine visited him and Goethe asked what he was writing, what he was working on. Heine answered that he was writing a Faust. Goethe got very quiet, and Heine disappeared. If Goethe had been less inflexible, he might have been able to think that Heine could have added something to his Faust, even though it was outstanding. The anguish of unsatisfied creation offers me a certain necessary fear. Neruda knew that every one of his verses was saying what he wanted to say, especially the Neruda of *Canto general.* But Neruda was usually right.

MGP: Like in the period of *Residencia.*

IV: Precisely. I also like *Extravagario* very much, but for another reason—because it achieves a sense of humor that doesn't diminish poetry, less dominant of matter. Maybe with art I like to feel that there is something that hasn't had a chance to quite make it. I like primitive sculpture, Etruscan, for example, more than classical Greek sculpture, or I prefer the Middle Ages more than the Renaissance, with exceptions, of course. I think that when everything is perfect, when everything is done, the reader is a mere overwhelmed spectator. Perfection is a closed circle. Or is it? I'm thinking of César Vallejo. His poetry, compared with that of others, doesn't seem to be closed; is it possible to think in terms of "virtuality" and "act"? Poetry is something one can barely pretend to reach—I mean its purpose.

MGP: Is it an aspiration?

IV: Of course it's an aspiration, but with the awareness that you can't attain it.

MGP: Not to be as arrogant as a Huidobro, perhaps?

IV: Do you think Huidobro is arrogant? He's a man who's looking for a form.

MGP: Huidobro is on a more permanent search that leads him to experiment with different forms and even different mediums, even the poem to be worn on a dress.

IV: That's right, and maybe there's more doubt with someone I'm thinking of—an Argentine whom you haven't mentioned. It's Oliverio Girondo. In *Campo nuestro* a loose, calm Girondo appears, but in *Masmédula* anguish and utter doubt about language in the coming century win out, whether it will reach total disintegration. But I'm afraid that the way of the future might be the way of the already convinced, of inertia.

MGP: Along the same lines, in an interview with Saul Yurkiévich in *Quimera* he says that "a new romanticism will follow the fatigue of relentless experimentation"—that is, a direct style will come back—"when figurative subjectivity reappears."

IV: Yes, it's possible. Neruda is a twentieth-century romantic. Lines can be extended, as Juan Ramón did. He's on the same line as Saint John of the Cross, as Adolfo Bécquer. There are others. Everything depends on what may prevail. If poetry accompanies the world in the midst of its disaster, it will end up on the level of patriotic songs. On a day when I'm feeling optimistic, I think everything has been preserved for centuries. But if I think of the atomic bomb and that, for the first time, man has the possibility of ending the human race, then I ought to think that poetry has no reason to have better luck.

MGP: I think there are some more positive signs in the novel as well, and I'm thinking of Vargas Llosa's last novel, in this particular case, of a renaissance of the historical novel.

IV: But poetry and novels can have different fates. Just as they have distinct inclinations—the novel to saturation and poetry to purification, the essential. It was after World War I, perhaps, that so many novels began to appear. Practically everyone showed off his or her Goncourt prize or Femina, or so many others, and most of them aren't read anymore. The belated *Gatopardo* may be an exception.

MGP: I was referring more specifically to our literature, Latin American literature, to set some limits for our discussion.

IV: I think that our literature is all literature. I resist admitting that I have to move within only one area. The truth is that my development comes from reading Homer, Dante, Virgil, Mann, Woolf, and many other Europeans. Why am I going to give this all back as European literature someday? I read much more European literature than Latin American literature. I began to read Latin American literature late, with an occasional exception like Machado de Assis. We had to read national writers when we were students, which got us to make a distinction between the national and everything else, even without thinking about it: Quiroga, Uruguayan and not Argentine; Acevedo Díaz, the best epic poet of Spanish America, practically unknown outside Uruguay. But although I read more writers from Spain and from other countries, I put the good national writers, without bias, on the same level as the others. That's why I was fascinated with a Greek mythology when I was little, which later allowed me to understand Garcilaso and read Homer with complete familiarity. Who reads a book on mythology today? Unfortunately, people must not think very highly of it. . . . Knowledge of mythology lets you understand the Greeks and the classics, Garcilaso, Quevedo, the Renaissance in general; that is, it assures continuity. Mythology is, at heart, an exemplification or consolidation of man's eternal problems, though the man in the street doesn't seem to have anything to do with mythology. Behind every problem, there's a myth; behind every myth, there's a situation everyone can understand. So when people would talk about whether Borges was an Argentine poet or a Latin American poet, it was a question that was passé, noxious, terrorist, an argument for mediocre people. Borges represents the best of Argentina and the Río de la Plata region. Besides admiration, it produces an infinite tenderness in me, not only because it's my world, the Río de la Plata again—not in vain he spoke so often about Montevideo—but also because he alone performed such a titanic task of cultural rescue and preservation that I'm afraid it began in America and still isn't finished. He suggests that literature is one, a continuum. It's one of his many lessons. Borges, as a native of the Río de la Plata region, shows that it is possible to develop a literature based on intertextuality with universal literature; that is, he reminds us that in southern literary writing, universality is one of its distinctive features. When I started reading without a guide, I read a lot of bad French literature. I went to a bookstore of old books (or used books) where I'd buy any book that said "First prize" for whatever. For five years, I read all the rubbish the French knew to convert into brilliant writers for export. When I read *Los premios* by Cortázar, I thought, at last a novel that takes place in the Río de la Plata that speaks in a language I understand and that mentions places like the ones I know, et cetera. But it was a false opposition, because I was comparing an excellent Latin American writer with mediocre French writers. It was also deceptive. Why did I have to read those people, whose names I'd just as soon not remember? But, of course, I still hadn't read Virginia Woolf. I hadn't discovered Nabokov. You have to compare things on that level. And if on some levels your formation has been the same as a European writer's or if an allusion to Icarus says more to me than an allusion to the history of, let's say, Ecuador, well, should I deny it? Of course, relationships aren't like that for everyone.

MGP: I think it's about rediscovering and vindicating Latin American culture and literary production, which are in a continuous process of defining themselves. And all of a sudden there are people who produce very important works, and they aren't recognized as innovators in Europe for a long time, for example. I even think it's considered doubtful that a man—not to mention the women who are little known in Europe at any rate, even today—coming from Latin America might come to be an influential writer. And Borges is considered an exception.

IV: It's hard for Europeans to become aware of other people's values, but once the ideas are revealed to them, I don't know if they make a distinction like the one we've been trying to make.

MGP: I think they do.

IV: The Europeans have been quite self-sufficient, but they once looked to the East for exotic things; today they look to Latin America. Once in awhile they wake up to some of our names. Borges, once again. But he doesn't always open up rapidly or for the best. We run the risk of being discovered for the *guajiro* or the *gaucho,* although the latter came too late to the Latin American boom.

MGP: I think that the practice of writing, the practice of painting, et cetera, results in the creation of cultural products, which eventually acquire universal value. That's a path people have to follow. That is, the *guajiro* today has a local voice, and maybe it's not interesting to some people. But it doesn't mean it isn't a human experience. Anyway, a practical task of reading and writing should be developed, one that is carried out slowly. The problem I see with the concept of the universal, according to what you've explained, is that it may bring the danger of nullifying the possibilities of development for many people in our America.

IV: The American integrates the universal. I don't think they're incompatible. I've insisted it is an enriching process to measure up to the best, wherever they come from. People talk about Latin American unity, and the reality is that such unity is relative. What's true for a Mexican isn't true for an Uruguayan. There is no generic norm. And vice versa. And I'd tell you that some Latin American countries that place great emphasis on their borders are as nationalistic as the Europeans, with the inevitable result that applying a formula implies. At any rate, there's a common, inescapable element, which is language. The panorama of the Spanish language is quite diversified, and it tends to be so more and more. For example, no

Latin American writer is close to Gabriel Miró, whom, years ago, I read quite extensively, using the dictionary almost as much as when I read my first novel in French. The first time I went to Europe, I stopped writing for about seven years. I felt I should change everything, that I had to write in a different way. Nor did I want the new poems to translate the diverse experiences of that period—positive but also negative—in an immediate form. Very few times I write a poem about some event. Once in a great while, a peaceful conversation that restates questions that touch on certain spiritual attachments can be immediately translated into a poem, but generally speaking, I need some time for a given experience to mature into a text. There are images that come to the surface with a somewhat absurd structure, and then I realize that they have to do with something lived and then forgotten many years ago until that precise moment. I have a bad memory. Maybe poetry is a way out, the place where things that stay submerged, apparently forgotten, can be kept safe. But that must happen to everyone.

MGP: Is poetry a way to recover the past?

IV: Yes, I think so, that it's basically as though poetry were between the past and the future. The present, everyone knows, doesn't exist. And it's also a way to stay longer in a future you like or of delaying or neutralizing an unlucky one. Basically, one must think of time as being cyclic, the way Borges wanted to.

✣ ✣ ✣

If so much is missing, it is because we had nothing

—*Gabriela Mistral*

Now
time used up must be paid for,
without delay,
rapture consumed
in walking through a garden of silica.
Once again we plowed the same furrow
for the fertility of misfortune,
and the letter,
the silence,
begin entering in with blood.

Years will come to graze on words
like dark pasture,
to throw small salamanders into the fire,
all the exorcisms,

barely memorial where there was once open air,
no longer a common place,
where no one
dreams or reads
for fear of crossroads.

Vague vans cross
toward
a past that crushes roots into dust,
that readies itself for mourning and bids us good-bye
[*"Jardín de sílice" from* Jardín de sílice].

✣ ✣ ✣

The future is the past. Down deep what are we but what we were in childhood? The future should be the development of what began in childhood, in adolescence. I think that's when people have the most important experiences.

✣ ✣ ✣

One memory dissolves spider webs,
others quickly breed them;
the swells in the ocean become a part
from summer to winter,
from verdant green to violent violet
in sinister disorder, without coming back.
It was a parched season
without respect for the dusty
reserve of not having drunk wine,
wine cellars of happiness, of times with light.
The quiet in the tornado's eye
dies of its own calm and oblivion,
like vertigo and the plunge
into the crevice.
There is nothing but to stop thought.
The obstinant accomplice echoes
draw an eschewed edge

But we walk, in silence, hearts inclined
[*"Mnemosine" from* Oidor andante].

✣ ✣ ✣

MGP: It's a somewhat deterministic theory, isn't it?

IV: Why deterministic?

MGP: Because you are saying that the future has already been forged in childhood.

IV: And don't some of our most important experiences take place during childhood? Psychoanalysts think so, don't they? Our lives have always been determined, and I prefer to think it's by our past and not by history. What's important isn't what happens to you, but rather how you handle what happens to you, what you turn it into. Depending on what elements one processes what I am receiving now. What determines whether I like Venice better than Florence and that I don't care for Rubens? How should I understand certain definitive loves, certain repeated rejections? I don't know. But maybe if I understood it all, I wouldn't write.

MGP: What role does poetry play in all this? What does writing poetry mean for you?

IV: I don't feel comfortable reasoning it out, but I know it's something I need. I suppose it's a way of getting to know myself and to know the world, of understanding the incomprehensible. I think that what I don't understand, I understand better when I write. And when I say "write," I refer to the actual activity of writing. I only write in front of a piece of blank paper. That's why whatever occurs to me when I wake up during the night is lost. I absolutely need to develop thoughts on paper. The poem is a form that I need to see and that almost always goes through numerous transformations. I could never be an oral poet.

MGP: Could you define your poetic practice? What themes do you write about?

IV: That's something the reader can see better.

MGP: Could you try to outline them?

IV: I'm already contaminated, because they've already been pointed out to me. Some change, others stay the same. I began to teach late, and naturally it was a new experience. Some of the poems in *Oidor andante* [The wandering listener] came out of my experience with the class, from the class readings, and even from the rejection of the pedagogical Ferris wheel. There's a poem called "Silencio" written in a burst of frustration, after a meeting where we heard people talk and talk, and one could feel the emptiness, the falsity of political formulas that don't mean anything or that cover up the perversion of language, . . . that mean one thing today and something else tomorrow. Naturally, poems are the "stars of possible meanings." After some Spanish professors took the poem and analyzed it as "the genesis of the word," one realized that texts have a life of their own and could take on additional interpretations. And since I mentioned *Oidor andante,* I think it was a book in which there was less distance between poetry and experience. It has less unity than others, because it responded to very different experiences. I wrote it more slowly. Time entered into it and made it less cohesive. Does poetry have to be only one poem or should it express many different things? Someone like Cavafy wrote only one poem, developed only one theme—his loneliness because of his homosexuality or because he felt estranged in his own world. By returning to the history of Byzantium, he is always telling himself.

MGP: What kinds of things interest you most for your poetry?

IV: What would interest me would be to find my just measure, whatever it turns out to be.

✣ ✣ ✣

We built the order of the table,
the foliage of the illusion,
a feast of light and shade,
the appearance of journeying in immobility.
We stretch a white field
so that the reverberations of thought
would shine within it
around the nascent icon.
Then we untied our dogs,
set them out on the hunt:
the most serene image, virtual,
falls into pieces
[*"Cuadro" from* Fieles].

✣ ✣ ✣

Sometimes I get my hopes up thinking that, with an imaginary reader, we are creating a space for rescuing a spiritual world that, on my bad days, I think is crumbling. These are my dreams of a doctrine. . . . But what appears most of the time is nostalgia for what is lost.

MGP: That aspect and tone can be seen strongly in *Jardín de sílice* [Garden of silica].

IV: The feeling of homeland, though it's been abused so much, doesn't appear in my first books, and landscape doesn't appear much either. The love theme appeared more frequently, also the theme of what I thought was difficult to reach or was already lost, as well as the theme of death. You never talk about death more than when you're an adolescent. Never you pursue so many things, sometimes so deceptively tempting. . . . What one longs for and doesn't have, one looks for in poetry. Of course, when I left Uruguay, it turned into the magical center of nostalgia.

MGP: So, getting back to what you said before, poetry is indeed a place of recovery of certain contexts and experiences for you.

IV: It's recovery, invention, or substitution:—disturbances that are overcome—thanks to a rhythm, an image. Poetry can emerge from a rhythm, through two or more words that are combined, and constitute a minimal reflection of the landscape. Then one must try to keep the rest of it from betraying the initial nucleus. But in the end, the origins are diverse and, for me, much more mysterious.

MGP: What kind of relationship do you have with painting in your poetry?

IV: It attracts me the way all unattainable forms of beauty do.

MGP: Any particular kind of painting? You have a poem dedicated to Magritte, for example.

IV: Although it's a bit deceptive, because a poem to Magritte is a poem to literature. Painters think that he "says" too much, that he's too literary, maybe because Magritte preferred to give his paintings poetic titles that he thought were compatible with the emotion produced by the picture. Every work that moves requires an homage to language, an impossible paraphrase. Translation is deceptive in this case, though more or less all translations are.

MGP: Deceptive?

IV: Yes, because it implies the illusion that you're being faithful to something, that you're preserving a whole, when all translation is really an entropy.

MGP: Are you particularly interested in Magritte because he was looking for the union of painting and poetry?

IV: Well, it wouldn't be right to say he's the painter who interests me the most. He doesn't interest me more than Klee, for example. He's a painter with excellent technique who, to the same degree he can make an absolute simulacrum of reality, he defends himself by taking a leap. I'm more eclectic with painting than with literature, though I reject some as strongly as literature.

MGP: Then there's nothing that particularly interests you for your poetry?

IV: When I'm attracted to something, I don't necessarily think about whether it will work in my poetry. The same thing happens to me with music. It's true that poetry sometimes manifests itself as a stupor and an immediate will to adherence. But one can't pretend it's mimetic, either. When I felt I needed music more, I studied voice for several years. But poetry and music are different fields. It's always by chance that distinct ways to touch beauty exist, and proposals for hybridization can be dangerous. Not even the famous vowel sonnet gives you the colors.

MGP: But that's an old obsession.

IV: Yes. You can try to search out rhythms or suggest the impression of color. My poetry should give off green or blue, not because that's what it suggests to me but because those are the colors that attract me in nature or in a silk fabric.

MGP: I've noticed that plants in your work are poetic material.

IV: They come from my childhood. My grandmother used to call plants by their botanical names. So did another aunt of mine, who died young and had been an assistant to the founder of the Montevideo Botanical Garden and had given my grandmother that double respect for plants and for the language that names them. Maybe I emphasize the word *aspidistra* or *drupa* in a poem. But they are words I use as easily as the words *wood* or *sky*. These recurring elements appear in certain poems and impart a specific symbolic worth that the reader may not realize. It could be an attempt to seize the natural world, but in any case, the presence of these elements is unconscious. Even within nature, we make choices. The forest attracts me more than the sea. The sea produces a painful sensation of infinity within me, a bit like Pascal's infinite spaces. Forests, on the other hand, have more human limits. Trees are more seizable. It's hard to think of them as enemies, as being dangerous. The sea confronts you with utter solitude. Plants and trees are individuals who can even establish a kind of dependence on us.

MGP: Which of your books do you consider most important?

IV: The last one.

MGP: Because it's the last one or because you feel it's the most successful?

IV: No. I always have a lot of misgivings when I'm writing—afterward, too. And as time goes on, I get more used to them and begin to feel worse about what they don't have. I ought to tell you that the first book is the most important one, because that was my point of departure. Obviously, I am too close still to the last volume I wrote, but there are some poems in all my books that seem to adhere better to their original ideal, and others I could have molded better.

MGP: Do you read over your poems much?

IV: No, I usually go through a period of pushing everything away. And I think about everything I would have to change. So I put them aside. Besides, there's always so much to read and so little time! Sometimes it upsets me to go back over recurring elements so often. Unless one gets it exactly right more than once, one of the versions will have to be the minor one, the weaker one, the unnecessary one.

MGP: Do you go back to texts the way Juan Ramón did?

IV: Juan Ramón lived with poetry in an atmosphere that had no gaps or interruptions. And he lived a very undivided life. Juan Ramón's experience would seem to be unique, continuous, without breaks. There is a break when he leaves Spain; it is breaking away from your language. But the most important breaks are, possibly, less geographically bound. . . . In my case, rewriting turned out to be too hard. Either I go back to being who I was in the moment I wrote the poem, or I correct it like a brand-new text. For a new edition that includes my early books, I've reworked *La luz de esta memoria* [The light of this memory] a bit, in order to salvage some already intolerably awkward parts, but that's not rewriting. What I do do is leave some poems on the back burner. But those are always poems in progress, poems I haven't finished yet.

MGP: What are you working on now?

IV: I've been writing a series of texts called "Léxico de afinidades" [Lexicon of affinities]. I explain there that it's like a bag full of fragments or scraps, that is, a putting together of dissimilar material in a circumstantial way. It's very different from poetry in that it responds to an idea, to something I've read or something that's happened. I mix tones that are very different, and I use a lot of humor.

✣ ✣ ✣

DAYS—The white days receive cautiousness, they clothe it, they throw over it, like cinnamon over a dish without flavor, the powder left behind by the black days.

The black days rise iridescent from a reflection of planetary death.

The white days are immune to the bone's lugubrious trumpetings, but they putrify hope by forcing it to practice a distending movement and then by caressing it.

The black days have the sinister courtesy of an executioner, the plush of academics.

The white days are forgotten, like the faces of insignificant people.

HISTORY—A thick sensation that oscillates between vertigo and excessive calm, with a leaden descending force that comes from pointing out a homogeneous mass of utterly impermanent adolescents, establishing a mirrored symmetry between the first Hellenes and ourselves, twenty cen-

turies before and after Christ, and in the middle, demented comprehension, all history, all culture, all fear, the uncontrolled whirlwinds, the unwound clockwork, the crazy machines that work beautifully at the beginning but suddenly get delirious when they move backwards and revise and repeat horrors that were once overcome, and they become simple, inept rough drafts.

And man, eager to leave a record of everything.

INCLEMENT WEATHER—There isn't any sigh that can stop it; autumn has come. The dry leaves fall so intensely that we constantly walk between their crackle and dust. Sometimes a genuine yellow blustery wind envelops us exactly between happiness and cold. Palm to palm, we walk through this space, which has taken on an air of a glass case displaying the first fruits, inch by inch we discover how it begins to share the seasons intentionally. We take out handkerchiefs of acceptance, books of rhythm measurement, anthologies of projects; we eat fruit, chocolates, snacks. But each time, our space gets more and more padded and rough, and between one caress and another, we look at the roof, from where more and more leaves keep falling [*From "Léxico de afinidades"*].

✣ ✣ ✣

MGP: Do you begin with a partial definition, for example?

IV: No. I generally start with something that comes to mind. Sometimes it corresponds to the need to explain to myself the word I started out with. The title "Léxico" is circumstantial, because the affinities are what I consider more important. Some texts are short, others are long, and there's poetry, too. The original format comes from the idea of a botanical dictionary in which the examples are certain kinds of seeds.

MGP: Once again the vegetable elements in your writing have surfaced.

IV: It's partly because of an aunt of mine who was a botanist. I inherited her room when she died, and she had a library that included a collection of stones, seeds, and other curious objects. There were small boxes with seeds, microscopes, et cetera. Besides, my grandfather was used to calling plants by their scientific names. What I mean is, it's a kind of beauty; the verbal and the resonant are ways of defending oneself from the world, from man, from people who don't make use of it very often. The dictionary is an idea for protecting things that get lost. Also, poetry does the same thing for me, because it's a kind of equation between the past and the future. This lexicon is still missing some letter entries. That's what ends up awaiting my attention because I've always resisted doing things intentionally.

MGP: Have you thought about putting together your abundant journalistic material in a book?

IV: Maybe it will make sense to do that.

MGP: Do you write all the time?

IV: I don't find it hard to write, but I do find it hard to put a book together because it involves a need for separation, for making a parenthesis out of everything and being completely dedicated to it. I try to forget I've written those texts. There always has to be a kind of unfolding, so the critic can get in and look at it as though it weren't mine or look at it as a mountain. That's why I have a hard time when I set about putting a book together. Another thing that happens is that I find out about things I never heard of before. By the way, I'm working on another book, a book of poems. Some of the poems in it have been published in *Vuelta,* to whose translations I also contribute.

MGP: Is it important to publish in certain kinds of magazines, so that your work is better known?

IV: When I publish something, I don't worry about who it comes out with or where it comes out. I think the text has to be able to defend itself. I think the only poem I published that was not part of a project was a poem about Darío.

✣ ✣ ✣

DARIO—The golden unicorn
clear clarinets
a dagger at the belt
ancestry Clavileño
sphinxlike sword
eternal uterus
panicked visionary.
But also a failure of crystals
thorn winter
erratic cadaver
horror
the how
the when
melancholy.

And even limits of wind
popular sea
canopy of sorrows

ambiguous father
bitter yellow mask
an eternity of the probable [*From "Léxico de afinidades"*].

✣ ✣ ✣

I'm putting together a hierarchy. Certain poems go into the book of poetry, and others stay outside. I'm talking about the enumeration that came from the dictionary—a poem made of words for different kinds of seeds. I wouldn't put it in another book because I think it's more circumstantial.

MGP: How do you decide? What is your criterion? Which texts do you call circumstantial?

IV: To my way of thinking, there are two categories. The first is the short poem, which has nothing to do with whether it's good or not. They're usually characterized by humor, and they are texts I'm not even sure can be called poems. This kind of writing doesn't appear in *Jardín de sílice,* for example. I view them as word games with a different tone. Prose is dominant in this kind of text, and when one of these poems appears, it's to give a certain continuity. This one is about childhood memories.

✣ ✣ ✣

There, in the hesitation
that led to the posthumous room of the dead woman,
they arranged the snow from the lilies of the valley.
I waited on my knees
to see if it would devote itself to singing meanings,
a lute that in infantlike nakedness
would tell stories without thinking,
would offer the trepidation of foreboding.
But it was a drop of silence,
to get us to be quiet,
                    simple,
sumptuously.
Its music,
          a constellation in white,
diamond,
            bell of peaceful silver
even touches transparently
above, against time,

between lights
[*"Música del invierno"*].

✣ ✣ ✣

MGP: Why did you decide to change your writing style?

IV: I like to write in prose because it's a different rhythm, a different kind of timing.

MGP: Is "Léxico de afinidades" the first prose you've written?

IV: Yes, if we don't count the critical notes. They're critical notes at first, for example, the notes on Felisberto Hernández.

MGP: What is the relationship between your critical activity and your poetical work?

IV: I feel very reticent about criticism. I try to approach authors who interest me or who are important to me and to do it in ways that contribute to their being understood better. I don't know whether or not that's criticism.

MGP: I think that's a fundamental aspect of the critical task.

IV: Yes and no, because there are many critical theories today. When I'm reading, which is what I dedicate most of my time to, I try to include authors that aren't well known in Mexico; for example, José Santos González Vera, a marvelous Chilean narrator who belongs to the Alone generation and hasn't been read enough. He won the Premio Nacional de Literatura after he'd only published two books, which caused a tremendous scandal in Chile. I knew him personally. He died when he was eighty, before the coup against Salvador Allende. He was never worried about writing too much, but he left humorous texts, including portraits of Gabriela Mistral and other people.

MGP: What kind of journalistic projects have you developed during your stay in Mexico?

IV: I've written for various magazines and dailies. I published articles in *Unomásuno* that were received very well. They are collections of texts to go with articles that have already been published. One can never pay the debt and establish clearly which ones left traces. Many other texts appear in *El sol*.

Selected Published Works

Allende, Isabel

1982 *La casa de los espíritus.* Madrid: Plaza & Janés. Translated by Magda Bogin, under the title *The House of the Spirits.* New York: Alfred A. Knopf, 1985.

1984 *De amor y de sombra.* Madrid: Plaza & Janés. Translated by Margaret Sayers Peden, under the title *Of Love and Shadows.* New York: Alfred A. Knopf, 1987.

1984 *La gorda de porcelana.* Madrid: Alfaguara.

1988 *Eva Luna.* Madrid: Plaza & Janés. Translated by Margaret Sayers Peden, under the title *Eva Luna.* New York: Alfred A. Knopf, 1988.

1990 *Cuentos de Eva Luna.* Buenos Aires: Editorial Sudamericana.

Angel, Albalucía

1970 *Los girasoles en invierno.* Bogotá: Editorial Linotipia Bolívar.

1972 *Dos veces Alicia.* Barcelona: Barral Editores.

1975 *Estaba la pájara pinta sentada en el verde limón.* Bogotá: Instituto Colombiano de Cultura, Subdirección Comunicaciones Culturales, División de Publicaciones.

1979 *¡Oh gloria inmarcesible!* Bogotá: Instituto Colombiano de Cultura, Subdirección de Comunicaciones Culturales, División de Publicaciones. The short story "Monquío," translated by Catherine Tinker, included in *Contemporary Women Authors of Latin America: New Translations,* ed. Doris Meyer and Margarite Fernandez Olmos. Brooklyn, N.Y.: Brooklyn College Press, 1983.

1982 *Misiá señora.* Barcelona: Vergara, Biblioteca del Fénice.

1984 *Las andariegas.* Barcelona: Biblioteca del Fénice.

Ferré, Rosario

1976 *El medio pollito: Siete cuentos infantiles.* Río Piedras, P.R.: Ediciones Huracán.

1976 *Papeles de Pandora.* Mexico City: Editorial Jorge Mortiz. The short story "Cuando las mujeres quieren a los hombres," translated by Cynthia Ventura, under the title "When Women Love Men," included in *Contemporary Women Authors of Latin America: New Translations,* ed. Doris Meyer and Margarite Fernandez Olmos. Brooklyn, N.Y.: Brooklyn College Press, 1983.

1980 *Sitio a Eros.* Mexico City: Joaquín Mortiz, 1980.

1981 *Los cuentos de Juan Bobo.* Río Piedras, P.R.: Ediciones Huracán.

1981 *La mona que le pisaron la cola.* Río Piedras, P.R.: Ediciones Huracán.

1982 *Fábulas de la garza desangrada.* Mexico City: Joaquín Mortiz.
1986 *Maldito amor.* Mexico City: Joaquín Mortiz. Translated by the author, under the title *Sweet Diamond Dust.* New York: Ballantine Books, 1988.
1986 *El acomodador: Una lectura fantástica de Felisberto Hernández.* Mexico City: Fondo de Cultura Económica.

Glantz, Margo
1971 *Onda y escritura en México: Jóvenes de 20 a 33.* Mexico City: Siglo XXI Editores.
1978 *Las mil y una calorías, novela dietética.* Mexico City: Premia Editores.
1979 *Repeticiones: Ensayos sobre literatura Mexicana.* Xalapa, Veracruz, Mexico: Centro de Investigaciones-lingüístico-literarias, Instituto de Investigaciones Humanísticas, Universidad Veracruzana.
1980 *Intervención y pretexto.* Mexico City: Universidad Nacional Autónoma de México.
1980 *No pronunciarás.* Mexico City: Premiá Editora.
1981 *Doscientas ballenas azules . . . y . . . cuatro caballos. . . .* Mexico City: Universidad Nacional Autónoma de México, Difusión Cultural, Departamento de Humanidades. An excerpt, translated by Magdalena García Pinto and Catherine Parke, included in *Formations* 3 (Fall 1986):21–24.
1981 *Las genealogías.* Mexico City: Martín Casillas Editores. An excerpt, translated by Magdalena García Pinto and Catherine Parke, under the title "The Genealogies," included in *Missouri Review* 7 (1985):156–166.
1982 *El día de tu boda.* Mexico City: Martín Casillas Editores. An excerpt, translated by Magdalena García Pinto and Catherine Parke, under the title "From *The Day of Your Wedding,*" included in *Artful Dodge* 14/15 (1988):85–87.
1983 *La lengua en la mano.* Tlahuapan, Puebla, Mexico: Premia.
1984 *Síndrome de naufragios.* Mexico City: Jorge Mortiz.
1984 *De la amorosa inclinación a enredarse en cabellos.* Mexico City: Ediciones Océano.
1984 *Erosiones.* Toluca: Universidad Autónoma del Estado de México.

Molloy, Sylvia
1972 *La Diffusion de la littérature hispano-americaine en France au XXe siècle.* Paris: Presses universitaires de France.
1979 *Las letras de Borges.* Buenos Aires: Editorial Sudamericana.
1981 *En breve cárcel.* Barcelona: Seix Barral. Translated by Daniel Balderston and the author, under the title *Certificate of Absence.* University of Texas Press, 1989.
1983 *Essays on Hispanic Literature in Honor of Edmund L. King.* London: Tamesis.

Orphée, Elvira
1956 *Dos veranos.* Buenos Aires: Editorial Sudamericana.
1961 *Uno.* Buenos Aires: Compañía General Fabril Editora.
1966 *Aire tan dulce.* Buenos Aires: Editorial Sudamericana.

1969 *En el fondo.* Buenos Aires: Editorial Galerna.
1973 *Su demonio preferido.* Buenos Aires: Emecé Editores.
1981 *Las viejas fantasiosas.* Buenos Aires: Emecé Editores.
1984 *La última conquista de El Angel.* Barcelona: Jorge Vergara. Translated by Magda Bogin, under the title *El Angel's Last Conquest.* New York: Available Press, 1985.
1990 *La muerte y los desencuentros.* Buenos Aires: Fraterna.

Poniatowska, Elena

1961 *Palabras cruzadas.* Mexico City: Ediciones Era.
1963 *Todo empezó el domingo.* Mexico City: Fondo de Cultura Económica.
1969 *Hasta no verte, Jesús mío.* Mexico City: Ediciones Era. Translated by Magda Bogin, under the title *Until We Meet Again.* New York: Pantheon Books, 1988.
1971 *La noche de Tlatelolco: Testimonios de historia oral.* Mexico City: Ediciones Era. Translated by Helen R. Lane, under the title *Massacre in Mexico.* New York: Viking Press, 1975.
1976 *El primer primero de mayo.* Mexico City: Centro de Estudios Históricos del Movimiento Obrero Mexicano.
1978 *Querido Diego, te abraza Quiela.* Mexico City: Ediciones Era. Translated by Katherine Silver, under the title *Dear Diego.* New York: Pantheon, 1986.
1979 *Gaby Brimmer.* Mexico City: Editorial Grijalbo.
1979 *De noche bienes.* Mexico City: Editorial Grijalbo.
1980 *La casa en la tierra.* Mexico City: INI-Fonapas.
1981 *Fuerte es el silencio.* Mexico City: Ediciones Era.
1982 *Lilus Kikus.* Mexico City: Editorial Grijalbo.
1982 *El último guajolote.* Mexico City: Cultura.
1983 *El domingo siete.* Mexico City: Ediciones Océano.
1984 *Confrontaciones.* Mexico City: Universidad Autónoma Metropolitana.
1984 *Pablo O'Higgins.* Mexico City: Fondo Editorial de la Plastica Mexicana.
1985 *¡Ay vida, no me mereces!: Carlos Fuentes, Rosario Castellanos, Juan Rulfo, la literatura de la onda.* Mexico City: Joaquín Mortiz.
1988 *La "flor de lis."* Mexico City: Editorial Era.
1988 *Nada, nadie: Las voces del temblor.* Mexico City: Ediciones Era.

Traba, Marta

1952 *Historia natural de la alegría.* Buenos Aires: Editorial Losada.
1966 *Las ceremonias del verano.* Havana: Casa de las Américas; Buenos Aires: Editorial J. Alvarez.
1967 *Los laberintos insolados.* Barcelona: Editorial Seix Barral.
1969 *Pasó así.* Montevideo: Arca.
1970 *La jugada del sexto día.* Santiago, Chile: Editorial Universitaria.
1979 *Homérica latina.* Bogotá: C. Valencia Editores.
1981 *Conversación al sur.* Mexico City: Siglo Veintiuno Editores. Translated by Jo Labanyi, under the title *Mothers and Shadows.* London: Readers International, 1986.

1984 *En cualquier lugar.* Mexico City: Veintiuno Editores.
1984 *Marta Traba.* Bogota: Museo de Arte Moderno de Bogotá, Planeta Colombiana, Editorial.
1985 *Historia abierta del arte Colombiano.* Bogotá: Instituto Colombiano de Cultura.
1986 *Bursztyn Obregón: Elogio de la locura.* Bogotá: Universidad Nacional de Colombia.
1986 *De la mañana a la noche (Cuentos norteamericanos).* Montevideo: Montesexto.
1986 *L. Caballero, me tocó ser así.* Bogotá: Editorial La Rosa.
1988 *Casa sin fin.* Montevideo: Montesexto.

Valenzuela, Luisa

1966 *Hay que sonreír.* Buenos Aires: Editorial Americalee. Translated by Hortense Carpentier and J. Jorge Castello, under the title *Clara: Thirteen Short Stories and a Novel.* New York: Harcourt Brace Jovanovich, 1976.
1967 *Los heréticos.* Buenos Aires: Paidos. Translated by Hortense Carpentier and J. Jorge Castello, under the title *Clara: Thirteen Short Stories and a Novel.* New York: Harcourt Brace Jovanovich, 1976.
1972 *El gato eficaz.* Mexico City: J. Mortiz.
1975 *Aquí pasan cosas raras.* Buenos Aires: Ediciones de la Flor. Translated by Helen Lane, under the title *Strange Things Happen Here: Twenty-six Short Stories and a Novel.* New York: Harcourt Brace Jovanovich, 1979.
1977 *Como en la guerra.* Buenos Aires: Editorial Sudamericana. Translated by Helen Lane, under the title *He Who Searches.* Elmwood Park, Ill.: Dalkey Archive Press, 1987. Also, by same title and same translator, included in *Strange Things Happen Here: Twenty-six Short Stories and a Novel.* New York: Harcourt Brace Jovanovich, 1979.
1980 *Libro que no muerde.* Mexico City: Universidad Autónoma de México, Difusión Cultural, Departamento de Humanidades.
1982 *Cambio de armas.* Hanover, N.H.: Ediciones del Norte. Translated by Deborah Bonner, under the title *Other Weapons.* Hanover, N.H.: Ediciones del Norte, 1985. The short story "Cambio de armas," translated by Lewald H. Ernest, under the title "Change of Guard," included in *The Web: Stories by Argentine Women,* ed. Lewald H. Ernest. Washington, D.C.: Three Continents Press, 1983.
1983 *Cola de lagartija.* Buenos Aires: Bruguera. Translated by Gregory Rabassa, under the title *The Lizard's Tail.* New York: Farrar, Straus, 1983.
1983 *Donde viven las águilas.* Buenos Aires: Editorial Celtia. The short story "Generosos inconvenientes bajan por el río," translated by Clementine Rabassa, under the title "Generous Impediments Float Down the River," included in *Contemporary Women Authors of Latin America: New Translations,* ed. Doris Meyer and Margarite Fernandez Olmos. Brooklyn, N.Y.: Brooklyn College Press, 1983.
1990 *Novela negra con argentinos.* Barcelona.

1990 *Realidad nacional desde la cama.* Buenos Aires: Grupo Editor Latinoamericano.

Vitale, Ida

1949 *La luz de esta memoria.* Montevideo: La Galatea.

1953 *Palabra dada.* Montevideo: La Galatea. The poem "Canon," translated by Darwin J. Flakoll and Claribel Alegría, included in *New Voices of Hispanic America.* Boston: Beacon Press, 1962.

1960 *Cada uno en su noche.* Montevideo: Editorial Alfa.

1972 *Oidor andante.* Montevideo: Arca. The poem "Answer of the Dervish," translated by I. Bradford, included in *Mundus Artium* 3 (1974).

1980 *Jardín de sílice.* Caracas: Monte Avila Editores.

1982 *Fieles.* Mexico City: Universidad Nacional Autónoma de México.

1984 *Entresaca.* Mexico City: Ediciones del Faquir, Editorial Oasis.

1988 *Sueños de la constancia.* Mexico City: Fondo de Cultura Económica.

Index